The Sister Fidelma
Mysteries

The Sister Fidelma Mysteries

Essays on the Historical Novels of Peter Tremayne

Edited by
EDWARD J. RIELLY *and*
DAVID ROBERT WOOTEN

McFarland & Company, Inc., Publishers
Jefferson, North Carolina, and London

ALSO OF INTEREST AND EDITED BY EDWARD J. RIELLY

Murder 101: Essays on the Teaching of Detective Fiction (2009)
Baseball in the Classroom: Essays on Teaching the National Pastime (2006)

An earlier version of "Sister Fidelma: A Woman for All Seasons" appeared in *The Brehon: The Journal of The International Sister Fidelma Society* 3.2 (May 2004): III–XIII. Used by permission of the publisher.

LIBRARY OF CONGRESS CATALOGUING-IN-PUBLICATION DATA

The Sister Fidelma mysteries : essays on the historical novels of Peter Tremayne ; edited by Edward J. Rielly and David Robert Wooten.
    p.   cm.
Includes bibliographical references and index.

ISBN 978-0-7864-6667-2
softcover : acid free paper ∞

1. Tremayne, Peter. Sister Fidelma novels. 2. Historical fiction, English — History and criticism. 3. Detective and mystery stories, English — History and criticism. I. Rielly, Edward J. II. Wooten, David Robert.
PR6070.R366Z86 2012
823'.914 — dc23
                                   2012028492

BRITISH LIBRARY CATALOGUING DATA ARE AVAILABLE

© 2012 Edward J. Rielly and David Robert Wooten. All rights reserved

No part of this book may be reproduced or transmitted in any form or by any means, electronic or mechanical, including photocopying or recording, or by any information storage and retrieval system, without permission in writing from the publisher.

Front cover images © 2012 Shutterstock

Manufactured in the United States of America

McFarland & Company, Inc., Publishers
   Box 611, Jefferson, North Carolina 28640
   www.mcfarlandpub.com

To Jeanne, whose support is never a mystery
Edward J. Rielly

For Kayleigh
"Fame is rot; daughters are the thing"—James Matthew Barrie
David Robert Wooten

Contents

ACKNOWLEDGMENTS ix

PREFACE
    Edward J. Rielly and *David Robert Wooten* 1

Sister Fidelma: A Woman for All Seasons
    Edward J. Rielly 5

Who Is Peter Tremayne?
    David Robert Wooten 20

The Impact of Sister Fidelma on Irish Crime Fiction
    John Scaggs 28

Teaching Sister Fidelma: Two Models
    Edward J. Rielly 33

Fidelma's Position in the Female Detective Genre
    Richard Dalby 44

Hidden from History: Fidelma of Cashel and Lost Female Values
    Christine Kinealy 50

Brother Eadulf: Monk of Saxmundham
    Mairéad Ní Riada 60

Fidelma Locations in Munster (Ireland)
    David Robert Wooten 68

Fidelma of Cashel and the Brehon Code
    Patrick O'Keefe 80

Druids and Brehons: Fidelma and the Druidic Tradition
    Anita M. Vickers 88

A Druid in New Guise
    Christiane W. Luehrs and *Robert B. Luehrs* 98

Fidelma of Cashel: The Plight of the Learned Lady
    Mitzi M. Brunsdale 109

Pursuing the Mystery of Religious Life
    Patricia C. Flynn 118

The Sister Is a Mother: Sister Fidelma and the Celtic Church
    Frank A. Salamone 130

Nothing Hidden That Shall Not Be Known: Mystery and Detection in the Sister Fidelma Novels
    John Scaggs 138

Lady Justice: Social Sleuthing and Sister Fidelma
    Jennifer Molidor 151

Fidelma and the Irish Language
    Anna Heussaff 160

Fidelma and the Celts of Brittany: Ancient and Modern
    Herve Latimier 172

Who Wears the Pants? Role Reversal in the Sister Fidelma Mysteries
    M.E. Kemp 182

The International Sister Fidelma Society
    David Robert Wooten 189

Féile Fidelma: Its Origins and History
    Seamus J. King 196

Interview with Peter Tremayne
    Edward J. Rielly 208

SISTER FIDELMA BIBLIOGRAPHY 221
ABOUT THE CONTRIBUTORS 223
INDEX 227

Acknowledgments

We gratefully acknowledge those who have contributed essays to this volume. Their insights have been equaled only by their courtesy, support, and patience. Without them, this volume, of course, would have been impossible. Above all, we are grateful to the man who gave us the many stories that inspired it: Peter Tremayne.

Preface

Edward J. Rielly *and* David Robert Wooten

Sister Fidelma, a seventh-century Irish religieuse, lawyer, and crime investigator, sprang into the world of crime fiction in 1993 in a series of short stories by Peter Tremayne, the fiction writing pseudonym of Celtic scholar Peter Berresford Ellis. At once, one critic of the genre perceived them as standing out from the usual historical crime thrillers. British critic and editor Richard Dalby, writing in *Book and Magazine Collector* that year, said: "Sister Fidelma promises to be one of the most intriguing new characters in 1990s detective fiction."

Based on these short stories, Jane Morpeth, the commissioning editor with Headline Book Publishing, London, offered the author a three-book contract to develop the character in full-length novel form.

When the first novel, *Absolution by Murder*, was produced in 1994, the London *Evening Standard* (October 3, 1994) saw Sister Fidelma as a competitor to Ellis Peters' bestselling Brother Cadfael. However, critics soon realized that Sister Fidelma was unique, representing a different culture and a period six centuries before Brother Cadfael. Critical praise for the characters and setting was prolific. Even leading novelists came forward to shower praise on the books—ranging from bestselling historical novelist Morgan Llywelyn to award-winning novelist and film and TV screenwriter Ronan Bennett.

By 2006 the French literary magazine *Livres Hebdo* (May 13, 2006) summed up the reaction to the Sister Fidelma Series as "Fidelmania—The Sister Fidelma Phenomenon."

By then Fidelma had made appearances in eighteen different languages and the author had won various accolades; among them an honorary doctorate of literature from the University of East London (2006), an honorary life membership in the Irish Literary Society (2002), a civic reception and presentation from the mayor and council of Cashel, County Tipperary (2004), and the Prix Historia du Roman Policier Historique (2010). One especially fascinating accolade was that from the London *Guardian* newspaper (February 28, 2009), listing Sister Fidelma as No. 9 in their Top 10 Literary Nuns.

Popular demand caused the establishment of a worldwide fan club — The International Sister Fidelma Society — in 2001, with a regular print journal entitled *The Brehon* issued three times a year, the Society's own website, and an Internet discussion group. The popularity of the series caused the Cashel Arts Festival committee, in Fidelma's "hometown," to launch an additional literary gathering in 2006 — an international meeting of Fidelma enthusiasts known as the Féile Fidelma. This has been held bi-annually since 2006.

So what is it that has caused "Fidelmania"—this Sister Fidelma phenomenon?

The current collection of essays from distinguished academics and literary scholars is an attempt to examine and explain this popular historical detective fiction. Each essayist has chosen areas of his or her own interests regarding the series to examine with widely varied self-explanatory titles. In addition, background essays are included: a biography of the author, the history of The International Sister Fidelma Society, the story of the Féile Fidelma, as well as methods of teaching the stories within a course on detective fiction.

If we, as editors, were to summarize the general conclusions of this volume — conclusions backed by nearly two decades of critical acclaim for the series — we would have to say that readers are primarily fascinated by the historical background of the novels and stories.

Peter Tremayne has presented us with an ancient world about which many of us, outside of certain universities, were unaware: the ancient law system of Ireland in the seventh century, the social system, the sophisticated philosophies and rich culture of that country. The author has presented us with an authentic look at this world using a knowledge gained from ancient sources, the law texts themselves, the annals and chronicles, and the rich textural evidence surviving from the seventh century, backed by recent archaeological finds. It is a world that has became obfuscated by the centuries of colonial destruction in Ireland.

But that alone is not what has attracted the wide readership of these books. After all, under his own name the author has published many serious nonfiction studies, which, while they have also sold well in several languages, have not produced the same degree of readership fascination and loyalty. Among those nonfiction works are *Celtic Women: Women in Celtic Society and Literature* (1995), *Celtic Inheritance* (1987), *The Ancient World of the Celts* (1998), *The Druids* (1994), *A Dictionary of Irish Mythology* (1987), *Celtic Myths and Legends* (1999), *Celt and Saxon* (1993), a *Guide to Early Celtic Remains in Britain* (1991), and many others.

So if it is not merely the revelations of this lost world, what else explains the impact the books and stories have had? The main ingredient has to be a good mystery, cleverly plotted and beautifully written, as the *Irish Independent* (August 21, 2010) describes the series. A leading Italian critic, Luca Crovi, went further when he said that the series "cannot be categorized as just genre fiction. It is literature. We can compare it to Umberto Eco's *The Name of the Rose*" (RAI2, March 21, 2009). Praise, indeed, from Italy.

Therefore, we have a fascinating background, a good, well-written mystery story, but then there is also the character of Fidelma herself and her relationship with the Saxon (beg pardon, Angle, as the author would point out) Brother Eadulf. Again, the books have surprised some readers by reminding them that not even the Roman Church regarded celibacy as essential to religious life until the dictums of Pope Leo IX in the eleventh century. Even then it took several centuries for the followers of Rome to conform to that ruling. But the author reminds us that Fidelma operates in what we now regard as the "Celtic Church," whose early conflict with the ideas coming from Rome were the subject of many councils. Whitby, the background for the first novel, *Absolution by Murder*, is the most famous, but there were many others, like Autun, which followed.

The author's recounting of the complex relationship between Fidelma and Eadulf, their differing personalities, the conflict of Fidelma's ambition, her unhappy affair with the warrior Cian before she meets Eadulf, all seem as eagerly followed as the mysteries themselves. There are Eadulf's concerns, coming from a pagan background and being converted to Christianity as a young man. There are the fascinating differences between Fidelma and Eadulf's two opposing cultures. All these are intriguing aspects for readers to follow. These are real people with real lives in a real environment, and the reader is inexorably caught up with them.

Perhaps the *Huddersfield Daily Examiner* (March 6, 2004) best summed it all up:

> Fidelma's popularity is almost entirely due to Tremayne's storytelling talents. His characters are vividly drawn. His narrative has pace as well as authority. He also tells stories that bristle with intrigue and human emotion. Escapism, yes. Well crafted whodunits, most certainly. But this is also fiction with a ring of real history about it.

With such a phenomenon as the Sister Fidelma Mysteries it has been surprising that she has not yet appeared on film or television, although rights were under contract for some years. Only German radio (WDR5) has actually broadcast a dramatization, and, of course, audio books have been issued in both English and German. As one of the founding members of the Fidelma Society, the late Irish writer Maurice McCann wrote in the 2006 Féile Fidelma program booklet: "It is unique that a series of crime thrillers could achieve such international popularity these days without having, so far, a media involvement in promoting them to the public." Certainly it is a question that regularly comes into the mailbox of the International Sister Fidelma Society — when is there going to be a film or television series?

Apart from anything else, it would be surprising if the Sister Fidelma Mysteries had not also had an influence on crime writing in Ireland. In 2004 the Irish *Sunday Times* observed that crime fiction had been undergoing a boom in Ireland. John Scaggs, then of the University of Limerick, who also contributes to this volume, pointed out, in 2006, "that far from being merely a part of the boom, the Sister Fidelma novels were one of the contributing factors that set it in motion." Apart from giving this boost to general Irish crime fiction, one obvious literary descendant of Sister Fidelma is a female Brehon named Mara. She first appeared in 2007 from the pen of Irish author Cora Harrison in *My Lady Judge*. By 2011 Cora Harrison had published six novels featuring her female sleuth, Mara, who works as a Brehon lawyer located in The Burren, County Clare, in northwest Munster, in the sixteenth century.

But if we were to sum up the entire Sister Fidelma Mysteries series, we could do no better than repeat the line from the *Belfast Telegraph* (September 8, 2001): "This is masterly storytelling from an author who breathes fascinating life into the world he is writing about."

Sister Fidelma:
A Woman for All Seasons

Edward J. Rielly

Sister Fidelma is a seventh-century Irish religieuse who solves complex mysteries through an engaging mixture of imagination, reason, and methodical use of probing interviews. That, however, is only part of the story. Sister Fidelma is also an extraordinarily independent woman who exercises considerable power throughout Ireland and beyond, even into Britain and Rome. She is a dálaigh, or advocate of the law courts of Ireland, empowered to gather evidence and identify what crime has been committed and the perpetrator of the crime. Fidelma therefore is both a religious figure and a highly educated and powerful professional woman whose job calls her far afield from her home base at the abbey of St. Brigid in Kildare.[1]

Peter Tremayne, a pseudonym for the historian Peter Berresford Ellis, makes Sister Fidelma work effectively as the protagonist of his detective stories by bringing into congruence several narrative elements: a vividly drawn heroine who is a complete person, a time and place that permit her not only to function as a detective but to develop her considerable intellectual talents, the author's expert knowledge of the historical period in which he places her, and interesting mysteries that unravel slowly for both Fidelma and the reader.

Sister Fidelma lived at the right time to become the strong and complete person that she is within Tremayne's stories. The Christian Church in seventh-century Ireland was a Celtic Church, straining mightily against the advancing power of Rome that eventually would sweep Ireland also into a religious culture that made women subservient to men, banished women religious from the altar, and, while enforcing Augustine's primacy of the City of God over the City of Man, sought to banish sexuality from the heavenly skies of religious life. The Celtic Church was a product of the Celtic culture that spawned it, and both social and religious traditions offered women the chance to become a Sister Fidelma.[2]

Irish women at the time enjoyed protection under the law that, if not equal to what men enjoyed, was far superior to what women faced elsewhere at the time, or would face in a future Ireland. Tremayne summarizes women's legal protections in a historical introduction to his first Fidelma novel, *Absolution by Murder*, where he states that under the Brehon Laws

> women occupied a unique place. The Irish laws gave more rights and protection to women than any other western law code at that time or since. Women could, and did, aspire to all offices and professions as the coequal with men. They could be political leaders, command their people in battle as warriors, be physicians, local magistrates, poets, artisans, lawyers and judges.... Women were protected by the laws against sexual harassment; against discrimination; from rape; they had the right of divorce on equal terms from their husbands with equitable separation laws and could demand part of their husband's property as a divorce settlement; they had the right to sickness benefits [vi–vii].

The term "Brehon" comes from the word for a judge (*breaitheamh*). The laws also are referred to as the Laws of the Fénechus, the term meaning "free land tillers" (Ellis, *Ancient World of the Celts* 35).

Tremayne notes that "this background ... should be understood to appreciate Fidelma's role in these stories" (vii). Indeed, Fidelma's accomplishments would be wildly unbelievable without this background; while within this historical and cultural setting, she is a great woman in a world that permitted women to be great.[3]

What Tremayne presents in summary fashion in this introduction, he develops in convincing detail, under his actual name, in *Celtic Women: Women in Celtic Society and Literature*. Another, certainly crucial, right relates to education. As Ellis demonstrates, women in Ireland were able to attend the bardic and ecclesiastical schools that prepared them to be judges, advocates (like Fidelma), and scholars. To cite just a few examples, Ulluach, a tenth-century woman poet, was elected "the chief bard in Ireland"; Bríg Briugaid, a judge, is recorded as correcting a mistaken ruling by a male judicial colleague; and Darí, a legal scholar, authored the Cáin Darí laws (116).

Sister Fidelma is justly proud of her education and position, and she is not bashful about stating her qualifications when confronted with a hostile witness or indignant official. In the short story "Hemlock at Vespers," Fidelma encounters Tírechán, the heir-elect of the Uí Failgi clan. When she takes a seat first and motions Tírechán to be seated across the table from her, he becomes outraged. Both she and the narrator quickly explain her role:

> "I am Sister Fidelma," she announced, quietly, before he spoke, for she saw the words forming to burst from his lips. "I am a *dálaigh* of the Brehon Court, qualified to the level of *Anruth*."
>
> Tírechán swallowed the words that had gathered on his lips and a look of

understanding mingled with respect, spread over his features. A *dálaigh*, an advocate of the Brehon Court, especially one qualified to the level of *Anruth*, could meet and be accorded equality with any provincial king or chieftain and could even speak at ease before the High King himself. An *Anruth* was only one degree below the highest professorship of *Ollamh* whose words even a High King would have to obey [13].

Similar situations occur in other stories, where Sister Fidelma presents her credentials, usually to a reaction of respect mingled with surprise at one still in her twenties having achieved such a high status. Her fame is such, however, that sometimes the presentation of credentials is done by someone else, as in *Absolution by Murder*, when Colmán, the Bishop of Lindisfarne, introduces her to Abbess Hilda of Streoneshalh not only by her title but as one who "was able to solve a mystery oppressing the High King of Tara" (44–45). Later in the story, after Fidelma's own Abbess of Kildare, Étain, has been murdered, she meets the Northumbrian king, Oswy, who has already learned of Fidelma's accomplishments. The king's task for Fidelma, of course, is to solve the murder.

Fidelma's fame spreads quickly and widely. In *Behold a Pale Horse* (as of this writing the most recent of the Fidelma novels but depicting action set chronologically in A.D. 664 after Fildema's exploits in Rome that are recounted in the second novel, *Shroud for the Archbishop*), Fidelma saves Magister Ado from an attack on the streets of Genua (Genoa). She accompanies Ado back to his residence, where Sister Gisa recognizes her name:

> "It was a week ago, just before we left the abbey to come to meet you [Ado], when one of our brethren returned with gossip from Rome. He spoke of a Sister Fidelma from a place called Cashel in Hibernia. She had solved a mystery of the murder of a Saxon bishop which had taken place. Even the Holy Father praised her" [9].

Arriving later at the abbey of Bobium, Fidelma finds that Abbot Servillius also has heard of her (69).

When Fidelma is especially provoked by a show of disrespect, or when she finds herself in a particularly dangerous situation, she may also announce her family background. Fidelma is the daughter of Failbe Fland, a former king of Cashel, the seat of Muman, one of the five kingdoms of seventh-century Ireland, and sister to Colgú, the future — and in later novels current — king of Muman. Faced with a lack of courtesy from Salbach, one of the villains in the novel *Suffer Little Children*, which Fidelma interprets to be "an insult to her sex," she reacts quickly:

> "I am Fidelma of the Eóganacht of Cashel, sister to Colgú, heir-apparent of Muman," she replied with a tone of steel. "I am qualified in law to the level of *anruth*" [130].

Attending dinner in the abbey of Lios Mór in *The Chalice of Blood*, set in 670, Fidelma dresses not as a religieuse but as a Muman princess, donning, in addition to other items, an ornate blue satin gown, a red satin cape edged with fur, bracelets, a band of gem-embedded silver in her hair, and around her neck a golden torc "which proclaimed not only her royal position but that she was of the élite Nasc Niadh of Muman, the bodyguards of the Eóghanacht" (183–84). Her appearance elicits a sharp outcry from Brother Lugna, the steward, labeling her attire as sacrilegious. She responds:

> "Do you insult the Eóghanacht? You have been too long in Rome, Brother Lugna. You are now in the kingdom of Muman and in the presence of an Eóghanacht princess.... I am Fidelma of Cashel," she went on in the haughty manner that Eadulf knew she could assume at will. "I am sister to Colgú, King of Muman. Have I not been requested to come to this place as the guest of your abbot, the Abbot Iarnla, who presides over this abbey and this *refectorium*? Am I not an honored guest in this abbey ... an abbey that, I must remind you, is part of my brother's kingdom?" [185–86].

That Sister Fidelma is a professional woman in an age that most people do not associate with professional women is one of the driving forces behind the Fidelma stories. The protagonist's popularity and success with readers, however, depends on both halves of the phrase "professional woman." Her role permits the movement from place to place and the accessibility to people and locations without which the stories could not exist. At the same time, however, she also is a fully realized woman whose completeness offers almost unlimited potential for plot complications and invites ever greater reader identification with her.

Along with being a highly educated and skilled dálaigh of the courts who studied law for eight years at the bardic school of Morann of Tara, Fidelma is a strong and assertive individual who is quick to defend the rights of women. She is horrified to learn in *Shroud for the Archbishop* that Saxon kingdoms have no laws against rape and proudly delineates legal protections accorded women in Ireland:

> "Not only does our law of the *Fenechus* protect all women from rape by force but even if a drunken woman is made to have intercourse then the offence is as serious. Our law protects all women. If a man dare kiss, or even touch a woman against her will, by the law of the *Fenechus* he can be fined two hundred and forty silver screpall" [135].

When Fidelma is concerned that Sister Necht, in *Suffer Little Children*, is being mistreated by the chief physician of the abbey of Ros Ailithir, Fidelma reminds her:

> "But no one, especially no woman, should put up with verbal abuse from others. The *Bretha Nemed* [an Irish law text] makes it an offence in law for

a woman to be harassed and especially to be verbally assaulted.... No woman need stand by and be abused by anyone," went on Fidelma. "And the abuse need not be a physical assault but if a person mocks a woman, criticises their appearance, draws attention to any physical blemish or wrongfully accuses them of things that are not true, then they have redress under the law" [233].

Fidelma's willingness to protect herself and others extends to physical defense. Her long list of abilities becomes even longer in *Shroud for the Archbishop* when she is attacked by an angry woman and has to defend herself by utilizing a means of defense called troid-sciathaigid, or battle through defense. As a religieuse, she does not carry weapons but has prepared herself nonetheless to meet physical dangers as effectively as possible. So she "reached out, caught the flailing arms and heaved her assailant into the air, over her hip and sent her cannoning into the wall on the other side of the room" (240). Fidelma almost daily practices this ancient form of self-defense, which helps to save her life in *Suffer Little Children*. Facing several armed men prepared to kill her and her companion, Cass, Fidelma is able to act instantly when Cass yells for her to flee the building. She races up the stairs and drops safely from the window ledge to the ground below (280).

Fidelma's ability at hand-to-hand combat also comes into play in the aforementioned rescue of Magister Ado in *Behold a Pale Horse* when she gets the better of a cudgel-wielding adversary. A sudden crouch sends him hurtling over her body (4).

This remarkably able religieuse is also quite attractive. Each story describes her beauty in words similar to those used in the story "Murder in Repose":

> Sister Fidelma, tall, green-eyed, stood before the Brehon with hands folded demurely in front of her. Her robes and hood, from under which wisps of rebellious red hair stuck out, scarcely disguised her youthfulness nor her feminine attractiveness [337–38].

Indeed, those same wisps of red hair continue to protrude from her hood in a number of stories, so that one wonders if that small portion of dishabille may be intentional on the young woman's part (*Absolution* 18, *Shroud* 9). Red hair, in fact, runs in the family: "Colgú ... ran a hand through his crop of red hair and gazed at his sister with a troubled expression" (*Chalice* 29). Sometimes, although the stray hair often remains, other details accrue to the basic description given above. Fidelma also possesses a "bubbling vitality and sense of humour" ("Hemlock" 1); she has a broad forehead (considered most beautiful in the Middle Ages) and "a faint hint of freckles" (*Suffer* 1); her figure is "well-proportioned" and her eyes, charged with emotion, seem to alternate between blue and green (*Subtle* 15–16).

Sister Fidelma's status as a complete woman includes attention to her sexuality. Fidelma admits to being sexually experienced in *Shroud for the Archbishop*, where she reflects on her life at twenty-eight, an "age when she considered herself long past the age for matrimony..." (288). She remembers, with some bitterness, an affair she had experienced with a young chieftain during her law studies at Morann's school. The affair, she recalls, "was no more than physical and the affair was passionate and intense" (288). The man had left Fidelma for another woman, and she "had never allowed herself to get close to a man again," although she had not refused "passing affairs" after that. The life of the ascetics, "who denied themselves such natural pleasures," was not for Fidelma (289).

That earlier lover shows up again in *Act of Mercy*, where Cian's capacity for seduction and betrayal leads to murder. Nonetheless, Fidelma reflects at the end of the novel that she is glad to have seen Cian once more, this time "in the maturity of her experiences," so that she could exorcise any vestiges of attachment through a final realization of just how immoral he really was. "Cian had no hold on her any longer, and she felt no sense of loss in that respect — just an enormous weight falling from her shoulders" (268).

Of great importance to Fidelma, though, is a young Saxon monk named Eadulf, who had been ordered by Oswy to collaborate with Fidelma in solving the murders in *Absolution by Murder*; and who had journeyed to Rome, the setting for *Shroud for the Archbishop*, shortly before Fidelma arrives there to present the new Rule of the Sisters of Brigid to the Pope. Eadulf becomes Fidelma's love interest, although the relationship maintains a subtle tension throughout the early stories. At the conclusion of *Absolution by Murder*, for example, Fidelma receives her mission to Rome with emotions that she does not fully permit herself to comprehend, although they are easily understood by readers who remember Eadulf earlier receiving his own Roman assignment and inviting Fidelma to accompany him, and the obvious pleasure she felt in thinking about accepting his invitation. So, with the fortuitous message from the Archbishop of Armagh,

> Suddenly Sister Fidelma found herself hurrying along the vaulted cloisters of the abbey back to the refectory. She did not know why her heart was beating more rapidly or what made the day so suddenly pleasant and the future full of excitement [272].

Fildema's feelings for Eadulf lead to the actions recounted in *Act of Mercy* and, ironically, to her reunion with Cian. Torn between her growing passion for Eadulf and her commitment to the religious life and needing an opportunity to consider her future, she embarks on a pilgrimage by ship to the Shrine of St. James in Spain, the voyage on which she encounters Cian. In the following novel, *Our Lady of Darkness*, she hurries her return from that pilgrimage on hearing that Eadulf has been arrested for murder in Laigin, one of the provincial kingdoms of seventh-century Ireland. She succeeds in her mission to save her more-than-friend, of course, and at the conclusion of the adventure accepts his request that she accompany him to Canterbury. At the conclusion of the still later *Smoke in the Wind*, the relationship moves forward yet another step, but this time into greater uncertainty. Fidelma and Eadulf participate in a ritual traditionally carried out on the eve of All Hallows Day: the eating of a piece of speckled cake. A ring is hidden in one piece, a hazel nut in another. According to the ritual, the person who receives the ring is destined to be married; the recipient of the hazel nut, however, will remain unwed. Eadulf smiles with the happy realization that he has received the ring before learning that Fidelma has the hazel nut. Her reaction demonstrates that she has much yet to puzzle out regarding the relationship: "Her features were formed in a smile and so Eadulf did not observe the serious look in her eyes" (267).

As the novels progress, Fidelma and Eadulf decide to marry, initially embarking on a sort of transitional marriage period, acceptable at the time, of living together for a year and a day before finalizing their marriage vows. They subsequently complete that trial period and their vows. In addition, they have a son, Alchú, who has reached the age of three by the time that the action chronicled in *The Chalice of Blood* occurs. Prior to then, readers had been following the progression of Fidelma and Eadulf's relationship through Fidelma becoming a mother in *Badger's Moon*, their son missing in *The Leper's Bell*, the permanent marriage temporarily delayed by a murder in *A Prayer for the Damned*, and wife and husband barely escaping death when their ship is captured by pirates in *The Dove of Death*.

Such a relationship between a religious sister and monk in most centuries and places would appear improbable and, were it to occur, decidedly sinful, but not in seventh-century Ireland. Here is another example of the author's successful union of time, place, and protagonist. Although many readers may assume that the love interest is introduced merely for commercial motives, this aspect of the story, like almost everything else in the Fidelma narratives, is historically credible. Celibacy, for members of religious orders in Celtic Ireland, was optional, even somewhat against the cultural grain, with men and women within orders often marrying. Some of the great religious houses of the time admitted both men and women, among them Fidelma's abbey of St. Brigid at Kildare. Although Rome was attempting to discourage clerical marriages, it had not yet forbade them. A general prohibition regarding marriage for religious would not be enforced until the eleventh-century papacy of Leo IX.[4]

Sister Fidelma, a historically credible early medieval religieuse, also appeals to readers because of her modernity, which is to say that Tremayne highlights ways in which the seventh and twenty-first centuries can harmonize, including impressive educational and professional achievements by women. Even Fidelma's experiences in love parallel those of large numbers of modern women, although they obviously do not coincide with typical experiences of modern nuns, who are expected to remain celibate.

Fidelma, however, for all her professional and worldly encounters, does not lose sight of her religious calling, although to be a religieuse in Celtic Ireland, as has been stated above, was (and remains) significantly different from living a vocation elsewhere and at other times. Even in spiritual matters, Fidelma appears as much twenty-first century as seventh, as when she reacts to a tour of supposed relics at the Vatican in *Shroud for the Archbishop*. A proud Roman Vatican guard, Licinius, rhapsodizes over the prized holdings, unaware of Fidelma's skepticism:

> "In there is a lock of the Virgin Mary's hair and a piece of her petticoat. That is a robe of Jesus sprinkled with his blood. That phial there has drops of his blood in it and in the other is some of the water which flowed from the wound in his side."
>
> Fidelma cast a distrustful glance at them.
>
> "And that old piece of sponge?" She nodded to an opened reliquary whose only content seemed a disintegrating piece of fibrous material which Fidelma identified as porous aquatic growth used for swabbing liquids.
>
> "The very sponge which was soaked in vinegar and given to Him on the cross," replied Licinius reverently. "And here is the table at which our Saviour ate the last supper...."
>
> Fidelma smiled cynically [251].

Fidelma's spirituality, however, is not built on the gullible sands of relic collecting. Hers is more profound and includes spiritual practices that also contribute to the historical milieu of the stories. Meditation is one such practice. Taking a break from her pursuit of several murders, she retreats into dercad, a meditative art practiced by the Druids long before Christians came to Ireland. This search for inner peace, or sitcháin, was supported by periodic visits to a sweat house constructed of stones. After an appointed time perspiring in this hut, the individual would leave and plunge into a pool of icy water, a practice that Fidelma had practiced since beginning her education (*Shroud* 214, *Suffer* 3).

Another spiritual ritual that Fidelma shares with her age is that of taking a soul-friend, or anamchara, a person not necessarily of the same sex who serves as a lifelong confidant and spiritual guide. Fidelma had chosen a childhood girlfriend, Liadin of the Uí Dróna (*Suffer* 107–08). The soul-friend also performed the role of hearing one's sins, a type of confession that influenced the Catholic Church as it gradually came to substitute personal confession to a priest for the earlier common practice of public confessions usually made just once during a person's lifetime. Thomas Cahill, in *How the Irish Saved Civilization*, offers the following provocative observation regarding private confession and the Celtic church:

> It is a shame that private confession is one of the few Irish innovations that passed into the universal church. How different might Catholicism be today if it had taken over the easy Irish sympathy between churchmen and laymen and the easy Irish attitudes toward diversity, authority, the role of women, and the relative unimportance of sexual mores [178].

All of the characteristics of the Celtic church that Cahill mentions and laments not finding in the modern church are both reflected by, and supportive of, Fidelma's roles and activities within Peter Tremayne's accounts of her detective work.

Fidelma, even regarding her basic roles — as religieuse, dálaigh, wife, mother, sister to her king — is far from a static character. As she and Eadulf sail for home at the conclusion of *The Dove of Death*, she is questioning her various relationships and roles. Eadulf also is engaging in serious self-reflection. He wants a more stable and conventional life, and worries that, given their many travels, their son barely knows them. Fidelma meanwhile is seriously questioning her role as a religieuse, acknowledging to herself that she "was no religious at heart" (368). However, she is far from desiring the settled, sedentary life that Eadulf envisions for them in the small gender-mixed Abbey of the Blessed Ruan.

Between the ending of that novel and the opening of the next, *The Chalice of Blood*, Fidelma and Eadulf have taken divergent paths in order to contemplate their futures. Eadulf has gone to the abbey north of Cashel for a period of discernment, and Fidelma is rethinking her future at Cashel.

One path seems clear to Fidelma. She has determined, as she tells Ségdae, Abbot of Imleach and Chief Bishop of Muman, "'I have come to you to announce my intention of withdrawing from the religieuse and to pursue my future as a layer unencumbered by other interests'" (*Chalice* 26). She also aspires to become Chief Brehon of the kingdom, an aspiration she shares with her brother as she further clarifies her choice of "'spreading the concept of truth and justice under the law'" rather than spreading the Christian faith (31).

Less clear in her own mind is her role as a mother. She feels guilty over what she now recognizes as resentment toward Alchú when he was born and her sense of freedom on leaving her son behind to face professional challenges. She also recalls feelings of depression after his birth, a response now known as postpartum depression (39).

Fidelma also is conflicted regarding her feelings for Eadulf in relation to her legal vocation. That she remains very fond of him is clear. She also recognizes that she has hurt him with caustic comments and bursts of anger but at the same time feels hurt by what she considers his failure fully to appreciate her deep commitment to the law (37–39). In a lengthy discussion in Chapter Nine, Fidelma and Eadulf share their feelings about these matters with each other and also consider the issue of equality. Eadulf expresses a sense of being subordinate, but Fidelma assures him that both she and her brother have great respect for him. They come to no definitive resolution of any of these matters, although Fidelma, readers learn, has come to a decision by the end of the novel, albeit one not yet shared with her husband or the reader. During this personal exchange between Fidelma and Eadulf, she states the choice that confronts her:

> "I do not want to lose you. You will forever be my soul mate, my *anam chara*, and if you go, my soul will die. But if I am constrained from doing what I need to do in life to be fully alive, my heart will die. So what is my choice?" [176].

Eadulf, who had been brought back to Cashel by Colgú to help Fidelma investigate a death at the abbey of Lios Mór — also an attempt by the king to reconcile his sister and brother-in-law — is likewise left with his own decisions to make.

Some readers may find Fidelma in *The Chalice of Blood* less likable than in earlier novels, even selfish, perhaps far from an exemplary parent. As a literary character, however, she may be better than ever: more fully realized, more compellingly developed as a multifaceted individual, more increasingly conflicted by a variety of goals, fears, desires, and ambitions. In other words, she seems more real than ever.

As compelling as Tremayne's depiction of Sister Fidelma proves to be, the stories also owe a great deal to the historical events surrounding her detective efforts. The historical environment is part of the charm of the narratives, and it is an integral part of the story itself, in both setting and plot. All of the stories combine historical verisimilitude through precise details and actual locales, buildings, and people. *Absolution by Murder*, the first Fidelma novel, may pose the most compelling historical setting of all the Fidelma stories. Ironically, the novel is not set in Ireland, although Irish affairs, especially those of the Celtic church, are at the heart of the situation.

The event that summons Fidelma to England is the Synod of Whitby, called by Oswy, King of Northumbria, in 664 to settle doctrinal disputes between the Roman and Celtic churches. Among the issues to be addressed at this important gathering of church leaders are the dating of Easter and the type of tonsure to be worn by monks.[5] Oswy had taken refuge on the island of Iona prior to his brother coming to the throne and had been strongly influenced by the Celtic churchmen who used Iona as a base from which to launch their missionary work, including their successful efforts to convert

Northumbria. Despite this background, and apparently for political as much as religious reasons, Oswy finds for the Roman positions.[6]

During the synod, several murders occur in the novel. Fidelma, in attendance as a member of the Celtic contingent, is asked by Oswy to solve the mysteries in partnership with Eadulf. From a historical standpoint, there is no evidence that the murders are anything but fictional, but much else in the novel conforms precisely to historical fact. In addition to Oswy, actual historical personages populate the novel. Among them is Hilda, Abbess of the abbey of Streoneshalh at Whitby, where the synod is held. Hilda, although Anglo-Saxon, was a protégé of the great Irish monk, Aidan of Lindisfarne, and was a strong supporter of Celtic practices. Her abbey, like that of Brigid at Kildare, was a double house for both men and women. The monastic school at her abbey was renowned for producing scholars, and students of literature recognize Streoneshalh as the site of England's first identifiable poet, Caedmon (Ellis, *Celtic Women*, 149–50; Sellner 19–20).

Also in attendance, among the many historical figures who populate the novel, are Colman, Bishop of Northumbria, Abbot of Lindisfarne, and a leader of the Celtic delegation; Deusdedit, the first native-born Archbishop of Canterbury; and Brother Wighard, designated by the Saxons as the successor to Deusdedit. Colman, consistent with fact, resigns his position after the verdict goes against him and returns to his native Ireland (Blair, *World of Bede* 101). Deusdedit dies of the Yellow Plague, which struck down as many as one-half of the Irish population as well as large numbers in England. The plague is usually noted as having developed shortly after the Synod, so the archbishop's death may have occurred after the Synod, rather than during it as in the novel. The Venerable Bede, for example, seems to place the Synod prior to the outbreak of disease but is not entirely clear on the chronology of those events and Deusdedit's death (185–95, 203). The *Anglo-Saxon Chronicle*, strangely enough, records the plague and Deusdedit's death in 664 but entirely ignores the important Synod of Whitby (34–35). Although Tremayne may take some liberties with Deusdedit's death, his fictional treatment is close enough to historical fact to be quite credible.

The role of Wighard becomes more important in the subsequent novel, *Shroud for the Archbishop*. Bede records the situation following Deusdedit's death:

> With the choice and approval of the holy Church of the English, the two kings [Oswy of Northumbria and Egbert of Kent] accepted the priest Wighard, one of Archbishop Deusdedit's clergy, a good man well fitted to be a bishop, and sent him to Rome to be consecrated bishop, so that, when he had received the rank of Archbishop, he could consecrate Catholic bishops for the churches of the English throughout Britain. Wighard arrived in Rome, but died before he could be consecrated... [198].

Bede's account of Wighard is consistently laudatory, and, of course, there is no mention of scandal or murder involving the Archbishop-designate. Bede says that he died of a plague (203), and that Pope Vitalian named Theodore Archbishop of Canterbury after Hadrian, an African, declined appointment (203–04). The novel includes the facts just mentioned but substitutes a different death for Wighard — murder — and a personal background for the would-be archbishop worthy of murder.

The use of a detailed historical milieu for the fictional exploits of Sister Fidelma continues throughout the stories so that any comprehensive account of the real historical details would be far beyond the scope of this examination of the stories. A few more examples, however, may be useful. As Sister Fidelma pursues the string of murders that follow the death of Wighard, she learns much about Rome from the young Vatican guard, Licinius, who temporarily becomes both her guide and assistant. Fidelma notes that many of the buildings are "curiously scarred as if by war" (100). Licinius responds by telling how Emperor Constans, earlier in the same year, had arrived with a large army for a state visit. After being greeted warmly by Vitalian, Constans was appropriately feasted and later went to the basilica of St. Maria Maggiore to pray:

> "While the Emperor was praying, his soldiers, at his order, began to strip the buildings of Rome of all metal parts; the bronze tiles, clamps and ties with which they were bonded; the great statues and artifacts which had stood since the days of the great Roman Republic. Never had there been such savagery which has reduced the city to the pitiful state you see today" [102].

In answer to Fidelma's questions regarding the emperor's purpose, Licinius explains that Constans wanted the metal to melt down for weapons. Ironically, it did him no good, for Arabian raiders intercepted the Roman ships carrying the confiscated materials and took all of it (102–03). Eamon Duffy tells the same story in his *Saints and Sinners: A History of the Popes* and recalls the satisfaction with which the author of the important history of the papacy, *Liber Pontificalis*, recorded that the emperor was murdered in his bath just a few years later (61).

The Constans story has nothing directly to do with the mysteries that Fidelma solves, but it has much to do, like so many other historical details, with creating a historically realistic environment for Fidelma and her readers. If at times Tremayne digresses from the requirements of the plot, as in this case, the reader is the beneficiary of his digressions. Another example of historical verisimilitude, this one more firmly rooted within plot, occurs in *Suffer Little Children*. Fidelma, seeking information needed to unravel one of her mysteries, journeys to the monastery of Fínán atop the steep cliffs of the island of Sceilig Mhichil some eight miles off the Southwestern coast of Ireland.

The description is detailed and vivid: the windswept, torturous climb up the rock; the collection of beehive huts; the birds that shared the heights with a group of hardy and pious monks (213–18). As Geoffrey Moorhouse points out, little is known of the history of this monastery, which, despite its most rugged of settings endured for about seven hundred years until its final abbot died in 1400 (195–97). The setting remains, like so many locations in Ireland, a testimony to the religious zeal that led monks to seek out the least habitable locales to worship their God.

Followers of Sister Fidelma find much more of the distant but enticing world of seventh-century Ireland: the libraries with their manuscript books cradled in hanging leather satchels ("Hemlock" 6; *Suffer* 13, 147–48); the ancient Ogham writing system still visible on stones and monuments in the Irish countryside over 1300 years later (*Shroud* 191–92; *Suffer* 84, 148; *Subtle* 10, 62); the water-clock, or clepsydra, by which members of religious communities attempted to organize their lives for God (*Absolution* 102; *Subtle* 101–02); remarkably modern bathing practices that were both cleansing custom and religious ritual (*Absolution* 59; *Subtle* 53–54); the gradual replacement of wooden monastic buildings with stone structures (*Chalice* 96–97); and a multitude of other aspects of Irish life in Fidelma's time.

Sister Fidelma is a woman of the seventh century and, in some major ways already adumbrated, a woman of the twenty-first century. Her character traits — her intellectual gifts, her determination, her refusal to let anyone usurp her proper role — as well as the historical events and the myriad of historical details surrounding her endeavors combine to make Sister Fidelma one of the most fascinating and engaging detectives currently involved in the business of solving crimes. She appears within a historical time and place that permit her to become what she is, yet she transcends the world of Celtic Christianity and seventh-century Irish life to become, as all great fictional characters, even in their historical credibility, must become — a person for all seasons.

Notes

1. Peter Berresford Ellis writes the Fidelma stories under the pseudonym Peter Tremayne. Under his real name he discusses an historical Fidelma who may well be at least a partial model for his fictional heroine: "Ethne was, of course, one of the two daughters of the Irish High King Laohhaire (or Loéguire macNéill, A.D. 428–C. 463). His other daughter was Fidelma. They had both been educated (fostered) by the Druids Caplait and Mael and therefore, with their religious background, were probably more interested than most in what Patrick had to say. The story of their conversion appears in Bishop Tirechán's seventh-century *Life of Patrick*, preserved in the *Book of Armagh*, compiled by Feardomhnach in about A.D. 807. Feardomhnach says that the two sisters had come to Clébac, near Tulsk, Co. Roscommon, 'as is the women's custom, to wash in the morning.' Ethne and Fidelma were converted, after their discourse with Patrick..." (*Celtic Women* 143).

2. While emphasizing the opportunities and freedoms accorded women within the

Celtic church, both Ellis (147) and Sellner (71–72) record, for example, that Brigid, the founder of the abbey to which Fidelma belongs, was consecrated a bishop. Ellis also considers her sexual relationships (148–49).

3. For a readable and informative overview of early Irish history, including Irish law and religion, see the early chapters in Moody and Martin. Also see Chadwick, chapter 7, on Celtic Christianity (190–223).

4. See Ellis, chapter 6, "Women in the Celtic Church" (142–71) for a discussion of the sexual freedom acceptable for religious in Celtic Ireland. Sellner also examines the "double houses" that admitted both men and women (18–20).

5. Useful discussions of the Synod of Whitby and its aftermath, and of differences between Celtic and Roman Christianity, include Edwards 53–62; Blair, *Roman Britain and Early England* 222–37; and Deanesly 29–54.

6. See Adomnán's *Life of St. Columba* for an extensive account of Columba and his founding of the monastery on Iona. Fidelma would have been a contemporary of Adomnán; the latter became abbot of Iona about fifteen years after the Synod of Whitby.

Works Cited

Adomnán. *Life of St. Columba.* Trans. Richard Sharpe. New York: Penguin, 1995.

The Anglo-Saxon Chronicle. Trans. G. N. Garmonsway. 2d ed. 1972. London: Dent, 1982.

Bede. *A History of the English Church and People.* Trans. Leo Sherley-Price and the Rev. R. E. Latham. New York: Penguin, 1968.

Blair, Peter Hunter. *Roman Britain and Early England 55 B.C.–A.D. 871.* 1963. New York: Norton, 1966.

_____. *The World of Bede.* London: Secker & Warburg, 1970.

Breatnach, Liam. "Lawyers in Early Ireland." *Brehons, Sergeants and Attorneys: Studies in the History of the Irish Legal Profession.* Ed. Daire Hogan and W. N. Osborough. Blackrock, Co. Dublin: Irish Academic Press in association with Irish Legal History Society, 1990. 1–13.

Cahill, Thomas. *How the Irish Saved Civilization.* New York: Doubleday, 1995.

Carr-Gomm, Philip. *The Elements of The Druid Tradition.* 1991. Boston: Element, 1999.

Chadwick, Nora. *The Celts.* Rev. ed. New York: Penguin, 1997.

Deanesly, Margaret. *A History of the Medieval Church 590–1500.* 1925. New York: Routledge, 1994.

De Breffny, Brian, and George Mott. *The Churches and Abbeys of Ireland.* New York: Norton, 1976.

Duffy, Eamon. *Saints & Sinners: A History of the Popes.* New Haven: Yale University Press, 1997.

Edwards, David L. *Christian England: Its Story to the Reformation.* 1980. Grand Rapids: William B. Eerdmans, 1983.

Ellis, Peter Berresford. *The Ancient World of the Celts.* 1998. New York: Barnes and Noble, 1999.

_____. *Celtic Women: Women in Celtic Society and Literature.* Grand Rapids: William B. Eerdmans, 1995.

Ginnell, Laurence. *The Brehon Laws: A Legal Handbook.* 1894. Littleton, CO: Fred B. Rothman, 1993.

Hughes, Kathleen. *Early Christian Ireland: Introduction to the Sources.* Ithaca: Cornell University Press, 1972.

_____, and Ann Hamlin. *Celtic Monasticism: The Modern Traveler to the Early Irish Church.* 1977. New York: Seabury, 1981.

Joyce, Timothy J. *Celtic Christianity: A Sacred Tradition, A Vision of Hope.* Maryknoll, NY: Orbis, 1998.

Kelly, Fergus. *A Guide to Early Irish Law*. Dublin: Dublin Institute for Advanced Studies, 1988.
Markale, Jean. *Women of the Celts*. 1972. Trans. A. Mygind, C. Hauch, and P. Henry. Rochester, VT: Inner Traditions International, 1986.
Matthews, Caitlin. *The Elements of The Celtic Tradition*. 1991. Boston: Element, 1999.
McNeill, John T. *The Celtic Churches: A History, A.D. 200–1200*. Chicago: University of Chicago Press, 1974.
Moody, T. W., and F. X. Martin, eds. *The Course of Irish History*. Rev. ed. Niwot, CO: Roberts Rinehart, 1994.
Moorhouse, Geoffrey. *Sun Dancing: A Vision of Medieval Ireland*. New York: Harcourt, 1997.
Otway-Ruthven, A. J. *A History of Medieval Ireland*. 2d ed. New York: St. Martin's, 1980.
Ryan, John. *Irish Monasticism: Origins and Early Development*. 1931. Ithaca: Cornell University Press, 1972.
Sellner, Edward C. *Wisdom of the Celtic Saints*. Notre Dame: Ave Maria, 1993.
Tremayne, Peter. *Absolution by Murder*. 1994. New York: Penguin, 1997.
_____. *Act of Mercy*. 1999. New York: St. Martin's Minotaur, 2001.
_____. *Badger's Moon*. 2003. New York: St. Martin's Minotaur, 2005.
_____. *Behold a Pale Horse*. London: Headline, 2011.
_____. *The Chalice of Blood*. 2010. London: Headline, 2011.
_____. *The Dove of Death*. 2009. New York: Minotaur Books, 2010.
_____. *The Haunted Abbot*. 2002. New York: St. Martin's Minotaur, 2004.
_____. "Hemlock at Vespers." *Murder Most Irish*. Ed. Ed Gorman, et al. New York: Barnes & Noble, 1996. 1–27.
_____. *The Leper's Bell*. 2004. New York: St. Martin's Minotaur, 2006.
_____. *The Monk Who Vanished*. London: Headline, 1999.
_____. "Murder in Repose." *Great Irish Detective Stories*. Ed. Peter Haining. New York: Barnes & Noble, 1993. 337–58.
_____. *Our Lady of Darkness*. London: Headline, 2000.
_____. *A Prayer for the Damned*. 2006. New York: St. Martin's Minotaur, 2007.
_____. *Shroud for the Archbishop*. London: Headline, 1995.
_____. *Smoke in the Wind*. 2001. New York: St. Martin's Minotaur, 2003.
_____. *The Spider's Web*. New York: St. Martin's, 1997.
_____. *The Subtle Serpent*. London: Headline, 1996.
_____. *Suffer Little Children*. 1995. London: Headline, 1996.
_____. *Valley of the Shadow*. London: Headline, 1998.

Who Is Peter Tremayne?

David Robert Wooten

Peter Tremayne was actually "born" on Friday, November 12, 1976. That was the date of the first published use of the pseudonym for a book review in the weekly London-based newspaper *The Catholic Herald*. It was to become the fiction writing name of Peter Berresford Ellis.

The editor had suggested to Peter, who had written feature articles and reviewed for the newspaper, that he needed a new name to write some special reviews. The editor wanted him to review some books by the writer Ellis Peters. That year she had published a book entitled *Never Pick Up Hitch-hikers!* Ellis Peters was, in fact, the pseudonym of Edith Pargeter (1913–1995). The editor felt that readers might think that Ellis Peters was reviewing her own book if it appeared under Peter's own name. As it turned out, Peter, using his new Tremayne persona, did not review an Ellis Peters book until he reviewed the first Brother Cadfael novel for the newspaper in 1977. This was *A Morbid Taste for Bones*. The story is told by Peter in *Past Poisons: An Ellis Peters Memorial Anthology of Historical Crime*, edited by Maxim Jakubowski (Headline, 1998).

August 1977 marked the first appearance of a book under the Peter Tremayne pseudonym.

What made Peter Berresford Ellis choose Tremayne as a pseudonym? Peter had lived in St. Ives, Cornwall, in the late 1960s, and he recalled a little hamlet called Tremayne ("the place of stone" in the Cornish language), near Newbridge in West Penwith. There he had fond memories of Enzo's Restaurant, which he regarded as the best Italian restaurant in all Cornwall.

At the time of this writing (spring 2012), Peter Tremayne has published 51 books, 22 of which are Sister Fidelma stories. Of his 96 short stories, 34 are Sister Fidelma tales. Peter has also published 8 novels as "Peter MacAlan," and 34 nonfiction titles under his own name. As for pamphlets, papers, and signed articles, it would probably take a bibliographer many years to track them all down.

When the word "prolific" has been used to describe his work, Peter has always been disarming about his output. "'Prolific' applies to the romance writer Kathleen Lindsay (1903–1973), who produced 904 books under eleven pseudonyms," he responds. "And even if limited to mystery writers, there is John Creasey (1908–1973), with 564 published titles; Georges Simenon (1903–1989), claimed as producing 500 titles, with 75 novels and 28 short stories featuring his famous sleuth Commissioner Maigret; while Nigel Morland (1905–1986) had 300 titles published. Compared to writers like those, my output is meager."

What cannot be argued is the eclectic range of Peter's work. Historian, literary biographer, novelist, and short story writer, he is also proud to be called a journalist. But in addition, he is a contributor of many scholastic studies, papers, and articles in the area of Celtic Studies in which he has a First Class Honours Degree and a Master's Degree. His work has caused him to be elected by his peers as a Fellow of the Royal Historical Society and as a Fellow of the Royal Society of Antiquaries of Ireland. He was also awarded a Doctor of Literature (*honoris causa*) by the University of East London in recognition of his work.

So who is Peter Tremayne? First we have to seek out Peter Berresford Ellis.

Peter Berresford Ellis was born on March 10, 1943, in Coventry, Warwickshire, England. His father was an Irish journalist who had settled in England in the 1920s, and his mother was from an old, established family in Sussex, England.

The Ellis family had first appeared in historical record in Cork in the thirteenth century, when documents refer to Richard, son of David Elys, as holder of the lands of Elystoun (later Ballyellis) in North County Cork. They were originally Breton merchants. Peter's father started his career on *The Examiner* in Cork before eventually arriving in London's Fleet Street, then the center of the newspaper world in England, as a crime reporter. At the time of Peter's birth, his father was a freelance journalist also doing part-time volunteer war work as an armaments inspector.

Peter's mother had been the wardrobe mistress in London's West End theatre-land, in a repertory company run by Matheson Lang, a famous actor-manager and film actor. His mother's family, the Randells, can trace a direct line from the sixteenth century, and a broken one to the thirteenth century, all in the same area of mid–Sussex. They were mainly involved in small business enterprises. Peter's mother wrote an autobiography, *Daisy: Growing up in a Sussex Village 1897–1919*, charting her first twenty-one years of life. It was published posthumously, in 2003, after being kept in a Sussex library. She died in 1991. Her mother had also descended from a Breton family. Peter has frequently said: "With uncles and aunts who were Irish, Welsh, Breton, and Scottish, it was obvious that I would develop an interest in matters Celtic."

At the end of World War II the family moved to Sussex so that Peter's father could be near London's publishing world again. Peter was the youngest of six siblings, three sisters and three brothers. He grew up primarily in the Sussex countryside, but also surrounded by books. The family library was immense, he has told me. When Peter left college, he decided to follow his father into journalism, becoming a trainee reporter on an English south coast weekly newspaper — the *Brighton and Hove Herald*. However, he had always been fascinated by history, particularly Celtic history. A friend of Peter's father was the well-known surgeon and archaeologist Eliot Cecil Curwen (1895–1967), author of such works as *Archaeology of Sussex* (1937), who was impressed by Peter's schoolwork and showed it to Ivan D. Margary (1896–1976), the leading authority on Roman-British roads. Both distinguished experts proposed Peter for membership in both the Sussex Archaeological Society and Sussex Archaeological Trust when he was only sixteen. Peter used to go on "digs" when the opportunity occurred, especially those involving Celtic (Iron Age) sites, and remained a member for many years. Using his knowledge of such fieldwork, Peter compiled the Constable *Guide to Early Celtic Remains in Britain* (1991).

By early 1964 he had moved to London and was an assistant editor on a weekly publishing trade magazine. Although it was a full-time job, he also found time to earn extra money by freelance reporting and writing feature articles for some of the major newspapers. In addition to this, his ambition was to be a fiction writer, and he had started writing novels and plays at the age of fifteen. "These efforts were quite rightly rejected, but they constituted part of my training for the future," he has commented.

He had become a frequent visitor to his father's homeland of Ireland. In the fall of 1964 he was in Belfast, Northern Ireland, to report on the General Election there, and witnessed the first major riots arising from the sectarian nature of its government and lack of civil rights for Catholics. "It was a learning curve," he has commented. He was a regular contributor of feature articles to Belfast newspapers, as well as to other journals. A sign that he was already interested in the ancient Irish law system, the Brehon Laws, has been pointed out by one of the members of The International Sister Fidelma Society, who found an article by Peter in *The Irish Weekly* (Belfast) of April 25, 1970, entitled "The Irish National Health System 300 B.C." It was an article relating to medical practices in the Brehon Law system.

In 1966 he met his future wife, Dorothy, who had just returned to London after working in Rome, Italy. Her mother was Italian. They had a whirlwind romance, and have been together ever since. 1966 was an important year for his career, as well as for his personal life. That year Peter sent a manuscript to Michael Thomas of A.M. Heath & Co Ltd., one of the oldest literary agencies in London, founded in 1919. Thomas was impressed with his work and offered to represent him. The company has represented him ever since.

His first published book, a journalistic account of the rise of the Welsh independence movement, *Wales — A Nation Again*, was published in early 1968. A foreword was contributed by Gwynfor Evans, the first UK Member of Parliament for Plaid Cymru (the Party of Wales). Peter had just celebrated his twenty-fifth birthday when the book was published.

Peter and Dorothy had moved to St. Ives, Cornwall, where he started his researches on the Cornish language and its literature. In June 1968, *The Cornish Times* commissioned him to write a series of weekly articles, "Our Language," which ran for nine weeks. This formed the basis of a pamphlet history, *The Story of the Cornish Language* (1971). He wrote several other articles, and an academic paper, on aspects of the language and its history before producing *The Cornish Language and its Literature* (Routledge & Kegan Paul, 1974). It was regarded as the then definitive history of the language and became a standard text for the exams of An Kesva an Tavas Kernewek (The Cornish Language Board). An Kesva an Tavas Kernewek later published three of Peter's stories in Cornish as *An Gwels Nownek ha hwedhlow erell* (*The Hungry Grass and other Tales*), in 1996, and another short volume, *Li an Sows* (The Oath of the Saxon), in 1997.

Peter's work was honored with a bardship of the Cornish Gorsedd. The Cornish Gorsedd was founded in 1928 as a nonpolitical and nonreligious body to promote the study of literature, arts, and the Cornish language. It was sponsored by the two elder Gorsedd organizations — the Gorsedd of Wales, founded in 1792, and the Gorsedd of Brittany, founded in 1902. Bardship of one of the Gorseddau (plural) is given either by examination in the language or as an honor for contributions to the national arts, language, and literature of Wales, Brittany, or Cornwall. None of the three Gorsedd are connected to the various "New Age Druid" organizations.

Leaving Cornwall, he was invited to become deputy editor of a weekly Irish newspaper, *The Irish Post*, to be launched in February 1970 as "the voice of the Irish in Britain." At the time, Peter had just finished his second book, co-authored with a Scottish colleague — the first detailed account of the Scottish insurrection of 1820. In 1989 Peter was appointed Honorary Life Chairman of the Scottish 1820 Society, founded in 1970 to commemorate and research this last major insurrection in Scotland.

While deputy editor of *The Irish Post*, he was working on his fourth commissioned book, and eventually felt he had to resign from the newspaper to devote full time to it. It was a wise move, for it was the book that made his reputation as an historian. *A History of the Irish Working Class* (1972) is still regarded as a classic of Irish historiography (*History Ireland,* September 2010). It even became a bestseller in Japanese translation and has recently appeared in a Spanish translation as well.

After its publication he was persuaded to return to journalism full time, when, in 1974, a London-based major magazine company offered him the chance to launch a weekly publishing trade magazine, *Newsagent and Bookshop*. Having devoted two years as editor to making the magazine a success, he resigned to pursue his writing career again.

By the time he resigned the editorship he had published seven nonfiction works under his own name, including his best-selling *Hell or Connaught: The Cromwellian Colonisation of Ireland 1652–1660* (1975). This was followed by his account of the famous battle of the Boyne, *The Boyne Water,* published in 1976. These books further enhanced his reputation as an historian. As a result, he was called upon to appear as an expert witness on the battle, giving evidence to the Supreme Court of Ireland on battlefield locations when there was some contention about the location of a particular cavalry charge.

In later years, other nonfiction books increased Peter's reputation in the field, including *The Celtic Empire: The First Millennium of Celtic History* (1990), the aforementioned *A Guide to Early Celtic Remains in Britain* (1991), *Dictionary of Celtic Mythology* (1992), *Celt and Saxon* (1993), *The Druids* (1994), *Celtic Women: Women in Celtic Society and Literature* (1995), *Celt and Greek: Celts in the Hellenic World* (1997), *Celt and Roman: The Celts in Italy* (1998), and *The Ancient World of the Celts* (1998).

He was invited to lecture, not only in the UK and Ireland, but also in France, Spain, the United States, and Canada. He also taught short courses on the ancient Celts at a London university. He was appointed organizing chairman of Scrí-Celt, the first-ever Celtic languages Book Fair, in 1985, and again in 1986. In May 1989, he was asked to chair a meeting of London academics and teachers specializing in Celtic Studies and language teaching. The purpose was to form the London Association for Celtic Education (LACE), of which he was asked to remain chairman. However, he insisted on resigning after the association was successfully established, becoming vice-president from 1990 until 1995, and was then made an Honorary Life Member. Unfortunately, a lack of funding has recently hit the association, and it has become moribund. From 1988 to 1990 he was also elected international chairman of The Celtic League, originally formed in 1962, with branches in all the Celtic countries, as well as in London and New York. He has frequently broadcasted on radio and television in several countries.

Peter also continued with his journalism until very recently. From October 1987 until June 2007, he was best known to Irish readers for his polemic *Irish Democrat* column, "Anonn Is Anall" ("Here and There"), and another column, "Anois agus Arís" ("Now and Then"), which ran in the weekly *Irish Post* from May 27, 2000, to July 26, 2008.

In 1989 his work was recognized with an *Irish Post* Award.

An Honorary Life Membership of the Irish Literary Society (founded in 1892 by, among others, the Nobel Literary Laureate W.B. Yeats) was bestowed on him in 2002 by the then Honorary President of the Society, Nobel Literary Laureate Seamus Heaney.

In December 2006, he was awarded a Doctorate of Literature (*honoris causa*) in recognition of his work by the University of East London.

But it was back in 1976 that he devised the Peter Tremayne pseudonym. Peter felt that his writing talent and imagination needed a new direction. He had always been in love with fiction. His first unsuccessful attempts at getting published had been with fiction stories. He now saw the accidental creation of "Peter Tremayne" as a means to write popular fiction. From the start, he made it clear that his stories were meant as entertainments. He turned to one of his boyhood fascinations — supernatural fiction. He personally considered *The Hound of Frankenstein* (1977) a "pot-boiler." It was a short novelette set in his favourite location, Cornwall. He never expected it to continue to be reprinted twenty years after its first publication, let alone be translated in other languages, from Italian to Japanese. Soon after it appeared, however, the novels comprising his "Dracula" trilogy were published (*Dracula Unborn*, 1977; *The Revenge of Dracula*, 1978; and *Dracula My Love*, 1980). These, he has said, were written to answer questions he felt Bram Stoker had not answered in his original 1897 novel. The trilogy secured his recognition in the genre.

He also produced numerous supernatural tales, as well as turning to heroic fantasy themes, both as novels and short stories. Of note was his Lan-Kern trilogy: *The Fires of Lan-Kern* (1980), *The Destroyers of Lan-Kern* (1982), and *The Buccaneers of Lan-Kern* (1983), all published by Methuen in London. These were set in a once and future Cornwall using Celtic mythological themes. He returned to Cornwall as a setting for other novels and short stories. This trilogy was followed by an unconnected series of novels again based on Celtic legends: *Raven of Destiny*, *Ravenmoon*, and *Island of Shadows*. Indeed, Celtic myths and folklore were essential to most of his early popular fiction. They were well greeted with enthusiasm by the fans and critics alike.

In October 1979, Peter was invited as a guest to the fifth World Fantasy Convention in Providence, Rhode Island, on the strength of his "Dracula" books. He was Guest of Honour at the British Fantasy Convention VII in 1981, Guest of Honour at the Count Dracula Fan Club gala dinner in 1984, and a guest at the tenth World Fantasy Convention in Ottawa, Canada, also in 1984. In March 1984, the British Fantasy Society published a booklet tribute to him and his work as *Masters of Fantasy 1: Peter Tremayne*. An introduction was written by the bestselling horror-fantasy writer Brian Lumley.

Although Peter has written occasional supernatural short stories for anthologies, following the emergence of the first Sister Fidelma stories, his books in the supernatural genre culminated with his short story collection *Aisling and other Irish Tales of Terror* (1992). When the Japanese translation came out, its translator, Professor Marie Kai of Tokyo, had no hesitation in describing these stories as something more than mere horror-fiction, declaring that they should be regarded as literature.

In 1984 Peter gave a series of lectures at St. Michael's College, University of Toronto, at the invitation of Professor Robert O'Driscoll, chair of the Celtic Studies Department. The talks included the role of women in society, and literature in ancient Ireland. During question time, a student mentioned to Peter the notion that women, allowed to be advocates of the ancient Irish law system, would make an exceptional background for historical mystery stories. Peter thought no more about the idea.

However, it was in 1993 that Peter's friend, the anthologist Peter Haining, asked him if he had ever written a crime story with an Irish setting. An idea naturally came to Peter, and he submitted the story "Murder in Repose." Haining liked the story, but not the name that had been given to the sleuth. She had been called Sister Buan. Haining asked Peter to reconsider the name. He did so, and Sister Fidelma was born. Haining felt the new name was perfect, and thereafter, Peter hailed Peter Haining as Sister Fidelma's "godfather."

Peter felt inspired by the character that he had created. He wrote no fewer than four mystery short stories within a few weeks. They were all published in October of that year, 1993 — "Murder in Repose" in Haining's *Great Irish Detective Stories*; "The High King's Sword" in *The Mammoth Book of Historical Whodunnits*, edited by Michael Ashley; "Hemlock at Vespers" in *Midwinter Mysteries 3*, edited by Hilary Hale; and "Murder By Miracle" in *Constable New Crimes 2*, edited by Maxim Jakubowski. The editors snapped up the stories as soon as they read them.

Critics immediately noticed that Fidelma had arrived, and Richard Dalby, author and leading critic of the UK monthly *Book and Magazine Collector*, wrote that Fidelma promised to be the most interesting sleuth of the 1990s. Editor Jane Morpeth, of UK's Headline Publishers, contacted Peter's agent with the proposition of a three-book contract.

U.S. rights deals soon followed, and then German, Italian, French, and Spanish, until Fidelma stories have, at present, made appearances in a total of eighteen languages. The demand for Fidelma short stories was almost equal to the books. Anthologists were eager to commission short stories. Magazines, including *Ellery Queen Mystery Magazine, The Strand*, and other journals, were publishing them. Not only were these stories in demand, several were selected for reprinting in "Best Story" collections. Boxed sets, audio books, and even a two-hour play adaptation of *Suffer Little Children* on German WDR5 radio supported the demand for the stories.

The Sister Fidelma website went online in 2000, followed by the launch of The International Sister Fidelma Society in 2002, with its print magazine *The Brehon*, while the first Féile Fidelma in Cashel, Ireland, was held in 2006. The histories of the Society and the Féile are recorded in this volume.

The French book magazine *Livres Hebdo* called this amazing reaction to the character "Fidelmania — the Fidelma Phenomenon." Among recent awards for his work, Peter received the *Prix Historia du roman policier historique* from France — *Historia* magazine's award for the best historical mystery of 2010. This was for the Fidelma novel *Master of Souls*.

One of the Society's founding members, Maurice McCann (1938–2011), writing in the first program booklet of the Féile Fidelma in 2006, made an interesting point: "It is unique that a series of crime thrillers could achieve such international popularity these days without having, so far, a media involvement in promoting them to the public. There have been neither movies nor television series of the Sister Fidelma Mysteries that have brought them to public attention."

To date, Tremayne has not had his work adapted for the small or big screen, although two of his previous novels, one of which was *Dracula, My Love*, were optioned for film. Even the Fidelma series was optioned for some years by a Dublin production company, though progress was never made with them, and rights were finally withdrawn.

Peter and Dorothy have made their base in a Victorian house in North London, where they can have access to Ireland or Italy as the mood takes them, or, indeed, to other countries. Peter is as active as ever he was, and he shows no sign of being unable to come up with exciting and well-plotted stories. On a personal level, I have found, in my dealings with Peter over the years, that he is the most accessible and tolerant author I have met. In spite of continuing publicity demands and interview requests that have met his success, he exhibits no "airs and graces." Despite some of the misinformation that appears online now and again, he has quoted from Oscar Wilde's *A Picture of Dorian Gray*: "There is one thing in the world worse than being talked about, and that is not being talked about."

I think we can leave it to Peter to sum up how he sees his work: "I write the Sister Fidelma Mysteries primarily as entertainment. If readers are not drawn into the story and carried along with it, then I have failed in what I set out to achieve. Everything else is superfluous."

The Impact of Sister Fidelma on Irish Crime Fiction

John Scaggs

There are two questions that need to be asked from the outset. The first—"Who is Sister Fidelma—in the present company requires no answer. The second—"What is Irish crime fiction?"—is the one that demands a little more attention at this point, and I want to briefly consider what seem to me to be the three main reasons for identifying something as an example of "Irish crime fiction." It is only by considering what we mean by the term that we can really understand the impact that Sister Fidelma has had.

1. Crime fiction written by Irish writers or writers of Irish descent.
2. Crime fiction featuring Irish characters, history, politics, and culture.
3. Crime fiction set in Ireland.

Crime Fiction Written by Irish Writers or Writers of Irish Descent

In this particular category, it seems to me that Peter Tremayne is in good company, coming as he does from Irish stock. Edgar Allan Poe, generally recognized as the "grandfather" of the mystery story, also had Irish roots. The Poes were, according to Peter Haining in his introduction to *Great Irish Detective Stories,* tenant farmers in County Cavan until John Poe, Edgar Allan's grandfather, emigrated to the New World in 1750. Poe himself, however, never visited Ireland. Some readers may have noticed the significance of Haining's book, *Great Irish Detective Stories.* This collection of short stories includes one of the first Sister Fidelma stories, "Murder in Repose" (1993).

Wilkie Collins, author of *The Moonstone* (1868), which none other than

T.S. Eliot described as "the first, the longest, and the best of modern English detective novels" (Introduction), also had Irish roots. There are aspects of the sensation novel, of which *The Moonstone* is an example, which are evident also in the Sister Fidelma novels.

Sir Arthur Conan Doyle, creator of Sherlock Holmes, was born in Scotland of Irish parents — Mary Foley and political cartoonist John Doyle. Doyle, as most are well aware, is a good Irish name. Not only that, but in the Holmes canon, the great detective is said to have visited Ireland several times on cases, and certainly Dublin, Belfast, Waterford, Maynooth, and (strangely) Skibbereen, are mentioned in this regard.

I mention these writers not just to indicate that Peter, whose family hails from Cork, is in good company (as if it weren't enough of a blessing to have Irish roots in the first place!). No, I mention these three writers because there is, in Peter's Fidelma novels, a re-engagement with the themes, techniques, and devices of these writers that forms an important part of contemporary crime fiction. This is something that I cover in a separate essay — "Nothing Hidden That Shall Not Be Known — Mystery and Detection in the Sister Fidelma Novels" — elsewhere in this collection.

There are other writers with Irish roots, of course, some more contemporary than Poe or Doyle. Raymond Chandler's mother, for example, was Irish, and Chandler's letters reveal that he was proud of his Irish ancestry — and why wouldn't he be? More recently there is Dublin-born Ruth Dudley Edwards, whose crime novels are in the tradition of the great Golden Age writers like Dorothy Sayers, Margery Allingham, and Ngaio Marsh. Again, the writers of the Golden Age are invoked here because the Fidelma novels, as I will outline shortly, revisit the themes, techniques and devices of the classic whodunit, albeit by reinventing them and relocating them in seventh-century Ireland.

However important the "Irishness" of the crime writer might be in identifying what exactly constitutes Irish crime fiction, there are still two more reasons that a novel or a story might be characterized as such, and the first of these is how prominently Irish characters feature in the story — and, by extension, how prominently Irish history, culture, politics, and so on, feature.

Crime Fiction Featuring Irish Characters, History, Politics, and Culture

There is a sense in which novels featuring Irish characters, history, culture, politics, and so on, can be considered Irish crime fiction, but it's difficult to know where to draw the line. Certainly, without these elements it's difficult to identify something as "Irish" crime fiction, but even with these elements in place it can be difficult. Peter Lovesey's *Invitation to a Dynamite Party* (1974), the plot of which revolves around the attempts of a group of Fenians to use a bomb to assassinate the Prince of Wales in 1884, while it features Irish characters and turns on the political question of Home Rule, could hardly be described as Irish crime fiction. A novel like Les Roberts' *The Irish Sports Page* (2002), set in Cleveland and featuring a Slovenian PI, but whose plot focuses around the Irish community in Cleveland, would similarly be difficult to describe as an example of Irish crime fiction.

Of course, neither Lovesey nor Roberts has Irish roots, so perhaps it is a combination of the three points mentioned before, rather than the presence of merely one or two of them, that can help us to define what it is about Irish crime fiction that makes it *Irish* crime fiction. In which case, the third situation, that the novel or story be set in Ireland, is clearly significant to our understanding of Irish crime fiction.

Crime Fiction Set in Ireland

What is interesting here, in relation to the Fidelma novels, is that the novels are not always set in Ireland. In fact, it is not until the third novel in the series, *Suffer Little Children* (1995), that we are treated to the first novel to be entirely set in Ireland, and it is not until the fourth novel in the series, *The Subtle Serpent* (1996), that the Fidelma/Eadulf partnership is featured in an Irish setting. The first novel in the series, *Absolution by Murder* (1994), is set at the Synod of Whitby in what is now England, while *Shroud for the Archbishop* (1995) is set in Rome. Despite this fact, few would disagree with the identification of these, and all of the Fidelma novels, as Irish crime fiction. So clearly the requirement of the story being set in Ireland is not set in stone. Again, this reinforces the point that we tend to identify Irish crime fiction not by one element alone, but by the relationship between the three elements outlined above.

It is at this point that we can begin to understand the central importance of the contribution to Irish crime fiction that Peter's Fidelma novels have made, and it is this: It is only in the last ten or twelve years that a recognisable body of Irish crime fiction began to develop, and the Sister Fidelma stories were in the vanguard of this development. *Absolution by Murder* in 1994, *Shroud for the Archbishop* in 1995, and so on. A quick survey of what little critical commentary there is on the field reveals that the overall consensus is that Irish crime fiction, until recent years, has been very thin on the ground, and that even now there is far less, per capita, than in the United States, Britain, or elsewhere in Europe.

Bob Flynn, writing about Ken Bruen's first Jack Taylor novel, *The Guards* (which is set in Galway), says that it has "few, if any antecedents," and describes it as "one of the curiously rare Irish crime novels." Flynn was writing his review of Bruen's novel in 2001— not so long ago, although crucially, in terms of highlighting the importance of the Sister Fidelma series, *seven years* after the publication of *Absolution by Murder*. Gerry McCarthy, writing three years later in *The Sunday Times* in a review of Cormac Millar's *An Irish Solution* (2004), points out that crime fiction "has been undergoing a boom in Ireland," and I think it is important to note that far from being merely a part of this boom, the Fidelma novels were one of the contributing factors that set it in motion.

There is another key point to make here. The two novels by Bruen and Millar mentioned above, frequently cited as key texts in the developing field of Irish crime fiction, are both contemporary novels. They are novels which are set in, and reflect on, an Ireland characterized by increasing affluence, a fast-growing multi-cultural population, rapidly expanding urban centres, and increasing levels of violent crime. When James Joyce wrote, in "The Hanging of Myles Joyce," that there is less crime in Ireland than in any other country in Europe, his observation was far from prophetic. Importantly, the Fidelma novels offer an insight into an Ireland before the arrival of the Celtic Tiger, even before the destructive forces of foreign occupation, political upheaval, and civil war. Interestingly, though, the world that the novels depict is not so different in many ways from the Ireland of today. There is a simple reason for these similarities. As Gerry McCarthy points out, in his review of Millar's novel, crime fiction tends to flourish "in a society with a pervasive aura of corruption, where nobody can be trusted." Speaking of the Ireland of today, he identifies how the country "is steeped in chicanery and broken promises," and how it offers "an ideal backdrop for genre fiction."

The importance of the Fidelma novels, then, is that they reflect both on Ireland's past and on her not-so-different present. Significantly, as the Fidelma novels make clear, particularly in the way that their plots crucially depend on events, hidden or otherwise, in the past, Ireland's present is a child of its past. In this way, despite the fact that they are historical novels, the Fidelma stories are also a part of Ireland's Celtic Tiger present (political double-dealing, civil war, and even hunger strikes are also alluded to, or form the focus of the plot, in most of the Fidelma novels).

The Fidelma novels contribute to the growth of Irish crime fiction in other ways too. In general, as Bruen's Jack Taylor novels make clear, hard-boiled detective fiction, normally identified as a distinctly American genre, is popular with Irish crime writers. This has something to do with the identification that the Irish feel with rule-breaking, anti-authoritarian, individualistic, and often heavy-drinking hard-boiled private eye heroes in the mould of Raymond Chandler's Philip Marlowe, Dashiell Hammett's Sam Spade or Continental Op, and Robert Parker's Spenser. It also has something to do, I think, with the Irish abhorrence of the spy and the informer — something instilled in the Irish mindset by what Bruen describes as a tortuous history of betrayal. Significantly, the figure of the amateur detective, as he or she appears in the Golden Age fiction between the two world wars, has much in common with the figure of the spy and the informer.

What the Fidelma series has done is to reinvent the figure of the analytic detective for the contemporary reading audience, by reinventing her in the figure of Sister Fidelma. As a *dálaigh*, or lawyer of the Brehon system, she represents the forces of law and order, but she is no slave to the ruling elite. On the contrary, she is presented as fiery, independent-minded, and not easily swayed by the consensus, and her appearance reinforces this, with "rebellious" strands of red hair which frequently escape from the confines of her headdress (*Absolution by Murder* 2, *Shroud for the Archbishop* 9, and so on). Her rebellious nature is attractive to a people who pride themselves on that same quality.

This is important because what it allows the Fidelma novels to do is to re-engage with a tradition of crime writing which, for various reasons, has been long overlooked by Irish writers — the Golden Age whodunit. The whodunit, of course, drew on an even older tradition of crime fiction established by Edgar Allan Poe, and taken up some fifty years later by Sir Arthur Conan Doyle.

Works Cited

Bruen, Ken. *The Guards*. Dingle: Brandon, 2001.
Eliot, T. S. Introduction. *The Moonstone*. By Wilkie Collins. World's Classics. London: Oxford University Press, 1928.
Flynn, Bob. "Down the Mean Streets of Galway." *The Guardian* 8 June 2011.
Haining, Peter, ed. *Great Irish Detective Stories*. New York: Barnes & Noble, 1998.
Lovesey, Peter. *Invitation to a Dynamite Party*. London: Macmillan, 1974.
McCarthy, Gerry. "Millar's Crossing." *The Sunday Times* 4 April 2004.
Roberts, Le. *The Irish Sports Page*. New York: Thomas Dunne Books/St. Martin's Minotaur, 2002.
Tremayne, Peter. *Absolution by Murder*. London: Headline, 1994.
_____. *Shroud for the Archbishop*. London: Headline, 1995.
_____. *The Subtle Serpent*. London: Headline, 1996.
_____. *Suffer Little Children*. London: Headline, 1995.

Teaching Sister Fidelma: Two Models

Edward J. Rielly

I first taught a novel by Peter Tremayne in the fall of 1999 in a course called Religion and Literature. Tremayne and his protagonist initially came to my attention on a trip to Ireland, where I purchased, as I recall, three of the Sister Fidelma novels. From that point on, I followed each new book in the series, a series that interested me both for its literary quality and its historical underpinnings. In addition, as a Celtic religieuse, Sister Fidelma obviously was part of the early stages of Christianity in Ireland. So as I planned my course, I decided to incorporate one of the Fidelma novels into it.

Saint Joseph's College of Maine is a small Catholic liberal arts college sponsored by the Sisters of Mercy. Religion naturally enough plays important roles at many levels in the life of the college, so it seemed appropriate to me to fashion a course that explored the intersection of religion and literature. The course would offer my students a reading list that consisted entirely of outstanding literature, all of it dealing at least in part with the experience of religious faith. My objectives were small in number but expansive in scope. "Students will explore how writers have expressed religious beliefs and issues of spirituality in a variety of literary genres, including the essay, short story, novel (and in subgenres of the novel such as science fiction and detective fiction), memoir, and poem," the syllabus stated. Further, "because this is a literature course, students will improve their ability to read, reflect on, discuss, and analyze works of literature. In addition, students will have opportunities to reflect on the importance of spirituality in their own lives."

The literary possibilities for inclusion in this course were virtually limitless, stretching back close to two thousand years even with a primary focus on Christianity. I briefly considered selecting literature that also reflected other world religions but gave up that attempt as something like attempting to fit the universe within a teacup. The great problem was to narrow down the options to a number manageable for the students within the framework of one semester. I finally settled on Dorothy Day's memoir *The Long Loneliness*, Graham Greene's novel *The Power and the Glory*, C. S. Lewis's science fiction novel *Out of the Silent Planet*, the medieval poem *Pearl*, selections from the anthology *Shadow and Light*, and two novels set respectively in the early and late Middle Ages: Peter Tremayne's *Absolution by Murder* and Ellis Peters' *A Morbid Taste for Bones*. The choices were admittedly subjective, but they all passed the test of literary excellence while offering a reasonably wide range of literary genres.

So how did *Absolution by Murder* fit in this course? The short answer is quite well. A complete analysis of the course is well beyond the scope of this essay, so the focus will stay with Sister Fidelma for the moment. As popular culture studies have blossomed in colleges and universities, and organizations such as the Popular Culture Association have grown in popularity, literature that once upon a time, despite its considerable literary merit, would have been consigned to the arenas of light reading and guilty pleasure, has been accepted into the world of real literature. So genre fiction, including detective fiction, has become quite academically serious and acceptable while remaining as enjoyable as ever.

Absolution by Murder offers in Sister Fidelma a vibrant and compelling protagonist, clever and sufficiently evil villains, a challenging plot, richly described scenes, dramatic conflict, believable dialogue, and an interesting historical context. It offers all of these characteristics of fine literature while being about many things, including the history of Christianity in England and Ireland. The novel invites — even when it does not explicitly mention — consideration of a wide range of pivotal moments in Christian history: the temporary and partial conversion of England to Christianity after the fourth-century conversion of the Roman emperor Constantine, the gradual conversion of Ireland starting in the fifth century, the withdrawal of the Roman legions from Britain in the early fifth century and the subsequent arrival of Germanic peoples (Angles, Saxons, and Jutes) with a general shrinking of Christian influence, the arrival of Augustine in 597 to attempt the reconversion (ultimately successful) of Britain, the history of Iona in the sixth and seventh centuries, the important religious and cultural roles of monasteries, and the growing tensions between monastic and diocesan Christianity (with the issue of largely local autonomy versus centralized control from Rome contributing heavily to these tensions). A work of literature is like a pond into which a large rock is thrown. The ripples flow outward, ever widening. So discussing a literary work leads in the classroom to considering many matters not directly presented within its pages, in the case of the Tremayne novel, some of the historical events mentioned above.

The novel itself, of course, focuses quite directly on an enormously important event in the history of Christianity: the Synod of Whitby, held in Northumbria in 664. This gathering of Church leaders considered a range of issues dividing Celtic and Roman Christianity. It attempted to settle such matters as how to date Easter, the type of tonsure to be worn, the appropriate day of rest (Sunday for Rome or the Celtic preference for Saturday), and even the proper method of using fingers to convey a blessing. Over and above specifics, however, the overriding issue was whether Rome would rule the Christian world — whether in matters both doctrinal and liturgical, the pope, based in Rome, was to be obeyed by Christians everywhere.

The novel also raises issues that were being hotly debated in the late twentieth century and continue to arouse high passions today, such as the role of women in the Catholic Church and in other Christian denominations, and whether celibacy should be required for Catholic clergy. The political and religious conflicts that Sister Fidelma must attempt to navigate raise the question of how separate the political and religious realms out to be. It is the Northumbrian king, Oswy, who sits in judgment during the Celtic-Roman debate, while the United States generally accepts as a fundamental principle of individual freedom that church and state must be separate. That principle of separation, my students come to understand, is not true in all nations today, as it was not true even in England until modern times. In Ireland, one might argue that genuine separation of church and state has developed only quite recently.

Murder, political machinations, and the threat of warfare all occur within this religious-historical context and are inseparable from it. Further, Sister Fidelma is not only caught up in all of this but plays a crucial role in untangling skeins and solving mysteries, although even she cannot change the powerful religious current that is establishing a centralized, Rome-dominated Christianity. As a brave, intellectually gifted dálaigh (an advocate in the law courts), she performs a public role that also merges church and state, inviting discussion about the current roles of Catholic nuns as religious orders generally decline in numbers. Yet even as the number of nuns declines (Burns 70–71), recent decades have seen many new religious communities. Given the importance of women as religious leaders in Celtic Ireland and the existence of communities consisting of both women and men (Ranft 16–18), it is interesting to note that 27 percent of the emerging religious communities in the United States since 1960 have included both women and men (Froehle and Gautier 125–39). As Sister Fidelma continues her efforts in Ireland, England, and on the continent through the many subsequent novels, she comes seriously to question her role as a religieuse as she recognizes in her position as a dálaigh her primary purpose in life.

Considering the centralizing results of the Synod of Whitby also invites some reflection on another important gathering of Catholic Church leaders in the 1960s: the Second Vatican Council. In some ways Fidelma, while faithfully representing her own times, also comes across as post–Vatican. The Second Vatican Council, called into session by Pope John XXIII, summoned the Catholic Church to become more attuned to and involved in the modern world — without, of course, sacrificing core religious values (D'Antonio et al. 116–17, Abbot 201–02). It also placed greater emphasis on the role of women within the Church, although without granting women the opportunity to be ordained as priests. As Tremayne has shown in both his Sister Fidelma novels and in his nonfiction (under his real name, Peter Berresford Ellis), the Celtic Church of Fidelma's time was much more open to leadership roles for women as well as to marriage by clergy and religious sisters than was Rome. These issues also are highly relevant to the ultimate jurisdictional decision emanating from Whitby, as that decision helps to establish the foundation for Rome's enforcing a celibate and all-male clergy (as well as celibacy for women who enter religious orders), requirements that remain in effect within Catholicism into the twenty-first century despite Vatican II.

The Religion and Literature course was something of a transitional course for me in three ways. I began to incorporate more technology into my teaching, adding an online discussion group for my students in order to maintain course-based dialogue between class meetings. In addition, I added service-learning as an optional component, with students who chose that option (rather than a traditional research paper) working with youngsters at after-school education centers operated by the Portland (Maine) Housing Authority. Since religions typically encourage helping others, the service-learning project seemed fitting for a course that involved religion; and the fact that much of the assistance with homework that my students would be providing involved helping younger students with reading and writing made the service-learning also relevant to the literary side of the course. Finally, the course marked my first serious work with Sister Fidelma, who has proven a fine companion through many hours of teaching (and even more hours of reading) over the years.

My most recent assignment of a Peter Tremayne novel again was *Absolution by Murder*. I taught the novel during the fall semester of the 2011–12 academic year in Detective Fiction from Sherlock Holmes to the 21st century. This was a new course at my college, one that I had been thinking about offering since editing *Murder 101: Essays on the Teaching of Detective Fiction*, which was published by McFarland in 2009. A new course, as most faculty know, takes a great deal of planning. There is not even someone else's syllabus to provide a starting point.

Settling on a focus for the course was challenging, given the extraordinary number of accomplished authors who have produced detective fiction. A comprehensive history of detective fiction appeared simply too much of a reach for a one-semester course, yet I wanted my students to at least sample a range of ways in which literary detectives have fought crime, helped victims, and furthered the cause of justice. Consequently, I decided to begin with two classics of detective literature and then move into the present with enough contemporary novels to at least hint at the wide range of detective fiction being written.

We began by reading and discussing several Sherlock Holmes short stories ("A Scandal in Bohemia," "The Red-Headed League," "The Five Orange Pips," "The Man with the Twisted Lip," and "The Adventure of the Speckled Band"), followed by Dashiell Hammett's *The Maltese Falcon*. In these early readings, we examined two basic types of detectives: the detective who depends on observation and, to use Arthur Conan Doyle's term, deduction (although Holmes's approach actually is induction), and the hardboiled detective in Sam Spade. Then came Tremayne's *Absolution by Murder*, to give us the historical detective (from our twenty-first century perspective), a type of detective examined in the two *Detective as Historian* volumes edited by Ray B. Browne. Then the class read Rhys Bowen's *Murphy's Law*, Laurie King's *A Letter of Mary*, Margaret Coel's *The Story Teller*, and Dana Stabenow's *A Cold Day for Murder*. We discussed these works collectively as a class. In addition, the students read Steve Hamilton's *A Cold Day in Paradise* and Nevada Barr's *Track of the Cat* on their own and wrote a paper on each.

The selections offered considerable variety in crime-fighting techniques, types of detectives, and settings. *Murphy's Law* is the first novel in a series featuring the Irish fugitive from justice Molly Murphy, who arrives in New York City in 1901 and becomes a rarity in early twentieth-century America, a female private investigator. Laurie King's series of novels with Mary Russell as heroine is set in post–World War I England. A protégé of the retired Sherlock Holmes, Mary becomes the wife of the much older Holmes, and the two are caught up in a new set of adventures, as in *A Letter of Mary*. The Mary letter refers, not to Mary Russell, but to Mary Magdalene, a letter that, if genuine, could well turn Christianity upside down.

We then moved to novels set in contemporary times: the duo of an Arapaho attorney, Vicky Holden, and a Jesuit priest, Father John O'Malley, on the Wind River Reservation of Wyoming in *The Story Teller*; Alex McKnight, a former Detroit policeman now living in upper Michigan in *A Cold Day in Paradise*; Kate Shugak, an Aleut facing dangerous criminals amid the rugged Alaskan terrain in *A Cold Day for Murder*; and Anna Pigeon, a park ranger patrolling the West Texas Backcountry in *Track of the Cat*.

All of the stories assigned in the course are parts of series, a deliberate choice, for encouraging further reading is an endless process for teachers of literature. My hope was that students taking the course (and twenty-three did during this first offering of it) would connect with one or more of the authors, want to read additional works by the authors, and be able to find them. Only Sam Spade, among the investigators, does not appear many times, making just three more appearances, all of them in short stories. Further, the emphasis in the course was on private investigators, although official police officers make their appearances from time to time in the stories, quite positively in the Coel, Stabenow, and Bowen series (in the latter as Molly Murphy's love interest). Sister Fidelma, as a dálaigh, may be the most official of all the detectives in the course. Once I gave up attempting a truly comprehensive approach as unrealistic, I found it easier to justify excluding certain types of detective fiction, including police procedurals.

We spent five classes on *Absolution by Murder*. For part of the first class meeting, I lectured on the early history of Christianity in England and Ireland, including the first conversion of England to Christianity under Constantine; the invasion of the Angles, Saxons, and Jutes, with the subsequent decline of Christianity in much of Britain; the conversion of Ireland; the following two-pronged reconversion of Britain — by Irish monks in the north and the Roman mission led by Augustine in the south. We also acquainted ourselves with the geography, including the location of Iona and Whitby.

Once we started discussing the novel, we approached it not only in terms of the story itself (and the many ingredients that go into making it successful, such as the characters and plot) but also tried to understand how one goes about writing a detective novel. None of the students had read any of the Fidelma stories before taking the course, but I gave them also a brief introduction to the author and the Fidelma series. Consequently, we could examine not only how one writes a detective novel but also how the author may position the protagonist for subsequent appearances.

Initially, we see a group of travelers coming upon the disconcerting scene of a body hanging from an oak tree. At that point, we do not know who the protagonist is; in fact, the main character could even be Brother Taran. We might be watching the scene unfold from among the surrounding trees, and only gradually do we come to understand the make-up of the group. An interesting and telling detail, however, as some of the students quickly saw, was the willingness of one of the women in the party to approach the corpse. We note that she seems unafraid of the body; we also see what she looks like — all this before even knowing her name. Only after that first view do we hear someone refer to her by name — Sister Fidelma. Further, her ability to confront the obviously dangerous Wulfric and his men tells us more about this religieuse. The first chapter offers a useful lesson on how to begin a novel in order to gain the reader's interest quickly. There is no lengthy presentation of the protagonist's background. Instead, we are led immediately into the story and learn about Fidelma by observing her in action.

The second chapter appears to move away from Fidelma just as we are expecting to see more of her, so we consider why. Again there is a party approaching the Abbey of Streoneshalh, this one by boat, so we conclude that most likely one or more of the members of this party will prove to be important. An obvious choice is Eadulf, about whom we learn quite a bit in this chapter. The second chapter also offers a prophecy of death, as Canna foretells that "on the day the sun is blotted from the sky, blood will flow" (29). We appreciate the relevance of such a prophecy to the mystery novel and assume, rightly it turns out, that we will be encountering additional murders before long.

Fidelma reports the murder that she encountered on her journey in the third chapter, but we suspect that whatever mystery may engage her primary attention will not be that early death, but rather one associated with the great gathering of Christian leaders who have come together to attempt to bridge the differences between the Celtic and Roman churches. By this time, we have progressed far enough to consider how a writer concludes chapters. Chapter Three, for example, ends dramatically with a restatement of Canna's prophecy, this time specifically noting that the following day will see his prediction come true — an approach that makes the reader want to continue reading. Chapter Four also ends dramatically — and ominously — as a solar eclipse occurs, "a harbinger of evil on these proceedings" (69). And sure enough, in the next chapter, the assembly is interrupted when Oswy, the king; Hilda, the abbess of Streoneshalh, the abbey at which this religious council, known to history as the Synod of Whitby, is occurring; and many of the other dignitaries present hurry from the room. Shortly afterward, Fidelma is summoned to appear before Oswy, Hilda, and Bishop Colmán to learn that her friend, the abbess of her home Abbey of Kildare, the learned and beautiful Étain, has been "most foully murdered" (75).

One of the happy characteristics of my class was that several of the students were majoring in criminal justice. Another was that several were seriously interested in writing. Examining how a writer works therefore was especially interesting to the future writers in the course; and exploring such concepts as motive and means, as well as being suspicious of anyone who might have had the opportunity to commit the murder, directly related to the sorts of issues that a number of the students would actually be facing in their future careers.

We recalled, after learning of the death of Fidelma's friend, who had been the cause of Fidelma's coming to the synod, that she had earlier told

Fidelma of her plans to marry and to resign her position as abbess at Kildare. Perhaps, we conjectured, passion, possibly a spurned lover, might be the motive. Or, since Étain was to give the opening address on behalf of the Celtic delegation, her murder could be the result of political and theological intrigue. As Oswy points out in Chapter Six, the religious issues dividing the Celtic and Roman factions also related to political issues and potential plots, including political machinations of his children.

We agreed that a talented writer of detective fiction would likely offer up a wide array of potential suspects, for part of the experience of reading detective stories is to pit one's ability at crime-solving against the fictional detective. We also agreed that fairness is necessary in detective fiction. The writer may make it hard for us to solve the crime, as it may be difficult for his or her detective to unravel the mystery, but there should be no tricks. What the detective sees, we see, although we may not see as clearly or perceptively as, in this case, Sister Fidelma.

Then there is Brother Eadulf, who is charged by Oswy to assist Fidelma in finding the murder in order to convey a sense of impartiality — one Celtic detective (Fidelma) and a Roman one (Eadulf). By this time, we have come to the conclusion that Eadulf is going to be an important character in the novel. In fact, I offer my own prophecy, that Eadulf will be making many appearances within future Fidelma stories. Furthermore, I suggest that we pay close attention to the relationship between these two people. With that suggestion in mind, we look back to the first time that Fidelma encountered Eadulf, before she even knew his name. As she rounded a corner, she ran into Eadulf. "For a moment the young man and woman stared at each other. It was a moment of pure chemistry. Some empathy passed from the dark brown eyes of the man into Fidelma's green ones" (50). Thus is laid the first brick in the foundation that will be the Fidelma-Eadulf relationship.

My students must develop, I tell them, the ability to read (and observe) not as laypersons but as detectives. Any word, no matter how casual, any gesture, no matter how seemingly innocuous, and any action, despite its apparent triviality, may offer an important hint of what is to come. It may help lay bare the mystery. A good detective novelist presents readers with many hints; the readers must learn to look for them. We see, of course, in the first encounter between Fidelma and the Saxon brother, the beginning of something personal (as well as professional) that will bring them together, although the writer will surely develop that relationship through many twists and turns. Another apparently minor detail that I point out to the students — the sort that nondetecting readers might quickly pass over — is a small descriptive detail concerning Deusdedit, the Archbishop of Canterbury: "An elderly man came next, his face yellow and glistening with sweat" (65).

We later talk about the Yellow Plague, what it likely was (an especially virulent version of yellow fever), and that the illness and the archbishop's death have nothing to do with the primary story line of the novel. Then, we wonder, why include the Yellow Plague? In response, I ask whether it would be feasible for someone to write a story set in New York City during September 2001 without mentioning the terrorist attacks. Not likely, my students agree, as something that momentous anyone living in the city at the time would certainly mention. Similarly, we conclude that to write about an actual event that occurred in England in 664 without mentioning another event as significant as the plague that caused widespread death there and elsewhere in Europe would seem to suggest that the writer was simply unaware of the actual history of that time. That a respected historian such as Peter Berresford Ellis would be so unaware of the Yellow Plague would be difficult to fathom. Hence, although from a strict plot perspective, the plague could be deemed irrelevant, it provides part of the fabric of the age and is appropriately included.

As we continue through the novel, the plot, as the saying goes, thickens. Sometimes it proves difficult for students to follow, especially when we read about the brooches and love poems. Staying up with Fidelma is a challenge. We soldier on, though, considering various theories and suspects as do Fidelma and Eadulf, and consoling ourselves that they sometimes get off on the wrong track as well. During this winding journey toward a solution, we discuss the technique of misdirection: so ordering the story that we — and our detectives — pursue what appear to be solid leads but that turn out to be unproductive after all. Étain's intended, Athelnoth, looks suitably suspicious, especially as he is less than totally honest with Fidelma about his having known Étain before. Yet he turns out to have truly cared for the murder victim, and had even been a loyal servant to Oswy, riding out to ascertain details of a plot against the king when his apparent flight from the abbey suggested to readers the possibility of his guilt.

The murders multiply. Athelnoth is found hanged. Seaxwulf asks to talk with Fidelma and is then found drowned in a cask of wine. Who is this murderer? Who is he? As we deliberate on that question, we note the small but important correction offered by Fidelma when Eadulf refers to the murderer by that masculine pronoun *he*. "'He or she,' corrected Fidelma" (207). By the time that we reach this point, most of the students have finished the book and know the identity of the murderer. Few, however, initially saw Sister Gwid as the criminal. Even more likely, some asserted, was the king's sister, Abbe, Abbess of Coldingham. After all, when Fidelma and Eadulf interviewed her, Abbe had acknowledged arguing with Étain about the murder victim's willingness to negotiate a compromise with the Roman faction. And then there was that moment of what seemed like pure hatred when Abbe looked at Eadulf: "The glance Abbe cast at Eadulf was unguarded for a moment. A look of venomous hate. The features froze in a Medusa-like graven image. Then the look was gone and the abbess forced a cold smile" (167). If looks could kill! Another misdirection?

We also consider the final explanation of the crimes. The students appreciate how more dramatic it is to have Fidelma recount her findings to a gathering of officials and suspects rather than simply report in private to Oswy and then have Sister Gwid arrested. In fact, we agree that if Gwid denied the accusations, there might not be enough proof to convict her beyond a reasonable doubt. Although Oswy would not have needed that level of certitude, he would have wanted it in order to convince all parties, political friend and foe alike, that he did indeed have the murderer — and that she was not killing in the service of either religious faction. We also like that moment when Gwid convicts herself by attempting to murder Fidelma — and how fitting it is that Eadulf saves her.

A few pages of prose cannot lay bare every strand of our classroom conversations regarding *Absolution by Murder*, but what has just been presented conveys something of the range of the approaches that we took and the subjects that we discussed. Overall, my students in Detective Fiction from Sherlock Holmes to the 21st century found the novel challenging, enjoyable, and instructive. Sister Fidelma at the end of the novel finds "the future full of excitement" (272). That she will be reuniting with Brother Eadulf is no small part of what makes that future exciting for her. In addition, Fidelma may well find that on her future adventures she has some unexpected companions from Saint Joseph's College.

Works Cited

Abbot, Walter M. "The Pastoral Constitution on the Church in the Modern World." *The Documents of Vatican II*. New York: Guild Press, 1966.
Barr, Nevada. *Track of the Cat*. 1993. New York: Berkley Books, 2003.
Bowen, Rhys. *Murphy's Law*. 2001. New York: St. Martin's Press, 2002.
Browne, Ray B., and Lawrence A. Kreiser, Jr., eds. *The Detective as Historian: History and Art in Historical Crime Fiction*. Bowling Green, OH: Bowling Green State University Popular Press, 2000.
_____. *The Detective as Historian: History and Art in Historical Crime Fiction*. Vol. II. Newcastle, Great Britain: Cambridge Scholars, 2007.
Burns, Robert A. *Roman Catholicism after Vatican II*. Washington, D.C.: Georgetown University Press, 2001.
Coel, Margaret. *The Story Teller*. 1998. New York: Berkley Prime Crime, 1999.
Conan Doyle, Sir Arthur. *The Adventures of Sherlock Holmes*. 1892. New York: Tom Doherty Associates, 1989.
Day, Dorothy. *The Long Loneliness: The Autobiography of the Legendary Catholic Social Activist*. 1952. New York: HarperOne, 1996.

D'Antonio, William V., et al. *Laity: American and Catholic: Transforming the Church.* Kansas City: Sheed and Ward, 1996.
Froehle, Bryan T., and Mary L. Gauthier. *Catholicism USA: A Portrait of the Catholic Church in the United States.* Maryknoll, NY: Orbis, 2000.
Greene, Graham. *The Power and the Glory.* 1940. New York: Penguin Classics, 1991.
Hamilton, Steve. *A Cold Day in Paradise.* 1998. New York: St. Martin's Press, 2000.
Hammett, Dashiell. *The Maltese Falcon.* 1930. New York: Vintage Crime/Black Lizard, 1992.
King, Laurie R. *A Letter of Mary.* 1996. New York: Picador, 2007.
Lewis, C. S. *Out of the Silent Planet.* 1943. New York: Simon and Schuster, 1996.
Pearl. Trans. Marie Borroff. New York: Norton, 1977.
Peters, Ellis. *A Morbid Taste for Bones.* 1977. New York: Mysterious Press, 1994.
Ranft, Patricia. *Women and the Religious Life in Premodern Europe.* 1996. New York: St. Martin's Press, 1998.
Stabenow, Dana. *A Cold Day for Murder.* 1992. New York: Berkley Prime Crime, 1993.
Tippens, Darryl, Stephen Weathers, and Jack Welch, eds. *Shadow & Light: Literature and the Life of Faith.* Abilene: A.C.U. Press, 1997.
Tremayne, Peter. *Absolution by Murder.* 1994. New York: Signet, 1997.

Fidelma's Position in the Female Detective Genre

Richard Dalby

Sister Fidelma is currently, in this author's opinion, the most fascinating, compulsive, and unique character in the long line of female detectives which have greatly entertained devotees of crime and mystery stories for over one hundred and fifty years. This article takes a brief look at some of the best lady investigators, from the most famous to the far lesser known but equally talented examples.

While Edgar Allan Poe was still alive, there were several plucky heroines who attempted to solve crimes on an amateur basis when the police were unable to help. One of the best examples is the protagonist in Catherine Crowe's *Susan Hopley, or Circumstantial Evidence* (1841), in which an enterprising maid tracks down the murderer of her brother. This novel achieved considerable popularity and was reprinted many times during the latter half of the nineteenth century.

The most famous recent example of the enterprising maid-detective came in the Oscar-winning screenplay of Julian Fellowes for *Gosford Park* (2001), which sees Maggie Smith's maid Mary MacEachran (Kelly Macdonald) solving the murder of Sir William McCordle (Michael Gambon), in place of the doltish Detective Inspector (Stephen Fry)—a standard feature of the amateur sleuth triumphing over the professionals.

The first professional female sleuth was Mrs. Paschal in the *Revelations of a Lady Detective* (1861, "by the author of *Anonyma*"), followed closely by the very similar (but nameless) *The Female Detective* (1864), by Andrew Forrester, Jr., appearing exactly halfway between Edgar Allan Poe's first detective story in 1841 and the debut of Sherlock Holmes in 1887.

In her debut appearance Mrs. Paschal related how, suddenly finding herself devoid of income after the death of her husband, and "verging on forty," she was unexpectedly offered a job that was remarkable, exciting, and very mysterious. She immediately accepted and became "one of those much-dreaded but little known people called Female Detectives." She confidently proclaimed her intention to rely on the powers of her "vigorous and subtle" brain, and her talents as an actress, to enable her to get to the truth of seemingly difficult cases.

Like Mrs. Paschal, the unnamed "Female Detective" of 1864 decided to become a full-time sleuth as a means of avoiding the undesirable state of "genteel poverty," and managed to join the London Metropolitan "secret police" force. She reminded the reader that only women can successfully undertake certain types of cases in order to arrive at the correct solution. "But without going into particulars," she adds, "the reader will comprehend that the woman detective has far greater opportunities than a man of intimate watching, and of keeping her eye upon matters near where a man could not conveniently play the eavesdropper."

Both these collections were bestsellers in their mass-produced "yellow-back" format, and were reprinted several times. One of the first American women sleuths was *Clarice Dyke, the Female Detective*, created by Harry Rockwood (pseudonym of Ernest A. Young), published in 1883 as a companion volume to the exploits of her husband *Donald Dyke, the Down-East Detective* (1882). The book's cover blurb stated:

> As the wife and confidante of one of the most skillful detectives living, she has become an enthusiast in the profession. More than once has her wit and forethought proved themselves equal to Donald Dyke's, and more than once has she rendered him substantial aid in the ferreting out of mysterious crimes.

Clarice Dyke was quickly followed by a long line of equally resourceful but now completely forgotten American women detectives. Many of these were reissued in London by the prolific Aldine Publishing Company which flourished in the last two decades of the nineteenth century specializing in cheap (two-penny) paperback editions of short dime thrillers and a long-running series of "Detective Tales," which included *Lady Kate, the Dashing Female Detective* (Lady Kate Edwards), *The Actress Detective* (Hilda Serene), *Sarah Brown Detective*, *Kate Scott: The Decoy Detective*, and *Mura: the Western Lady Detective*. Most of these stories were set in America, usually New York, and all were anonymous, although the author of *Sarah Brown Detective* was cited as K(ate) F. Hill in a 1901 reprint. Notable among other American sleuths of this period was C. Little's *Laura Keen: The Queen of Detectives* (1892), who always took two pistols and a bowie knife, in her Midwestern adventures.

As Mrs. George Corbett's *Adventures of a Lady Detective* (featuring Annie Cory; 1890?) is a legendary lost volume, not located in any library, the first genuine full-time professional lady detective of the Holmesian era is now regarded to be Loveday Brooke, originally created by Catherine Louisa Pirkis for a series of six adventures which ran in *The Ludgate Monthly* from February to July 1893. She quickly rose to become one of the most intuitive and brilliant investigators in London, able to assume a multitude of disguises and with ratiocinative powers rivaling those of the great Holmes himself, perceiving vital clues invisible to others. A seventh story was added to the 1894 first edition of *The Experiences of Loveday Brooke, Lady Detective*, which had the bonus of having her personal calling card affixed to the front cover.

George R. Sims, best known for his plays, urban ballads, and numerous works on poverty in London, produced two popular bestselling series of *Dorcas Dene, Detective—Her Adventures* in 1897 and 1898. Dorcas was an actress who leaves the stage to earn money as a detective when her artist husband becomes blind. She is a mistress of disguise, and "has been mixed up with some of the most remarkable cases of the day."

Also in 1898 Fergus Hume, author of *Mystery of a Hansom Cab* (1886), created *Hagar of the Pawn-Shop* in which the vivid Romany heroine solves twelve different mysteries of which each focus is an object brought in for pawning, including an early edition of Dante, a silver teapot, a jade idol, a Persian ring, and an amber and diamond necklace.

Two other female detectives in the last years of the eighteenth century gained a very large readership—like Sherlock Holmes—in *Strand* magazine serials: Lois Cayley in *Miss Cayley's Adventures* (March 1898 to February 1899) and *Hilda Wade*, subtitled "A Woman with Great Tenacity of Purpose" (March 1899 to February 1900). Both these were written by Grant Allen, who had achieved his greatest success with *The Woman Who Did* (1895), the most notorious of the "New Woman" novels. The final two Hilda Wade stories were completed by his friend Arthur Conan Doyle, after Allen's sudden illness and death.

Like many of the best female detectives, Hilda Wade (whose real name was Maisie Yorke-Bannerman) worked largely through her capacity to harness "the deepest feminine gift—intuition," plus the bonus of a photographic memory and "a mesmeric kind of glance that seems to go through" nearly everyone, especially her devoted male admirer, Dr. Hubert Cumberledge, who narrated the twelve episodes.

Matthias McDonnell Bodkin's *Dora Myrl, the Lady Detective* (1900) featured another feisty heroine who worked as an independent professional detective-consultant, an opponent of the chauvinistic protagonist of *Paul Beck, the Rule of Thumb Detective* (1898) before they eventually married ten years later.

Anna Katharine Green has been described variously as the "mother, grandmother and godmother of the detective story" and her first novel, *The*

Leavenworth Case (1878), was one of the most popular and bestselling detective novels ever written. Her most durable police detective, Ebenezer Gryce, made his debut in this classic work, and he was later joined by the redoubtable Miss Amelia Butterworth, who narrated both *That Affair Next Door* (1897) and *Lost Man's Lane* (1898). This aristocratic spinster was the prototype of the elderly busybody female sleuth, an important seminal figure in the genre thirty years before the advent of Jane Marple, Maud Silver, and Hildegarde Withers. Green created a younger detective in *The Golden Slipper, and Other Problems for Violet Strange* (1915).

Two other early American detectives, Frances Baird and Marilyn Mack, were both based on factual investigators. In Reginald W. Kauffman's introduction to *Miss Frances Baird, Detective: A Passage from her Memoirs* (1906), he revealed that this case was selected from one of many related to him by a dear friend who was a real-life professional sleuth.

Hugh C. Weir's *Miss Madelyn Mack, Detective* (1914) followed the example of Sherlock Holmes very closely with Mack's ingenious logic and deductions, and even resorted to drugs ("those horrid cola-berries") whenever she felt in need of artificial stimulation. Weir added a lengthy dedication to a Mary Holland, which began: "This is your book. It is you, woman detective of real life, who suggested Madelyn. It was the stories told to me from your own notebook of men's knavery that suggested these exploits of Miss Mack. None should know better than you that the riddles of fiction fall ever short of the riddles of truth."

Two of the most popular British female detectives who gained a very wide readership in monthly magazine serializations were Baroness Orczy's Lady Molly Robertson-Kirk and Richard Marsh's Judith Lee. The "Adventures of Lady Molly of Scotland Yard, as related by her friend Mary Granard" first appeared in twelve episodes in *Cassell's Magazine* from May 1909 to April 1910. The publisher's blurb proudly declared that "Lady Molly, who out-Sherlocks Sherlock Holmes, is an outstanding example of the superb value of a woman's intuition in the detection of crime."

Richard Marsh, best known for his much reprinted horror—mystery novel *The Beetle* (1897), created the unusual and memorable detective Judith Lee, who worked with deaf people as a teacher of lip-reading, and applied this talent to solving crimes. The first twelve stories were serialized in the *Strand* magazine as "Judith Lee—The Experiences of a Lip-Reader" from August 1911 to August 1912, and a further nine adventures were published in 1916, shortly after the author's death.

Arthur B. Reeve's scientific detective Craig Kennedy—regularly called the "American Sherlock Holmes"—became one of the most popular detectives in U.S. fiction for several years. Less known today is Reeve's *Constance Dunlap:*

Woman Detective (1916), presenting a notable criminal-turned-sleuth in the tradition of Maurice Leblanc's Arsene Lupin. Like Craig Kennedy, she employs pseudo-scientific implements such as a "detectascope" throughout the linked twelve stories. Constance Dunlap is a memorable example of an ex-criminal amateur sleuth overtaken by the philanthropic (and often nun-like) impulse to save others enmeshed in the downward spiral of terrible events which follow on their wrongdoing.

Three of the most famous and durable British female detectives all began their parallel investigative careers in the late 1920s. Agatha Christie's Miss Jane Marple first appeared in six stories published in the *Sketch* (1928), based around weekly "Tuesday Club" meetings of Jane and four close associates in their supposedly peaceful village of St. Mary Mead; and these were later expanded into *The Thirteen Problems* in 1932. There were a dozen Marple novels from *The Murder at the Vicarage* (1930) to *Sleeping Murder* (1976). Jane Marple was the archetype "old maid of the village who knows everything and sees everything and hears everything." Agatha Christie implied that Miss Marple was based on her own grandmother — a Victorian lady not unacquainted with the depths of human depravity — but it is equally likely that she was partly inspired by Anna Katharine Green's stories of Amelia Butterworth thirty years earlier.

Patricia Wentworth's equally memorable spinster Maud Silver — like Jane Marple — "plays her part in restraining the criminal and protecting the innocent" throughout the villages and country houses of England. Unlike Miss Marple, Miss Silver is a professional detective who charges for her services. Originally a governess, she is described in her debut novel, *Grey Mask* (1928), as "a sleuthess — a perfect wonder [who] had old Sherlock boiled.... " She was sometimes compared to a nun in her appearance: "A little person with no features, no complexion, and a great deal of tidy mouse-coloured hair done in a large bun at the back of her head." Miss Silver continued to solve many more crimes and mysteries in over thirty novels from *The Case Is Closed* (1937) to *The Girl in the Cellar* (1961).

The ageless Mrs. (later Dame) Beatrice Adela Lestrange Bradley holds the record as the most long-lived and prolific of all women detectives, appearing in sixty-six novels by Gladys Mitchell from 1929 (*Speedy Death*) to 1984 (*The Crozier Pharaohs*). As a consultant psychiatrist to the Home Office, Dame Beatrice was a vivid eccentric of enduring appeal. She resolved many of her cases with explanations of the murderer's psyche, and the alleged supernatural figured prominently in her investigations, leading to the widespread description of Mitchell as "a fantasist of genius."

These three leading lights of the genre were followed by an ever-growing number of brilliant women detectives during the 1930s, 1940s and beyond.

Some of the best short stories of their exploits were published in these anthologies: Ellery Queen's *The Female of the Species* (1943) and Michele B. Slung's *Crime on Her Mind* (1975).

While Ellis Peters (Edith Pargeter) was writing her celebrated Brother Cadfael series, the similarly pseudonymous Elizabeth Peters (the qualified Egyptologist and archaeologist Dr. Barbara Mertz, a.k.a. Barbara Michaels) created a long series of exciting period mysteries featuring Victorian archaeologists Amelia Peabody and her husband Radcliffe Emerson, who solved strange mysteries among the ancient temples and tombs of Egypt, beginning with *Crocodile on the Sandbank* (1975) and *The Curse of the Pharaohs* (1981). Coincidentally, Ms. Peabody shared her first name with a real-life prominent Victorian archaeologist and mystery writer, Amelia B. Edwards.

Closer to the medieval world of Cadfael is the fifteenth-century physician and apothecary Kathryn Swinbrooke, living in the environs of Canterbury Cathedral, who solves several crimes and murders in novels ranging from *The Eye of God* (1994) to *Saintly Murders* (2001), written by C.L. Grace (Paul C. Doherty). The stories are full of recondite information from ancient coins to homeopathic cures.

Another recent historical addition to the genre is the Elizabethan mystery *Face Down* series featuring Susanna, Lady Appleton, by Kathy Lynn Emerson. Susanna is both tough and compassionate, wily and appealing, ideally suited to the violent milieu of the 1560s and 1570s.

Many Fidelma devotees have also been attracted to the crime novels featuring Dame Frevisse, set in a Benedictine priory in Oxfordshire in fifteenth-century England (specifically the 1430s), beginning with *The Novice's Tale* (1992) and *The Servant's Tale* (1993), by Margaret Frazer (pseudonym of Gail Frazer & Mary Monica Pulver). After the first six novels, *The Prioress's Tale* (1997) and subsequent books were written by Gail Frazer alone.

Although many of the above women detectives have their legions of admirers, the unique Sister Fidelma will always retain the Number One position as my own personal, completely unexcelled favorite.

Hidden from History: Fidelma of Cashel and Lost Female Values

Christine Kinealy

IRISHMEN AND IRISHWOMEN: In the name of God and of the dead generations from which she receives her old tradition of nationhood, Ireland, through us, summons her children to her flag and strikes for her freedom.

The 1916 Proclamation of the Irish Republic addressed men and women equally. By the standards of earlier revolutionary declarations, acknowledging women as agents of change was unique. And, even by the standards of the early twentieth century, this was a remarkable declaration. It was a short-lived aspiration as the Easter Rising failed. However, recognizing women as the equals of men — as political partners in a mutually beneficial enterprise — was central to the vision of Irish nationalists in 1916.

Political changes did follow. In 1918, Irish women of property aged over thirty, by virtue of Ireland remaining part of the United Kingdom, received the right to vote in parliamentary elections and to stand for parliament. In the election that followed, Countess Constance de Markievicz, a hero of the Easter Rising, became the first female MP elected to the British House of Commons. She declined to take her seat, preferring to sit in the (then illegal) *Dáil Éireann*. In 1920, the British government passed legislation that provided for the partition of Ireland. As a consequence, twenty-six counties of Ireland were designated a "Free State." Neither the state nor the Irish people were truly free from British rule. The important role to be played by Irish women, however, appeared to have been recognized by the *Dáil*. The Irish Constitution, enacted in June 1922, gave women in the Free State equal suffrage rights with men (Ryan and Ward xxi). In the United Kingdom (of which the newly created statelet of Northern Ireland remained part), this right was extended only to woman aged over twenty-one in 1928. Furthermore, the new Irish government was the first in the world to appoint a woman to an executive position when Countess de Markievicz was made Minister for Labour. It appeared that Ireland, after centuries of political domination by "the stranger," had a view of independence that encompassed men and women equally. This aspiration proved to be illusionary.

Disappointingly, the 1937 Constitution deemed that an Irish woman's place was in the home. Forty years later, the pioneering historian Margaret MacCurtain admitted that she was bewildered by the role played by women in twentieth-century Ireland:

> Her public face is that of wife and mother, enshrined in the 1937 Constitution ... her private face is that of one who has been offered no place at the conference tables and who, increasingly, knows she has been hidden from history [Owens xii].

Short-lived though the ideals of 1916 proved to be, they provide insights into the ideals of a generation of men and woman who wanted to co-exist as equals. In this way, they had more in common with Sister Fidelma's Ireland of the seventh century, than with the one that emerged under the leadership of Eamon de Valera.

Women who had chosen a life of devotion to God fared little better in post-independence Ireland. Pioneering religious women who did not fit easily into a "feminist equal-rights paradigm" have frequently been invisible in academic studies (Daly 105). One consequence, as the scholar Mary Cullen suggested, is that "historians of religious congregations regularly have to decode the language of self-effacement in which women religious attributed their own initiatives to male ecclesiastics" (9).

Women's studies as an academic discipline also came late to Ireland. The groundbreaking *Irish Women's History* edited by Margaret MacCurtain and Donnchadh Ó Corráin, appeared only towards the end of 1978, while specialized studies in Irish women's history only began to appear in the 1980s (MacCurtain, Foreword). It was not until the 1990s that real progress was made, with Irish women gaining some social autonomy and sexual freedom, and with women being written back into the history of the nation (Kinealy).

The Fidelma Mysteries reveal that the Celtic Church not only allowed women to play a role equal to that of men but, as a consequence of the Brehon Laws, Irish women had more rights, respect, and protection than women in the rest of Europe. As Fidelma's creator, Peter Tremayne, points out:

> Women were protected by law against sexual harassment; against discrimination; against rape; they had the right of divorce on equal terms from their husbands, with equitable separation laws, and could demand part of their husband's property in a divorce settlement; they had the right of inheritance

of personal property and land and the right of sickness benefits when ill or hospitalized [Historical Note to *Absolution by Murder*].

It is perhaps no coincidence that Fidelma of Cashel had her literary birth in 1993. Fidelma is the creation of Peter Tremayne, the pen name of Peter Berresford Ellis, a scholar of Celtic Ireland. She is a seventh-century detective *cum* legal advocate. Her double role both as a religious (*religieuse*, as Tremayne prefers) and as a *dálaigh*, an interpreter of law, is made possible due to the existence of the Celtic Church and the Brehon Laws, two institutions that made Irish society and culture unique. Working within the framework of the Brehon Laws, Fidelma crosses boundaries between the religious and the secular worlds. Under this system, men and women could work equally as judges, legal advocates, and makers and interpreters of law.

Being an island, off the coast of a larger island, at the edge of a continent, gave Ireland's institutions a distinctiveness and distance from those of its neighbours. The brilliance of Ireland's culture was rendered all the more dazzling because the backdrop was the "Dark Ages" in the rest of Europe. Although Ireland was situated on the periphery of Europe, culturally and intellectually it was at the heart of it, largely as a result of the learning of its church. People came from all over Europe to the great ecclesiastical sites of Ireland, which were famed as centres of scholarship and teaching (Cahill).

By the standards of Europe in the seventh century, Irish society was enlightened, structured, and cultured. At that stage, Celtic culture existed only in scattered pockets. According to the scholar Jean Markale, it had been at its height in the third century B.C. when a "Celtic Empire" had loosely covered all of Europe. The Romans had been the main beneficiary of its slow decline (Markale 26–8). Ireland avoided Romanization, thus allowing the continuation of Celtic society and Druidic practices. However, it did not escape Christianity, associated with Patrick's mission in the fifth century. Yet Christianity in Ireland, in contrast to other Celtic strongholds, did not destroy Celtic customs or traditions (Markale 28). It was into this world, in which Christian and Celtic practices coexisted, that Fidelma was born. Although the Mysteries take place two centuries after Patrick, the ongoing tensions between Druids and Christians is a constant theme (*Chalice of Blood* 226).

Early Irish society was also distinguished by its sophisticated legal system. The Brehon Laws had been codified and written down in the fifth century, a process that possibly involved Patrick. The laws were unique to Ireland, and they had no basis in Canon Law. For the twelfth-century Anglo-Norman invaders, the laws were a challenge and a threat to their authority. They also gave lie to the myth that the Celts were uncivilized. By the fifteenth century, the Brehon and English legal systems operated in distinct and separate spheres, reflecting the political divisions within Ireland. The Brehon Laws provided a powerful medium for traditional Irish culture and for some female autonomy to survive (Knox 15–19). The Reformation, Tudor expansionism, Spanish aggression to England, and the failure and final defeat of Hugh O'Neil's rebellion in 1603 changed the balance of power in Ireland, while making the complete subjugation of Ireland a necessity and a possibility. As a consequence, by the middle of the seventeenth century, English law had been imposed on Ireland, and the conquest that had commenced in the twelfth century was complete (Ohlmeyer 158).

Fidelma lived in a society in which women had many of the same rights as men. Seventh-century Ireland was hierarchical, with a king at the top, but a king who was expected to govern in the interest of his people and who was answerable to his people, the continuation of his kingship depending on a combination of hereditary factors and electoral support. Within this society, women had more rights and more opportunities than was to be the case for many centuries.

Fidelma was an "anruth," an upholder of the law and a legal advocate who pleaded in court. Within Irish society, anruth was below an "ollamh," or professor, who was the equal of kings. Fidelma had studied for eight years to reach this position and it required not only being conversant in Brehon law, but also in poetry, literature, and medicine and to be fluent in writing and speaking. Despite her achievements, in a number of the mysteries, male condescension is evident, both in regard to Fidelma's gender and to her youth in attaining such a position (*Hemlock at Vespers* 3). Her position as anruth, however, ensured that her decisions were always respected.

Fidelma belonged to the Celtic Church. In the seventh century, the Celtic Church still retained much of its autonomy from the Church in Rome. The Celtic Church differed from Rome in a number of ways — crucially over the issue of celibacy and the fact that religious men and women coexisted. In the Celtic Church, unlike the Roman Church, women were priests and could celebrate mass. In Ireland, there existed double houses, where men and women lived side by side, and in some cases, raised their children in Christ's service.

The Church in Ireland did not follow the teachings of Rome regarding issues to do with liturgy and ritual. In the Fidelma mysteries, we learn about the theological disputes between Rome and Ireland. Rome, in turn, was anxious to bring such a powerful member of the Christian church under its orbit. The Celtic Church proved resistant but found it difficult to hold out against the twin forces of political and ecclesiastical incursions. An example of the latter occurred in 1155 when Henry II of England schemed with Pope Adrian IV, a union that resulted in the *Bull Laudabiliter*, authorizing an invasion of Ireland.

The autonomy and freedom enjoyed by women at the time of Fidelma was gradually being eroded. The coming domination by the Roman Church signaled the triumph of a patriarchal system in both religious and secular matters. Fidelma, who observed this arrangement first-hand during a stay in Rome, opined, "This is a sad city for women" (*Shroud for the Archbishop* 13–14). Nonetheless, by the later medieval period, when the Irish Church had become more Romanized and patriarchal, women who chose a religious life were increasingly invisible, living in separate and enclosed communities (Hall 17).

Fidelma uses her equal ranking in positive ways. It gives her the freedom to bring what some writers of women's history have identified as "female values" to her role as legal advocate. As the power of the Church in Rome increased and Irish society became more patriarchal, these values were lost. It was not until the early twentieth century that a new generation of Irish feminists "anticipated that women's admission to citizenship would bring new standards of morality, compassion, equality and justice into public decision making" (Cullen 15). They were to be disappointed. Fidelma, in her constant pursuit of the truth, exemplified these ideals of meaningful participation, although they eluded women of later generations (Cullen 16).

Throughout the mysteries, Tremayne interweaves his fictional creations with real characters and events. We are told that Fidelma had been a member of the community established by Brigit in Kildare, but that she had left on a point of principle. But was Brigit any more real than Fidelma? For centuries, Brigit, and even her very existence, had been a contested topic in Irish history. Scholarship over the last forty years has generally reached a consensus that she *did* exist and that the document of her life written by Cogitisus is genuine. Historian Margaret McCurtain, speaking in 1999, suggested that "Brigit is very central to the retrieval of Irish women's history these years" (Interview 1999). Within a fictional context, the same could be said of Fidelma.

Fidelma of Cashel belongs to the genre of medieval fictional detectives. Yet she is different from her literary counterparts by virtue of her gender, lineage, religious standing, and intellectual training. Fidelma's value in bringing women back into medieval studies was discussed at the 1999 Medieval Studies Conference at Western Michigan University, which included a section on "Cadfael's Companions: Strategies for Writing Women into History through Detective Fiction" (Merivale 289). In this way, Tremayne's Fidelma has proved trail-blazing. As the critic John Scaggs argues, "The simultaneous awareness of past and present evident in historical crime fiction seems to offer a means of gaining a new perspective on the present through the lens of the past" (134).

Tremayne's ability to combine scholarly details with entertainment — authoritative knowledge with medieval mystery — has inevitably led to comparisons with Umberto Eco. Eco's first novel, the much-acclaimed *The Name of the Rose*, is an historical murder mystery set in an Italian monastery in 1327.

The world created by Eco is a traditional male-dominated one. His unfamiliarity with the role played by women in the Celtic Church is suggested by a 1998 article in which he speculates on the reasons for excluding women from the priesthood. According to one commentator, Tremayne's book *Absolution by Murder* is something of a feminist take on Eco (Merivale 288). The feminist theme has been taken up by a number of reviewers. As one such Irish reviewer succinctly stated, "Fidelma is a feminist with a cool brain — a nun with a male companion" (*Irish Independent*).

Unusually, the Fidelma Mysteries are written by a man. The contribution of men to women's studies has not always been recognized. However, a recent review of a feminist text was criticized for not mentioning "the existence of potentially feminist historical Mysteries by men eg Peter Tremayne's Sister Fidelma's titles" (*Choice* 1172). Why did Tremayne choose a female character? His answer is "I chose a female protagonist because this was the most intriguing aspect of the seventh-century Irish system which placed women in a co-equal role to men." Moreover, it was inevitable that she had to be a religious for, in pre–Christian days "all the professionals and intellectuals were part of the Druid caste" (Drew 384).

Making his hero female is particularly appropriate for Tremayne, who acknowledges that the main influence on his interpretation of Celtic Ireland was a woman, Dr. Sophie Bryant. The largely forgotten Bryant was the first woman in the United Kingdom ever to obtain both a Bachelor of Science degree (in 1867) and a Doctor of Science degree (in 1884). According to Tremayne, Bryant "made a ground breaking analysis of the ancient Irish (Brehon) law system from a feminist viewpoint" (Interview). Bryant had been born in Dublin in 1850. Despite there being a female monarch on the throne, women throughout the United Kingdom had few legal rights. Bryant campaigned both for women's suffrage and Irish independence. In 1918, limited voting rights had been granted to women. When Bryant died in a mountaineering accident in 1922, the partitioning of Ireland was in process.

The world in which Sophie Bryant lived was vastly different from Ireland in the seventh century. For women, it was far more restrictive and patriarchal than the world inhabited by Fidelma. Bryant, like a number of other Irish nationalists, hoped that Irish independence would be accompanied by a return to the precepts of the Brehon Law. The new Free State, however, adopted English Statute and Common Law, which was an easier option in a time of so much uncertainty. Her legacy lives on, though, because, as Tremayne acknowledges, "Without Sophie Bryant, her work on Brehon Law and women's place within it, my alter ego, Peter Tremayne, might never have created the 7th century Irish sleuth and lawyer, Sister Fidelma" (Interview).

Similarly to Brigit, regardless of Fidelma's achievements and status, her attributes have been gendered. As we learn from Fidelma's experiences, despite the Brehon Laws there is a concern that she is transgressing gender roles. Significantly, on a number of occasions, Fidelma is asked to show her credentials — sometimes quite literally ("Murder in Repose" 3). In search of truth (rather than simply justice), Fidelma uses her reason and logic, which are often seen as male attributes. In contrast, part of the charm of both Fidelma and Brigit has been their adherence to "womanly ways." As historian Lisa Bitel explains, typical feminine traits "praised by Irish gnomic literature and canons of the period [state] a good woman was sensible, prudent, modest, well-spoken, delicate, mild, honest, wise, pure and smart. A bad woman was promiscuous, stole and lied, chattered and argued" (6). Clearly, Fidelma is both a feminist and feminine. Rather than ignore Fidelma's femininity, Tremayne celebrates it. We learn that Fidelma has green eyes, red hair and pale skin. Physically, she embodies the ideal of Irish womanhood. The Celtic Church did not demand celibacy, and Fidelma has low-key, but important, relations with men. As a young student, she loved the warrior Cian, her intellectual inferior. She wanted to marry, but he did not (*Act of Mercy* 52–4). Later, her constant companion is Eadulf, a Saxon monk. Their meeting is described as a "moment of pure chemistry" (*Absolution by Murder* 50). As a French review makes clear, Fidelma's appeal transcends geographic borders:

> Cette jeune femme allie beauté à intelligence et érudition, humour et détermination à découvrir les coupables de crime. Elle est accompagnée d'un jeune moine d'origine saxonne, Eadulf [Sheherazade].

One of Tremayne's main achievements has been to write women back into medieval history. Fidelma belongs to a category of Irish women who controlled their own destinies and their own sexuality. Similar to her predecessors, including the warrior Queen Medb and Brigit, Fidelma is both a role model and an inspiration for the women who came later. Unfortunately, the important role of women in early Irish society was forgotten by subsequent generations. Anglo-Saxon and Anglo-Norman chroniclers despised the Celts and depicted their customs and laws as barbaric. Meanwhile, historians (generally male) ignored the role of women in earlier centuries. Individually and collectively, the memory of women as the equals of men was forgotten or denied. Lack of knowledge on this issue has led a small number of critics to ask of Peter Tremayne "Did Sister Fidelma's world really exist?" The author's succinct answer has been FIDELMA'S WORLD DID EXIST. Such questions also prompted him to include a "Historical Note" before each story. However, the Note also points out:

> The foregoing information may merely enhance your trip into Fidelma's world but, hopefully, a deep academic understanding of ancient Ireland should in no

way be a perquisite for what, after all, is primarily entertainment [International Sister Fidelma Website].

Was seventh-century Ireland a "feminist paradise"? Probably not. As one historian of Brigit points out, "All women in early medieval Ireland, including saints, were legally disenfranchised. No queens ruled on their own or in their own names. At best, Irish gender ideologies were generally ambivalent toward women and, at worst, rigorously misogynist." She does admit, however, that Brigit was not a "historical aberration" and that her achievements have not always been sufficiently celebrated (Bitel 2). Moreover, Alice Curtayne, biographer of many saints, has observed in relation to Brigit, "Women of early Christian Ireland were more emancipated than the women of 1933" (*St. Brigit of Ireland* 5). Almost thirty years later, she still believed, "There are many senses in which the women of early Christian Ireland were far more emancipated than we," although she points out that women who were bond-maidens or slave-women, had no rights and were treated cruelly (Interview). The literary Fidelma, like Brigit before her, is exceptional by any standards. However, they each suggest what women can achieve in a progressive society.

Inevitably, critics seek out modern comparisons. Tellingly, there are few. According to one Irish review written in 2010, however, "Fidelma is not *Murder, She Wrote*, although there is a slight similarity in the way both the Angela Lansbury character and Fidelma are treated with respect and listened to" (*Irish Independent*). Fidelma, metaphorically, has given birth in an unexpected way. In 2007, *My Lady Judge*, by Cora Harrison, was published. It was set in the sixteenth century, the final century when the Brehon Laws were in operation. With characteristic graciousness, Peter Tremayne provided an endorsement:

> Sr Fidelma would be delighted with her sleuthing "descendant"—a new female Brehon named Mara. Mara solves her cases under the ancient Irish laws in sixteenth-century Munster, nine centuries after Fidelma held legal sway there. Well researched and written [Quoted in Harrison].

Fidelma appeared in 1993 into an Ireland that was pre–Celtic Tiger and pre–Peace Process. Her arrival also predated the Irish cultural renaissance, typified by "Riverdance," Seamus Heaney, and U2, which put Irish dance, poetry, and music literally on the world stage. In 1993, the writing of Irish history was dominated by revisionism, an approach that was, at heart, antinationalist, at times driven more by a political agenda than a scholarly one (Meehan and Miller). The writing of Irish women's history was still relatively new. Peter Tremayne, through his mouthpiece Sister Fidelma, placed Irish cultural and intellectual heritage, and the equality of women, at the centre of his imaginative and engaging detective stories. He identified a gap in the Irish historical narrative and used literature as a way of filling it. As one critic has noted, "For Tremayne, Celtic Ireland was equivalent to civilization"; however, it was increasingly confronted with the twin evils of barbarism and narrow-mindedness (Browne and Kreiser 46). Fidelma's crusade against these evils in the seventh century mirrors some of the struggles taking place in contemporary Irish society. As the main churches in Ireland and elsewhere recover from multiple scandals and seek to find a role in the twenty-first, one Christian author has taken hope from Tremayne's portrayal of the Celtic Church and its emphasis on mission and community, even suggesting, "Sister Fidelma, the heroine, would be a great role model for women today" (Richardson 58).

So often women have been hidden from history; historical fiction can help to fill that gap. For the many people who do not read academic history books but who have an interest in the Celtic Church and the role of women within it, Fidelma performs an important function in retrieving women's history and the memory of women as the equals of men. By writing the Fidelma mysteries, Tremayne has helped to retrieve and make accessible seventh-century Ireland beyond the halls of the academy. In so doing, he has provided an invaluable service that is simultaneously entertaining and educational.

Works Cited

Bitel, Lisa M. "Gender, Authority and Worship in Early Ireland." *Irish Women's History*. Ed. Alan Hayes and Diane Urquhart. Dublin: Irish Academic Press, 2004.

Browne, Ray B., and Lawrence A. Kreiser, eds. *The Detective as Historian: History and Art in Historical Crime Fiction*. Bowling Green, OH: Bowling Green State University Popular Press, 2000.

Cahill, Thomas. *How the Irish Saved Civilization*. New York: Anchor Press, 1996.

Choice: Publication of the Association of College and Research Libraries, a Division of the American Library Association 44 (2007): 1172.

Cullen, Mary. "Feminism, Citizenship and Suffrage: A Long Dialogue." *Irish Women and the Vote: Becoming Citizens*. Ed. Louise Ryan and Margaret Ward. Dublin: Irish Academic Press, 2007.

Curtayne, Alice. Interview. *Saint Brigit. The Mary of Ireland*. 1960. Web. 5 May 2011. <http://www.catholicpamphlets.net/pamphlets/SAINT BRIGIT.pdf>.

_____. *St Brigit of Ireland*. Dublin: Browne and Nolan, 1933. Quoted in Ginna Sigillito. *Daughters of Maeve: Fifty Irish Women Who Changed the World*. New York: Citadel Press, 2007.

Daly, Mary E. "Oh Kathleen Ni Houlihan." *Gender and Sexuality in Modern Ireland*. Ed. Anthony Bradley and Maryann Gialanella Valiulis. Amherst: University of Massachusetts Press, 1997.

Drew, Bernard A. *100 Most Popular Contemporary Mystery Authors: Biographical Sketches and Bibliographies*. Santa Barbara, CA: ABC-CLIO, 2011.

Eco, Umberto. "The Exclusion of Women from the Priesthood According to Thomas Aquinas." *Catholic Internet Library*, 1998. Web. 15 Sept. 2011. <http://www.women-priests.org/theology/eco.asp>.

Hall, Dianne. "Necessary Collaborations: Religious Women and Lay Communities in Medieval Ireland, c. 1200–1540." *Irish Women's History*. Ed. Alan Hayes and Diane Urquhart. Dublin: Irish Academic Press, 2004.

Irish Independent. 21 August 2010.
Kinealy, Christine. *Ireland Since the 1960s.* London: Reaktion Books, 2010.
Knox, Andrea. "Testimonies in History: Reassessing Women's Involvement in the 1641 Rising." *Irish Women and Nationalism: Soldiers, New Women and Wicked Hags.* Ed. Louise Ryan and Margaret Ward. Dublin: Irish Academic Press, 2004.
MacCurtain, Margaret. Foreword. *Irish Women's History.* Ed. Alan Hayes and Diane Urquhart. Dublin: Irish Academic Press, 2004.
_____. Interview. 28 Jan. 1999. Web. 15 July 2011. <http://www.tallgirlshorts.net/mary-mary/margarettext.html>.
Markale, Jean. *Women of the Celts.* Rochester, VT: Inner Traditions, 1986.
Meehan, Niall, and Kerby Miller. "'For God and the Empire': An Irish Historian's Rapid Rise, Strange Fall, and Remarkable Resurrection." *Field Day Review* 7 (2011).
Merivale, Patricia. "Sub Rosa. Umberto Eco and the Medievalist Mystery Story." *From Arabye to Engelond: Medieval Studies in Honour of Mahmoud Manzalaoui.* Ed. A. E. Christa Canitz and Gernot R. Weiland. Ottawa: University of Ottawa Press, 2000.
Ohlmeyer, Jane. *Political Thought in Seventeenth-Century Ireland: Kingdom or Colony.* Cambridge; New York: Cambridge University Press, 2000.
Owens, Rosemary. Foreword. *Irish Women and the Vote: Becoming Citizens.* Ed. Louise Ryan and Margaret Ward. Dublin: Irish Academic Press, 2007.
Richardson, Rick. *Evangelism Outside the Box: New Ways to Help People Experience the Good News.* Downers Grove, IL: InterVarsity Press, 2000.
Ryan, Louise, and Margaret Ward, eds. *Irish Women and the Vote. Becoming Citizens.* Dublin: Irish Academic Press, 2007.
Scaggs, John. *Crime Fiction: The New Critical Idiom.* London: Routledge, 2005.
Sheherazade. *La Mort aux Trois Visages de Peter Tremayne.* Web. 20 June 2011. <http://www.livres-online.com/La-mort-aux-trois-visages.html>
Tremayne, Peter. *Absolution by Murder.* New York: St. Martin's Press, 1994.
_____. *Act of Mercy: A Celtic Mystery.* New York: St. Martin's Press, 1999.
_____. *The Chalice of Blood: A Mystery of Ancient Ireland.* New York: St. Martin's Press, 2010.
_____. *The International Sister Fidelma Website* Web. 2 Nov. 2011. <http://www.sisterfidelma.com/FAQS.htm#world>.
_____. Interview. *The International Sister Fidelma Society.* 2005. Web. 29 Aug. 2011. <http://www.sisterfidelma.com/FAQS.htm#BRYANT>.
_____. "Murder in Repose." *Hemlock at Vespers: Fifteen Sister Fidelma Mysteries.* New York: St. Martin's Press, 2000. 1–23.
_____. Quoted in front matter of *My Lady Judge*, by Cora Harrison. London: Macmillan, 2007.
_____. *Shroud for the Archbishop.* New York: St. Martin's Press, 1998.

Brother Eadulf: Monk of Saxmundham

Mairéad Ni Riada

Peter Berresford Ellis, the noted Celtic historian, under his fiction writing pseudonym, Peter Tremayne, has successfully created two of the most endearing fictional characters in English or Irish literature: Sister Fidelma and Brother Eadulf who appear in the Sister Fidelma Mysteries.

The two main protagonists of this series are Sister Fidelma, an attractive red-haired young lady with blue or green eyes depending on her emotional disposition, and Brother Eadulf, a brown-eyed, thickset and phlegmatic young man. They are from different cultural worlds. Fidelma is born into a royal family in Cashel, capital of the kingdom of Muman (modern Munster), and Eadulf is born in Seaxmund's Ham, in the land of the South Folk among the East Angles (modern Saxmundham, County Suffolk, East Anglia, England). They are first introduced to us in *Absolution by Murder*.

While much attention is given, quite naturally, to Sister Fidelma, I intend to examine the early life of Brother Eadulf: where he came from, what kind of an upbringing and education he had before going to the colleges of Ireland and Rome, and his subsequent meeting and life with Fidelma.

Some critics have unwisely likened Brother Eadulf as a Dr. Watson to Fidelma's Sherlock Holmes. This is entirely wrong; even if one goes back to the original Watson character as depicted by Conan Doyle rather than the Nigel Bruce bumbling character of the popular films that still creates the image of Watson for most of the general public. Eadulf is highly intelligent, perhaps not as assertive a character as Fidelma, but he often has a crucial input into resolving the mysteries. In *Valley of the Shadow*, for example, he is able to grasp the essential details of some obscure Irish law to defend Fidelma when she is wrongly charged with murder.

Brother Eadulf is not merely a fictional character living in seventh-century Ireland. Alongside his partner, Sister Fidelma, he is also a very important guide to that era. As an outsider, he is a valuable commentator and helps to explain matters for us as we enter this extraordinary world which was seventh-century Ireland. Eadulf comes to know and admire the Irish society in which he has studied and worked, and also points to the changes he witnessed in their land and how he reflected those changes himself.

Brother Eadulf is not just an appendage in the stories, a straight man to Sister Fidelma so that she can demonstrate her brilliance. He is very much an independent protagonist in the stories, which often leads to the tension between the two characters.

Early Life and Education

Eadulf, an Angle, was born and raised in Seaxmund's Ham. The town's name allegedly derives from the Anglo-Saxon "Seizmond's Home" in the land of the South Folk (Suffolk) ("Saxmundham"). It is situated in a valley between two hills on the road to London, and near a small stream which flows into the river Ore. Saxmundham is nineteen miles from Ipswich, thirty from Felixstowe. Walton Castle, once a Roman Fort, near Felixstowe, had an abbey within its walls, like Burgh Castle — St. Fursa founded his abbey within its walls in the seventh century. Saxmundham is also within easy traveling distance of Donmoc, now Dunwich, where it is said St. Felix founded his abbey (mentioned in *The Haunted Abbot*).

Why did the author choose Saxmundham for Eadulf's place of origin? The answer appears in *The Brehon* ("A Case for Sister Fidelma" XII), in that the author knows the area well and some of his wife's relatives live nearby. He once revealed that one of them, then a headmaster of a local school, suggested the town to him as being close to the famous Sutton Hoo seventh-century Anglo-Saxon royal burial site. This 91-hectare site has been described as "the greatest archaeological discovery of all time" centered around a 90-foot Anglo-Saxon ship burial.

Whether the Germanic peoples who settled in Britain were Angles, Saxons, or Jutes, to the Celtic population they were all termed Saxons. In Old Irish the word was written as *Saxanach* or *Sagsuin*, and today we say *Sasanach*. The British Celts called them Sais and *Saesneg*. For many of the books in the series, Eadulf was willing to go along with being called a Saxon. But when people annoyed him, he made a point of correcting them and saying he was an Angle from the land of the East Angles.

Eadulf's family were hereditary *gerefa* or reeves (magistrates: the modern word "sheriff" derives from "shire reeve") and consequently played an important role in the town and its neighborhood; consequently, young Eadulf would have been exposed early to the life of a Reeve as he listened to his father discuss work and saw him carry out his duties. His education at first would have been tailored towards this livelihood, his father ensuring that he would become well versed in the customs and laws of his people, handed down orally at that time. However, the young man felt a calling to the religious life and left home to follow his vocation.

Eadulf had become acquainted with the Irish scholar and monk Fursa who had come from Ireland as a missionary to East Anglia about A.D. 633 and established monasteries and schools in the region, under the patronage of East Anglian king Sigebert (A.D. 634–638) who had just ousted the pagan King Ricbert. See the Venerable Bede (d. 735), whose reference to Fursa (the name is also spelt as Fursey) is given in Book III.19 in *Bede's Ecclesiastical History*. Fursa provides an intriguing, but unexplored link, with Fidelma as he was a western Munster prince, the son of Fintan mac Fínloga and Gelgéis of the Uí Briúin. Fursa was therefore one of the Eóghanacht dynasty and must have been distantly related to Fidelma. He had already founded his own community not far from Inchiquin, County Clare, before arriving in East Anglia.

Eadulf studied under Fursa's care and became a convert to his religion. Seeing how apt a student this young man was, Fursa persuaded him to continue his studies in Ireland, both at Dharú, on the oak plain (Durrow, County Offaly), where Fursa had studied himself and later taught, and then at the medical college in Tuaim Brecain (Tomregan, County Cavan).

Durrow was founded by Colmcille and was famous for its school as well as its large library and scriptorium. Bede called it *monasterium nobile in Hibernia*, and this was the home of the spectacular *Book of Durrow*, compiled A.D. 650–700. This is where Fursa gained his love of classic learning. He was also known for his amazing visions of heaven and hell, which his contemporaries greatly admired (Tomassini 79, 83, 169).

Further Education in Ireland

Eadulf's time in the abbey of Durrow would have been a happy one, as he came in contact with the learned brethren that Fursa had told him so much about. He would have had a chance to study the books from their library, learn to speak Irish fluently, and improve his writing skills by observing the monks in the scriptorium as they transcribed and illustrated the Gospels on vellum. He would have had his choice of studies. Peter Berresford Ellis in his *Celtic Inheritance* (129, 137) reminds us that in the seventh century at the great ecclesiastical college of Durrow, no fewer than eighteen different nations were represented amongst the students. This is also outlined in the Fidelma short story "A Canticle for Wulfstan."

It is probably no coincidence that Peter Tremayne makes Fidelma's elderly cousin, Abbot Laisran, the abbot of Durrow at this time. Abbot Laisran first persuaded Fidelma to join the religious while Fursa sent Eadulf to Durrow to continue his education. Is this an indication that, at some point, the author might develop that connection?

The seventh century saw Ireland going through an intense phase of development in terms of education. Many of the monasteries had schools and well stocked libraries which attracted students from many countries. They are described in John Healey's *Insula Sanctorum et Doctorum: Ireland's Ancient Schools and Scholars*. As Bede mentioned, many Anglo-Saxon nobles sent their children to be educated in Ireland. This education not only produced Irish-trained monks and scholars for the Anglo-Saxon kingdoms but had many other effects on English learning which is generally outlined in Professor Charles D. Wright's *The Irish Tradition in Old English Literature*. Perhaps controversial for English perceptions is the claim by the famous Norwegian scholar C.W. von Sydow that the *Beowulf* poet was well acquainted with the Irish sagas and there are several close similarities between *Beowulf* and the early Irish saga *Táin Bó Fraoch*. Peter Berresford Ellis reminds us in *Celt and Saxon* (154) that Aldrith, King of Northumbria (A.D. 685–705), was not only a son of King Oswy, but his mother was Fin, daughter of a northern Uí Néill king who had been raised in Ireland and was bilingual in Irish and Anglo-Saxon. Three of his poems in Irish survive. He was a young man before being invited back to Northumbria to become king. It is said that *Beowulf* was composed under his patronage.

Durrow was just one of many fascinating centers of learning. Most of the books were on theology. The writings of the Desert Fathers and copies of the Gospels were to be found in Ireland, a subject reviewed in the *Atlas of Irish History*. A fascinating and visual survey of the books is *From Durrow to Kells: The Insular Gospel-books 650–800*, by George Henderson. This period has been described by Peter Berresford Ellis in his *Eyewitness to Irish History* as "Ireland's Golden Age of Learning" (4).

Tuaim Brecain

Having completed his studies at Durrow, Eadulf went to study medicine at Tuaim Brecain. This is sometimes written as Tuaim Drecain and is modern Tomregan, County Cavan. According to Dr. Eileen M. Hickey, "The country was then believed to be the most advanced in the civilization of the age. The school of Tuaim Brecain, near Belturbet, is of particular interest to us, as it appears to have been of medical character, and was founded by St. Brecain, a skilled medical practitioner, renowned above all for his skill in cerebral surgery" (71) St. Brecain died in A.D. 578.

Brecain's establishment also had three lay schools, each having its own professor:

> One a School of the Brehon Law [Fenechus]; another a School of Poetry and History and Classical Learning; and the third a School of Medicine. Brecain saved the life of a warrior named Cennfaeladh or Cenn Faelad, and in turn the warrior stayed on at the college and studied at all the three schools. He was a poet and a historian as well as a great lexicographer [Healy 602–04].

Aodh De Blacam credits Cenn Faelad with composing not only poems but a treatise on Irish grammar, traditional legal maxims, a history, and a dictionary in Irish, Latin and Greek. De Blacam identifies Cenn Faelad as being at the birth of Irish literature.

Eadulf studied medicine at Tuaim Brecain, especially the usage of medical herbs and other potions, leechcraft, bonesetting, surgery and many other areas of general medical care. He equipped himself with knowledge to enable diagnosis and treatment of many medical conditions and wounds. He would have studied and memorized many of the herbs and recipes for treatments in the college library, accrediting himself in his knowledge with his tutors. In many stories Eadulf is thus able to assist Fidelma when medical advice is need (for example, *Absolution by Murder* and *Valley of the Shadow*) and also uses his medical knowledge to save Fidelma's life when, during the Council of Autun, she is bitten by a snake (*Council of the Cursed*). There not being any poisonous snakes in Ireland, Fidelma was not aware of the danger, but there are adders in Britain.

Completion of Formal Education in Rome

Eadulf witnesses a growing dissention between some of the Irish Christian Religious communities and Rome, for example, discord over difference in theology, the types of tonsures the monks adopted, Rome's new date of Easter, and many aspects of the liturgy they followed. Having been educated in Ireland but being a firm believer in the Holy See, Eadulf decides to go on a pilgrimage to Rome to look for guidance. Once there he undertakes a course of studies to help clarify the theological issues raised on both sides. After two years of intense study Eadulf returns a supporter of Rome. But he has not become a fanatic. While he believes in many of the reforms that Rome was carrying out, his criticism of the "Celtic Church" hanging on to the original forms, very much like the Greek Orthodox churches were doing at this time, are mild. Can it be that Eadulf is uncertain or does not want to fall out with Fidelma who is certainly not enamored of Roman ways?

What come to life in the books are the fascinating revelation of Ireland as the place for Anglo-Saxons to study as well as the leading role that Irish missionaries played in bringing the Christian religion and literacy to the Anglo-Saxons. This fascinating period was outlined by Professor Dáibhí Ó Cróinín in his 2004 O'Donnell Lecture "The First Century of Anglo-Irish Relations (A.D. 600–A.D. 700)." Professor Ó Cróinín is regarded as Ireland's premier authority on Early Medieval Ireland. In his lecture, he points to Bede's *Ecclesiastical History* (Book III, chapter 27), where he acknowledges that the Irish taught the Anglo-Saxons "and also provided them with books to read and instruction without asking for any payment.... "Professor Ó Cróinín reviews the major sources, showing not only the work of the missionary Irish teachers in the Anglo-Saxons kingdoms but how both noble and common Anglo-Saxons went to Ireland to pursue their studies in the great Irish ecclesiastical and secular colleges. It was the verdict of Professor Julian Brown that "until A.D. 669 ... Anglo-Saxon England was a cultural province of Ireland, and evidently a province in which Latin learning flourished much less vigorously than in Ireland itself" (141–77).

For Professor Ó Cróinín, Brown hints at a sadness of how relations between England and Ireland were to develop in later centuries, for he ends his lecture with the observation that "it is that first century of Anglo-Irish relations, c. A.D. 600 to c. 700, that offers a model of how relations might be between the peoples of these islands" (Brown 16). One feels that thought is shared by Peter Tremayne in demonstrating the relationship between Fidelma and Eadulf.

Additional Studies

Having completed his formal education did not put an end to Eadulf's studies. In *Valley of the Shadow* we find him taking a short but highly intensive study of Laws of the Fenechus (Brehon Law) in order to support Fidelma, who had been charged with the murder of Brother Solin.

Eadulf had first met Fidelma when they both attended the Council of Whitby (Streoneshalh). When a murder of a leading delegate threatens to throw this important council into turmoil and warring factions, Abbess Hilda and King Oswy encourage them to work together in solving it. Abbess Hilda was born in A.D. 614 and was abbess from 657 to 680. She was a friend and follower of the Irish missionary Aidan. Hilda, while accepting the decision of the council to follow Roman usage, makes no attempt to hide the fact that she remained sympathetic to Irish liturgy.

Abbess Hilda and King Oswy decide that Fidelma, as an Irish lawyer, and Eadulf, as an Anglo-Saxon hereditary magistrate, are to make a join decision about the murdered delegate and therefore could not be accused of bias in one or other camp. When Fidelma and Eadulf first came together they clashed, both being each other's intellectual equal and used to making their own decisions.

Each was also familiar with the laws of their own countries. Eadulf had trained to take his place as hereditary *gerefa* before deciding to don the habit, and Fidelma was a fully qualified *dálaigh*. They also bonded as they instructed each other in their own laws and customs.

Eadulf's and Fidelma's relationship deepened over time, and in *Prayer for the Damned*, they enter into the Irish trial marriage for a year and a day in A.D. 667, during which time their son Alchú was born. The following year they entered a permanent marriage. They are portrayed in a very real manner with the weight of their family histories behind them. You can almost feel them calling on the collective unconscious of their peoples, both Celtic and Saxon. They are the products of great educational systems which had already been honed by generations of scholars.

During the series we see the couple as a team take on many cases to investigate and help resolve. We see them undergoing many difficulties, often faced with life-threatening situations and challenging adventures. We can empathize with their frustrations, joys and sadness too as they solve the mysteries and live their lives in exciting and dangerous times. The stories are thrilling and absorbing reads from a master storyteller.

Tremayne draws on his immense knowledge as an Irish/Celtic historian. He has achieved success in diverse disciplines. His scholarly and literary skills allow us to go on a journey with the time-traveler Peter Tremayne, shadowing Brother Eadulf and Sister Fidelma as they display their remarkable sleuthing skills and courtroom expertise in the many varied cases they undertake. We learn as we follow them and are enriched by what the author brings to his novels.

Works Cited

Bede, the Venerable. *The Ecclesiastical History of the English Nation*. London: J. M. Dent, 1930.

Brown, Julian. "An Historical Introduction to the Use of Classical Latin Authors in the British Isles from the Fifth to the Eleventh Centuries." *A Paleographer's View: Selected Writings of Julian Brown*. Ed. Janet Bately, Michelle Brown, and Jane Roberts. London: Henry Miller, 1983. 141–77.

"A Case for Sister Fidelma." *The Brehon: The Journal of the International Sister Fidelma Society* 10.1 (January 2011): XI–XIII.

De Blacam, Aodh. *A First Book of Irish Literature, Hiberno-Latin, Gaelic, Anglo-Irish, from the Earliest Times to the Present Day*. Dublin: The Talbot Press, 1934.
Duffy, Sean. *Atlas of Irish History*. 3rd ed. Dublin: Gill and Macmillan, 2000.
Ellis, Peter Berresford. *Celt and Saxon*. London: Constable, 1993.
_____. *Celtic Inheritance*. 1985. New York: Dorset, 1992.
_____. *Eyewitness to Irish History*. New York: John Wiley, 2004.
Healey, John. *Insula Sanctorum et Doctorum: Ireland's Ancient Schools and Scholars*. Dublin: Sealy, Bryers and Walker, 1890.
Henderson, George. *From Durrow to Kells: The Insular Gospel-Books 650–800*. London: Thames and Hudson, 1987.
Hickey, Eileen. "The Background of Medicine in Ireland." *Ulster Medical Journal* 8 (Nov. 1938): 66–83.
O'Cronin, Daibhi. "The First Century of Anglo-Irish Relations (A.D. 600–A.D. 700)." O'Donnell Lecture. National University of Ireland, Galway. 2004.
"Saxmundham." *The National Gazetteer of Great Britain and Ireland*. Ed. Nicholas E. S. Arm. 1868. London: British Library, 2011.
Tommasini, Anselmo M. *Irish Saints in Italy*. London: Glasgow, Sands, and Co., 1937.
Tremayne, Peter. *Absolution by Murder*. 1994. New York: St. Martin's, 1996.
_____. "A Canticle for Wulfstan." *Hemlock at Vespers: Fifteen Sister Fidelma Mysteries*. New York: St. Martin's, 2000. 183–217.
_____. Council of the Cursed. 2008. New York: St. Martin's Minotaur, 2009.
_____. *Valley of the Shadow*. 1998. New York: St. Martin's, 2000.
Von Sydow, C. W. "Beowulfskalden och nordisk tradition." *Yearbook of the New Society of Letters at Lund*. Lund, Sweden: University of Lund, 1923. 77–91.

Fidelma Locations in Munster (Ireland)

David Robert Wooten

To people reading their first Sister Fidelma story, it is not long before they realize how important and well defined the locations are. They contribute a visual intensity to Peter Tremayne's writing style, even to the point of being intrinsic to the plots. The settings show a deep familiarity not only with the landscape but its history. The author has always maintained that he does not write about locations with which he is not familiar, or has not visited. Perhaps, in this, lies the secret of the "spirit of place" that emerges in the Fidelma books.

I recently discovered that, back in 1968, Peter had interviewed Georges Remi (Hergé), the Belgian creator of the famous Tintin character (*Books and Bookmen*, Vol. 14, No. 2, November 1968). Remi prided himself on the meticulous accuracy of his settings. He told Peter that he had once crossed the North Atlantic in an old cargo boat to make sure the background was authentic. I have often wondered whether Peter was influenced by Remi's unique craftsmanship in his attention to location details.

The majority of the Fidelma mysteries are, of course, set in and around the town of Cashel, in the province of Munster in Ireland. Munster consists today of the counties of Cork, Kerry, Tipperary, Limerick, Clare, and Waterford. Munster is in the southwest of Ireland, forming the country's biggest province. In Fidelma's time it was a kingdom, one of the five kingdoms of Éireann. The modern Irish word for a province remains *cuíge*—a fifth. The five kingdoms of ancient Ireland were Muman, Ulaidh and Laigin, to which the Vikings added their word *stadr*, a place, making "ster" in English, and hence Munster, Ulster and Leinster. The name of the kingdom of Connacht was left alone, although sometimes Anglicized as Connaught. The fifth kingdom was the "middle kingdom," Midhe (middle), and today is comprised of

County Meath and County Westmeath. This was the territory in which the High King had his capital, Teamhair or Tara, and ruled over the five kingdoms.

So much do locations and their topographical descriptions play a part in the Fidelma stories that many years ago the Cashel Heritage Centre began to notice a growing number of tourists making inquiries about directions to specific Fidelma locations. The current manager at Cashel Heritage Centre, Olivia Quinlan, who also runs the Sister Fidelma Guesthouse in Cashel, is devising a plan for Fidelma locations tours or walks.

While this essay deals only with the locations in Munster, the Sister Fidelma Mysteries are, of course, not always confined to Munster or, indeed, to Ireland. Fidelma, like the Irish religious of her time, traveled, although in her case she was not exactly a typical *peregrination pro Christo*.

The first novel in the series, *Absolution by Murder* (1994), is set in Whitby (Streoneshalh) during the famous Synod of A.D. 664; *Shroud for the Archbishop* (1995) is set in Rome later that year. *Act of Mercy* (1998) starts out at Ardmore (Ard Mór), County Waterford, but is mainly confined on board a pilgrim ship heading to Santiago di Compostela. *Smoke in the Wind* (2001) has Fidelma and Eadulf shipwrecked on the coast of Dyfed (modern southwest Wales). *The Haunted Abbot* (2003) has Fidelma in Eadulf's own location, Seaxmund's Ham (Saxmundhams, in Suffolk, England). *The Council of the Cursed* (2008) is set in Autun, in Burgundy, France. *Dove of Death* (2009) is set in Morbihan, an area on the southern coast of Brittany, while *Behold a Pale Horse* (2011) is a retrospective novel set in Bobbio, in the Trebbia Valley of Northern Italy. This is the only novel out of sequence, as its takes Fidelma back to a period that fits between *Shroud for the Archbishop* and *Suffer Little Children*. The author has been to all these locations, and the books do follow his standards of attention to descriptive detail.

The other twelve novels in the series are firmly set in Ireland, and all but two are completely set in Munster.

Topography plays an important role in the stories. If a hill, mountain, or river is mentioned, the reader can be assured that it exists, and is placed accurately. Some readers are surprised when sophisticated roads are mentioned. The Brehon Laws, as the author points out, not only were very specific on the responsibility of road construction and maintenance, but they indicated locations of the major roads, bridges, and causeways. Although traces of ancient Irish roads have long been found, augmented by early textural references, it was only in 1985 that archaeologist Professor Barry Raftery (1944–2010) began to excavate a roadway in County Longford, which made those who believed that only the Romans built sophisticated roadways reconsider long held theories. This road had been preserved in the Corlea bog into which it had sunk. Like most roads in the Celtic world, it was a complicated structure of wood. It was carbon dated to the second century B.C., and represents sophisticated construction. Amazingly, after careful research it was discovered that the road was even mentioned in one of the Irish mythological tales, where the High King Eochaid charges Midir to build it. The details are given in Raftery's *Pagan Celtic Ireland* (1994).

Rivers like the Suir, the "sister river," where Fidelma learned to swim and fish with her brother, Colgú, the Blackwater (An Abhainn Mór), the Lee (Laoí), the Barrow (Bharú) and others are often mentioned. The author has often stated that he does not like to make allowances to modern anachronistic names, although he concedes the use of Cashel and Tara to help readers, rather than Caiseal Muman (Cashel) or Teamhair (Tara). So Kildare will be Cill Dara; Durrow, Darú; Ferns, Fearna; and so on. Sometimes, over the years, copyeditors have not agreed with the author's philosophy, and the modern Anglicized names have crept through.

Cashel is, of course, Fidelma's birthplace and is also the historic capital of the kingdom of Munster ruled by the Eóghanacht dynasty, the descendants of Eoghan Mór. During most of the stories, it is Fidelma's brother, Colgú, son of Failbe Flann, who rules Munster. He is a historical king whose dates of rule were A.D. 665–678. Colgú is listed as the twenty-second Munster King in descent from Conall Corc who founded the dynasty there. Fidelma is born there in 637. Caiseal Muman (stone fort of Munster), or the palace of The Rock and its surrounding township, is first introduced to readers in *Suffer Little Children*, where Tremayne vividly describes Fidelma's approach to the great palace to see her dying cousin, the King Cathal. Her brother is then heir apparent to the kingship and becomes king at the end of the story.

Cashel as a location is central, or referred to, in most of the stories. The great Rock of Cashel, on which the palace is located, is of limestone rising 200 feet from the plain of Tipperary and looks every bit a stronghold. The Eóghanacht built their capital there (reputedly) in A.D. 370. It is still an evocative place, although the current buildings on it date mainly from the Norman period. There is little sign of the royal capital because, in 1101, King Muirceartach gave the Rock and its buildings to the Church. Legends, such as the dubious visit of St. Patrick to The Rock to baptize the Eóghanacht King Óengus mac Nad Froích, and the magnificent church buildings, have caused a concentration by tourist guides on the Christianity aspects of The Rock.

Due to the demands of Sister Fidelma fans who wanted to know something of the early history of Cashel, Peter Tremayne wrote *Sister Fidelma's Cashel: The Early Kings of Munster and their Capital* (published by the International Sister Fidelma Society, 2008). Cashel and its story not only appear in the annals and chronicles, but also in an early text, *Senchas Faghbhála Caisil andso sis agus Beandacht*, or "The Finding of Cashel." According to Professor Myles Dillon (1900–1972) the text was set down in the early fifth century by Torna Eigeas (*Ériú*, No. XVI, 1952). The scribes and writers in ancient Cashel produced some impressive early Irish literary works. The first surviving dictionary of Irish was written in Cashel in the tenth century, *Sanas Cormac* or Cormac's Glossary, as the work is ascribed to the King-Bishop of Cashel, Cormac mac Cuuilleannán, born on The Rock in A.D. 836. He was known for his scholarship and his poetry.

As capital of Munster, Cashel is, of course, essential to the Fidelma stories.

More than once Fidelma has pointed out to Eadulf, as they passed the hill of Knockgraffon (Cnoc Raffan or Raffan's Hill), that this was the place of the coronations of the Eóghanachta kings of Munster before they decided on Cashel as their capital. Knockgraffon is fives miles southwest of Cashel. Four miles further south is Cahir (Cathair — a fortress), which is on the River Suir just south of the entrance to the Glen of Aherlow. These places are also mentioned in the stories.

In *Suffer Little Children*, Fidelma is sent southwest from Cashel on a mission to Ros Ailithir, the pilgrim's promontory, which today is called Rosscarberry, County Cork. It was here in the sixth or seventh century that St. Fachtna founded his religious community, which became famous for the quality of its teaching. The perceptive visitor may notice, on the wall of the surviving building of St. Fachtna's Cathedral, a plaque bearing the name of one of the author's forebears. Nearby is a stone megalithic circle called Reanascreena (Rae na Scríne — level place of the shrine), which Peter also uses as a location.

In this same story Fidelma has to follow some clues and takes a ship (*The Barnacle Goose*, which appears in several stories) to one of the most stunning locations. This is Na Sceallagha (The Skelligs) lying eight miles into the Atlantic at the end of the Iveragh Peninsula, County Kerry. They are sheer rocks jutting out of the Atlantic. On Skellig Micheal is a twin peaked rock where a sixth-century monastic foundation balances precariously at the top of a 724-foot climb on a rock face, with sides dropping like sheer cliffs. The ancient Irish monks had to cut stone steps in the rock to reach this place. Even so, the beehive shaped huts have a small garden and other outbuildings. Even in such an inaccessible place the religious were not safe from Viking raids, and the monks finally relocated to the mainland in the ninth century. The author and his wife have climbed the dangerous path in the footsteps of Fidelma to view the remains of the settlement.

In *The Subtle Serpent* Fidelma leaves Ross Aiithir to move further southwest to another of the author's favourite spots — the Beara Peninsula. It is a peninsula, with its roots at Glengariff on the south and Kenmare on the north, extending for 35 miles into the Atlantic with the Caha Mountains as its backbone. There is no other area in Ireland that contains such a proliferation of ancient sites. It is regarded in Irish mythology as the land of primordial beginnings and endings, where the ancient god of death, Donn, took the souls to rest on their journey to the Otherworld. It is the place where all the seven mythological invasions of Ireland made landfall. In 2007, the author, in his role as Celtic scholar, was invited to lecture the Beara Historical Society on the area — "The Peninsula of Primal Beginnings." His talk was regarded as so important that the local newspaper, *The Southern Star*, decided to print his text verbatim in the June 2, June 16, and June 23, 2007, issues.

Peter has written about his favorite spot, Dunboy, in a short story, "The Way of the White Cow," chosen for *Great Irish Stories of Childhood*, edited by Peter Haining (1997).

The author places his main Fidelma location in a spot where he once hired a house in an inlet beyond Castletownbeare, designated as The Abbey of the Three Wells. On the other side of the inlet was a favorite historical location — Dún Buidhe (Dunboy), a stronghold of the O'Sullivan Beare — which stood until 1602. It was regarded as the last castle to hold out against the Elizabethan Conquest. Sir George Carew, the English commander, pulverized it with cannon fire and then massacred all the inhabitants after they had surrendered. The location is a rich and impressive one.

At the end of *The Subtle Serpent* there is mention of an historical battle as an "off-stage" event, but it is central to the resolution of the novel. This is the Battle of Cnoc Áine (Knockainy — the Hill of Áine). It was fought by Colgú against the Ui Fidgente, who provide villains in this story and often in other stories as well. Knockainey is just west of Tipperary Town in County Limerick. It is an isolated hill standing 513 feet high, which was said to be the seat of the goddess Áine. Other stories claim her as a Munster princess of the second century, and the cairn on the summit is said to be her resting place. Until the nineteenth century the hill was the center of a festival in which men with flaming torches climbed to the top of the hill and circled the cairn. This, indeed, was the location, where the Uí Fidgente were defeated by Colgú of Cashel.

The Spider's Web (1997) starts out with Fidelma judging some minor cases in the abbey of Lios Mór (Lismore in County Waterford) south of Cashel on the river Blackwater (An Abhainn Mór) at the foot of the Knockmealdown Mountains (Cnoc Mhaol Domhnaigh or Hill of Maoldomhnach). Lismore is also the main location of *The Chalice of Blood*. The abbey there was founded in the seventh century by St. Carthach, who was given the pet name of

Mochuda. He died in A.D. 637, the year of Fidelma's birth. The site of the abbey is now lost, but a castle was built on the site in 1589 for the use of Sir Walter Raleigh, who had taken a lead role in the conquest of Ireland. The castle is now owned, as it has been since the mid eighteenth century, by the Dukes of Devonshire.

Lismore is a site which also occurs several times in the Fidelma stories. In *The Spider's Web*, after the initial opening, Fidelma is sent across the mountains into the village of Araglin, the valley of the river Ara. The Ara Valley runs towards Kilworth and Fermoy. The entire sequence of events takes place in this picturesque area, renowned for its scenic walks and equestrian territory.

Valley of the Shadow sees Fidelma and Eadulf pushing into an isolated area of the west to a place called Gleann Geis, the forbidden valley, where the clans have not yet converted to the Christian faith. It is clear, following the author's description, that we are now on the Iveragh Peninsula, County Kerry. Beyond the scenic Lakes of Killarney we rise into the highest mountain range in Ireland, the MacGillycuddy Reeks, which includes the tallest mountain in Ireland, Carrantuohill (Corran Tuathil or Tuathil's Sickle), at 3,414 feet. It is a deceptive place, where the climate seems mild, and there are many varieties of subtropical plants which grow in profusion on the mountainsides and near the lakes. But be warned. Many climbers and walkers, thinking the mountains are mere hills compared with many ranges, have met their death here in bad winter weather where temperatures drop to -20ºC. One German climber's body was not found for seven weeks, and another English climber went missing in September and his body was not recovered until the following April. For Americans, the mountain holds a special tragedy. In December 1943, a USAF DC3 (Dakota) with a five-man crew smashed into the top of the mountain and all were killed. The bodies could not be recovered until the following February. Deceptive at times, the area can be, as the author describes, a forbidden place.

It was obvious, given the period and topic of the series, that the author would take his characters to one of the most important seventh-century ecclesiastical sites in Munster. Imleach Iubair (Emly, Borderland of Trees) is modern Emly, in County Tipperary, eight miles west of Tipperary town itself. This is where the main action of *The Monk Who Vanished* (1999) is set. This was the site of a community founded by a pre–Patrician saint called Ailbe. Ailbe was the patron saint of the south of Ireland before St. Patrick took precedence. His foundation also became the main cathedral of the south, vying with Armagh for power. It was not until the reign of High King BríanBorú, who was a former King of Munster, that Armagh was accepted as the primacy of Ireland by those in the south of the country. Emly stayed a "Cathedral City" until 1587 when it was combined with the See of Cashel.

The original ancient buildings were replaced in the thirteenth century, and finally destroyed during the aftermath of the English conquest in 1607. The author himself took some of those attending the 2006 Féile Fidelma by coach to see the remains. The modern church was built 1882, although within its graveyard stands a yew tree, St. Ailbe's Well, and the remains of an ancient weathered stone cross claimed to be the marker on the saint's resting place dating to the sixth century.

There is a stop-off for Fidelma and Eadulf on their way to Emly at a tavern by Ara's Well (Tiobrad Árann, modern Tipperary). She comes there after crossing the river Suir at a ford by Athassael Abbey. The author believes the original name to mean the ford of the ass (Átha Assal), although some local people would dispute it. While Tipperary town, by the side of the River Ara, arose in the twelfth century, the author has located a small blacksmith and tavern there, which tavern occurs not only in *The Monk Who Vanished* but in *The Leper's Bell*.

Act of Mercy (1999) starts off in Ard Mór, Ardmore on the County Waterford coast but, of course, the main action is set on a pilgrim ship *The Barnacle Goose* sailing towards Santiago de Compostela. The author acknowledges that the course of the ship was carefully navigated by his friend, the composer Christos Pittas, on his yacht the *Alycone*, so that when the ship in the story comes into peril in a rocky area south of Cornwall and makes landfall on a Breton island of Ushant, these places actually exist. The author also uses his knowledge of the Muirbretha or "sea laws" from Brehon law. *The Barnacle Goose*, if one can regard the ship as a location, also occurs in *Suffer Little Children* and *The Dove of Death*.

Although the Ardmore location in *Act of Mercy* is confined to the opening chapter, it is a place that has occurred, or is mentioned, in other stories as, at this time, it is used as the closest sea port to Cashel. The author has used this location more than once, and it appears in his short story "Corpse on a Holy Day." Ardmore is a historic place where another pre–Patrician saint, Declan, founded his community in the fifth century. This was part of the subkingdom of the Déisi Muman. It was the Déisi who went to Wales and established the kingdom of Dyfed. As well as signs of the original foundation, St. Declan's Well, Ardmore has one of the oldest oratories, named after St. Declan. It measures 13 feet by 9 feet. There are Ogham-inscribed stones, a round tower, and a tenth-century cathedral still surviving. Perhaps there is no need to mention that Peter and his wife frequently stay there.

Our Lady of Darkness (2000) takes us from Munster, Fidelma having arrived back at Ardmore and then gone to Cashel before she crosses into the neighboring kingdom of Laigin (Leinster). This time Fidelma has to go to the then capital of the kings of Laigin, to an abbey in Fearna (place of the alder trees — modern Ferns), where Eadulf is being held prisoner by the cruel Abbess Fainder. The abbey at Ferns is said to have been founded by St. Aedh in A.D. 598. He is also known by his pen name Moaedhog (my little Aedh), who lived from 550 to 632. By the time of this story, the author has Abbess Fainder in charge of a mixed community. At this time another famous abbey had been founded nearby by St. Moling, who comes into later stories.

Badger's Moon (2003) brings us back to Munster, this time into West Cork where Fidelma and Eadulf have been sent by her brother. They stay en route at the abbey of St. Finnbar in what is now Cork City. St. Finnbar's abbey also occurs more than once in the Fidelma stories, such as in the short story "St. Finnbar's Bell." They then proceed west of the city, which one may still do, along the route N22, parallel with the river Bride (An Bhríd) before moving south to the main location of Rath Raithlen (Raheen). If you check the Irish names you will easily be able to follow the locations around the ancient hill fort, such as the settings along the river Tuogh and the bridge at Tuocusheen. In the old Irish references mentioned in the novel, this is the river Tuath, its full name explained to Fidelma as Tuath an Chúisnigh. This means the dividing market of the territory (Tuath) of Cúisnigh, one of the chieftains of the area. It is a fertile area, replete with ancient and even modern historical spots; not far away is Beal na mBláth, where on August 20, 1922, the famous Michael Collins was killed in an ambush during the Irish Civil War.

The end of the book includes a cliffhanger, as on the way back to Cashel Fidelma and Eadulf find a Cashel warrior waiting for them at a seventh-century monastery with the news that their son has been kidnapped, and their nurse, Saréit, has been killed. Ard Finnan (Finan's Height, now Ardfinnan, County Tipperary) is an abbey founded by Finn Lob hair, Finn the Leper, who died in A.D. 613. They cross by a ford over the river Suir. Ard Finan occurs in other stories, and in *The Chalice of Blood* they pass through it to find that a new bridge has been built across the river Suir.

The ending of *Badger's Moon* leads to *The Leper's Bell* (2004). As the search widens for the abducted Alchú, Fidelma's son, the locations take us from Cashel to the west once again. It's worth mentioning another location before we leave Cashel, which is Rath na Dríne, where Ferloga has his tavern. Rath na Dríne occurs several times in the stories and is situated along a minor road, a short distance due south from Cashel. It is between the two major roads that would take one the eight miles to Clonmel (Cluain Mela — the field of honey), where Fidelma also has associations.

In *The Leper's Bell* we are taken to Ara's Well (Tipperary) again, then the abbey of Imleach (Emly) to nearby Cnoc Loinge (Knocklong, County Limerick). Knocklong is another place of mythology and history. The Hill of the

Ship is said to have come from an early seventh-century battle when a Connacht army was defeated here — the encampment on the hill made it look like a ship under sail. On this hill it was said that the King of Munster consulted his Druid Mug Ruith when the High King Cormac Mac Art invaded the territory. We finally move on to the beginning of the Dingle Peninsula under the shadow of Sliabh Mis (Slemish Mountain). Here Eadulf finds the tower of Uaman, lord of the passes of Sliabh Mis. The tower is on an island, Inis, separated from the mainland at high tide by dangerous incoming tides. There is also quicksand. The area is easily identified even today. Inis is, of course, Inch, meaning "island."

The author does not move far from here for *Master of Souls* (2005), as it is thought that Uaman has not perished. The opening sequence is again at Inch. But Fidelma and Eadulf are at that time in the abbey of Ard Fearta — the hill with a grave. Ardfert, County Kerry, was a notable religious community founded by St. Brendan in the sixth century. The remains of the cathedral and monastery are among the most interesting in County Kerry, the visible remains dating back to the thirteenth century. But soon Fidelma and Eadulf have to leave there to solve their mystery. We are taken on a tour of the Dingle Peninsula. It is the most northerly and spectacular of the long Kerry peninsulas. It is mountainous and wild and there are many spectacular areas that Fidelma travels through from Daingean Uí Chúis (Dingle, or O Cush's fortess), now the largest town on the peninsula, where Fidelma is a guest of the local chief, Slébéne of the Corco Duibhne, and even sings for her supper. Not far away is the Gallarus oratory dating back to this period, a building of drystone masonry arranged to slope downwards to throw off the rain. Above the door are two corbels. The interior is as dry today as it was when it was first built. It is proof positive of the sophistication of the Irish ability to build in stone as described in the books.

There is another interesting location which the author uses in this story — the Magharee (Seven Hogs) Islands opposite Fahamoren. Fidelma sets off for the largest of them, Illauntannig, which has the remains of an early monastery and a ruined church, while on Illaimimil are a stone circle, a dolmen, and other megalithic remains.

A Prayer for the Damned (2006) starts off with an introductory sequence in Connemara. Then we are firmly back in Munster, with arguments over celibacy at a meeting in Imleach (Emly) before the main action, which occurs predominately in Cashel. There are excursions to the Valley of Eatharlaí (Glen of Aherlow). The river Eatharlaí, which runs through the glen, is a tautology as *eatharlaí*. The Glen of Aherlow is a valley about two miles wide at its mouth, narrowing to less than a mile. I was lucky to be on a coach with the author conducting us along this gentle and beautiful wooded and pastoral area. The river flows through the glen and the woods where there are ruined castles and a very early church with gravestones and St. Berrihert's Well. In fact, in this story, the author combines a historical account of three Saxon brothers — Berrihert, Pecanum and Naovan — who came to Ireland after Whitby and were allowed to settle in Aherlow, setting up their religious foundations there. Their sites are easily identified in the valley to this day.

In chapters fifteen and sixteen, Fidelma has a confrontation in a tiny glen called St. Patrick's Well. Again, this is an actual place, south of Clonmel (Cluain Meala — the "field of honey"), which Fidelma often refers to as a favorite bathing place on the river Suir. The hollow is situated just south of Clonmel, off the former main road to Cahir. It is a sheltered spot, easily missed if you are not looking for it. You enter by way of a long flight of stone steps to find yourself in a place with an old chapel, complete with a spring well from which a large volume of water continuously spurts. It is pure and clear. The quiet is incredible, and one is surrounded by amazing trees and undergrowth. Peter and his wife have often been to this spot, and the author is on record as saying the place is like a balm to the senses. Not so when Fidelma was fighting for her life there.

It was inevitable that Tara (Teamhair), the capital of the High Kings in County Meath, would enter into the stories. The author does not disappoint his readers; it is a setting for *Dancing with Demons* (2007) when the High King himself is assassinated and Fidelma is sent to investigate. Tara in all its glory is revealed in this book. Peter has often been there and has delivered lectures at Bellinter House, under its shadow, then run by the Sisters of Our Lady of Zion. He wrote an excellent defense of the Boyne valley against the Irish Government's plans to build the M3 motorway through the historic Boyne Valley which houses Tara — comparing it to knocking down the Egyptian pyramids to build a freeway ("Bridging the Past," *Irish Arts Review*, Autumn 2007).

Apart from Tara itself, Fidelma has to go to another nearby ancient site in County Meath. This is on Sliabh na Cailaighe (The Hag's Mountain) at Loughcrew. The author once called this site more fascinating than the sites at Knowth, Dowth, and Newgrange. Atop the hills are a series of fourth-millennium B.C. tombs, passage graves with petroglyphs, and astronomical alignments such as Cairn T where the sun of the Spring Equinox enters the passage and alights on the "Equinox Stone." The author uses these locations to great effect in an exciting sequence where Eadulf and Bishop Luachan are imprisoned in one of the tombs, and they are rescued by Fidelma. The author's wife, Dorothy, has told the story of how when she and Peter climbed up Sliabh na Caillaighe, she slipped twice on the descent, wrenching her ankle. Peter had to drive her to a doctor for attention. She commented: "The old hag obviously didn't like me."

Tara has also appeared in several Fidelma short stories such as "The High King's Sword" (1993) and "A Scream from the Sepulcher" (1998).

The Chalice of Blood (2010) has several fascinating settings: an opening at Bingium (Bingerbruck on the Rhine), then Cashel, passing through the Knockmealdon mountains and into Lismore. Lismore is the main location of the action, apart from a trip in search of answers to clues at Fermoy (Fhear Maighe — place of the men of the plain).

I have set myself to dealing with the main Munster locations in the novels, but, at this time of writing, there are also some 34 short stories, of which 30 have been gathered in two volumes — *Hemlock At Vespers* (2000) and *Whispers of the Dead* (2004). All these stories are set in Irish locations with one exception; "The Lost Eagle" is set in Canterbury in Kent, England, when Fidelma and Eadulf pass through to meet their adventure outlined in *The Haunted Abbot*. There is, perhaps, no need for me to recall that Fidelma began her "career" in short story form in 1993. Eadulf usually does not appear in these stories, and the locations vary across Ireland. Once more, the descriptions of locations are important to the stories. From Tara, Kildare, Durrow, even the islands in Roaring Water Bay off Baltimore, the Blaskets off Dingle, and among the mountains Comeragh and to Ferns, most stories have very identifiable locations.

It is not my intention to list them all. However, there is one Fidelma novella, "Night of the Snow Wolf" (*Historical Crimes*, edited by Mike Ashley, 2011), which is worth considering for its atmospheric location. In this story we can follow Fidelma's journey by horse during a winter blizzard, through the lonely Slieve Felim Mountains from County Limerick into County Tipperary, along deserted mountain passes, northward with the Keeper Hill (Sliabh Coimeálta) on her left and down to the river An Mhaoicheain. We can even pause by a standing stone which marks the spot where Fidelma is able to cross the river into the pass of Sliabh an Airgid, and the Silvermine Mountains, then to the town of Béal an Gabhann, known in English as Silvermines. It is a remote, trekking countryside, where the local place names have so far not condescended to being given English or Anglicized equivalents.

In examining the locations of the Sister Fidelma Mysteries there is an inevitable question that arises — one which I have found necessary to put to the author. "Which comes first, location or story? Do you go to a place and research it and say, 'This is a good place in which to set a Fidelma story'?"

Peter Tremayne responded for this essay:

> There has been only once where a specific location dictated an entire novel. That was, of course, in *Behold A Pale Horse*. I was visiting Bobbio in the Trebbia Valley in northern Italy, an abbey founded by the Irish missionary, Columbanus, in the early seventh century. I was asked to give a talk in the cloisters of the

abbey, at the end of which those gathered in the audience urged me to bring Sister Fidelma to Bobbio.

When I started to write the Fidelma Mysteries, I knew that she would be an Eóghanacht princess, and that meant only one major location — Cashel. I had known Cashel since I was a boy. I was, however, dictated by the annals and chronicles and the hagiographies. Often Fidelma has to set out across her brother's kingdom and even beyond. Without wishing to appear egocentric, I seemed to know the ancient geography of Munster as if all the modern towns and buildings did not exist. I could envisage Munster of Fidelma's day with its ancient fortress, abbeys, communities, mountains, rivers, hills, and its roadways. I have spent years exploring Munster, noting its topography, and I hope that I have succeeded in placing them correctly in the stories. When Fidelma sets out from Cashel, it is as if she leads me wherever the story should go. Often, she does not go where I expect her to. For example, in *The Chalice of Blood*, I had expected the story to be entirely set in the Abbey of Lismore. But something happened halfway through, and she ended up in Fermoy, where Fidelma found she had to consult a library, which I had vaguely remembered from an ancient text.

One gets the impression that the author, in these books, is preparing the way for adventurous modern-day tourists to come off the beaten track and start exploring the real Ireland. It is no wonder that the *Lonely Planet Guide to Ireland* (2010 edition) has quoted the Sister Fidelma novels. As a recent web reviewer says of *The Chalice of Blood*: "As always the setting comes to life in this strong historical series."

Fidelma of Cashel and the Brehon Code

Patrick O'Keefe

Like a Celtic knot, so intricate and tightly woven are the Sister Fidelma mystery novels of Peter Tremayne that it is sometimes possible to overlook the author's detailed familiarity with the Irish law of the seventh century. It would be an unfortunate mistake, however, to dismiss the leading character's exercises in legal reasoning as mere flights of literary license. Rather, they represent trenchant reflections on ancient Irish society presented by a trained and accomplished Celtic scholar, Peter Berresford Ellis, who in 1989 received the Irish Post award in recognition of his work in Celtic history. Deftly switching back and forth in his dual roles as storyteller and scholar, Tremayne/Ellis treats the reader to a fascinating, detailed, and entertaining immersion in a highly sophisticated bygone legal culture.

A key component of that legal culture, if not its very cornerstone, was the Brehon Code, so named in reference to the Gaelic word for judge—"*breitheamh*," though properly referred to as *Fenechas* or the law of the free soil-tillers. In his seminal work *The Celtic Empire*, Ellis maintains that the Brehon laws comprise the oldest formal law system in Europe. He notes that the legendary origin of the Brehon laws is attributed to Ollamh Fodhla who, when he became High King of Ireland circa 714 B.C., is said to have introduced the Brehon Law system (Ellis 183). It underwent an overhaul, as an ancient introduction to the Senchus Mor (a legal tract) maintains, in the year A.D. 438 when the then King of Ireland, Laegaire, appointed a committee of nine learned men, which included himself and St. Patrick, to revise the existing laws and compile a code. At the end of three years of labor the new code was presented at assemblies throughout Ireland where, apparently, it was met with nearly universal acceptance. Its popularity might be attributed partially to its characteristics as a genuine code. That is, it was a complete system of positive law, carefully arranged and integrated in order to address every sort of legal problem.

In this sense, the Brehon code was a true code and not merely a compilation of constitutions, edicts, and occasional legislation as were the Roman law Codex Gregorianus of A.D. 291 and the Codex Hermogenianus of 295. These privately published works apparently served as a sort of vade mecum, or handbook, for lawyers, merchants, and imperial administrators. It was not until the reign of the Emperor Justinian, nearly one hundred years after the Brehon Code, that a commission of ten learned men was appointed to prepare a true code for the Roman Empire. Published in 529, the Justinian Code replaced all prior imperial law, but it was supplanted in 534 by the Codex Repetitae Praelectionis.

The Brehon Code, by contrast, was intended to be modified, or updated, every three years following a *feis*, or festival assembly, at Tara where nobles, scholars, and the people together made any amendments deemed necessary. It might be supposed reasonably that this triennial gathering kept the code fresh and continuously useful. Tremayne makes reference to this law reform assembly in one of the short stories entitled "Gold at Night," which is included in the collection entitled *Whispers of the Dead*. Reference is also found in "The Fosterer" which is also included in *Whispers of the Dead*.

The Brehon Code, because it was comprehensive, responded to the entire spectrum of ancient Irish society and enumerated various rights and responsibilities. The relationships commonly established in human life — landlord and tenant, master and servant, husband and wife, etc.— were all carefully provided for (MacManus 129). The various professions and occupations were also the subjects of specific provisions in the law. For example, in "The Fosterer" Tremayne refers to "*brechbretha*," or the laws pertaining to beekeeping. In "Dark Moon Rising," another short story appearing in *Whispers of the Dead*, he makes reference to the provisions of the Leabhar Acaill, or the Book of Acaill, which specify that an employer is responsible for his workers if they are injured in his employ. It bears mentioning in this regard that these legal obligations preceded the contemporary concepts underlying modern workers' compensation laws by nearly two millenia.

Ancient Irish society was highly stratified; each inhabitant occupied a distinct rung on the social ladder, and the Brehon Code specified their reciprocal rights, duties, and privileges. There were five classes of people and rank was determined predominantly, though not entirely, by property. There was some fluidity of movement, driven largely by the acquisition of greater wealth and a demonstration of unimpeachable good character, such that one might rise to a higher status through diligence or good fortune. In the first rank were the kings, from the king of a *tuath* (a relatively small region) to the *Ard*

Ri, or High King of Ireland. At any point there were at least 100 kings of various ranks throughout the country. The next rank consisted of the nobles, called *flaith*, which included kings, followed by non-noble free men of property. This latter class included men who owned no land of their own but possessed moveable wealth, usually in the form of livestock. Tremayne frequently introduces a character called a "*bo-aire*," literally "cow-chief," as a petty magistrate. Such individuals were among this third class. Fidelma herself, as the biological sister of King Colgu of Muman, belonged to the high noble class, a fact which she used to advantage in several of Tremayne's stories.

Below these three classes of gentry were the non-noble freemen without property, or the *feine*, which comprised the bulk of the population. The literature suggests that this class was considered the bedrock of the community since they were both the governed and the ultimate source of law and authority. They were, in effect, the constituency. The final group consisted of the nonfree classes. This term does not necessarily connote slavery, though slavery was not wholly unknown in seventh-century Ireland. As an institution, however, slavery appears to have become neither as pervasive nor as economically essential as it was, for example, in Republican Rome (Cahill 148). In the main, the nonfree classes were individuals whose civil rights had been curtailed. The most serious disability associated with this status was that they had no claim on any part of tribe land, though they could be allotted small tracts for subsistence farming. Called "*fuidhir*," these individuals were often criminals or prisoners of war. Some were those who could not or would not pay fines or damages awarded against them by a judge. Tremayne alludes to this lowest class in *Our Lady of Darkness*, again in *The Spider's Web*, and also in "Who Stole the Fish," another short story in *Whispers of the Dead*.

An individual's standing in the societal hierarchy had to do with much more than just social status. In the construct of ancient Ireland, it determined his value and the amount of compensation due him in the event of a wrong or bodily injury. Professor Kenneth Nicholls observes in his book *Gaelic and Gaelicized Ireland in the Middle Ages* that the most unusual feature of native Irish law to the contemporary eye is the total absence of criminal law as we know it (59). Instead, the Brehon Code provided an elaborate system of compensation to the aggrieved party if injured and to his family in the event of death. Known as an "*eraic*" fine or "honor price," it established the amount of damages, in silver or in cattle, according to the rank of the injured party; the higher his social rank, the greater the damages. Body parts if injured had assigned values and, again, the amount varied from one social class to another. Since most of the Fidelma mysteries involve murder and mayhem, the concept of the honor price payable for wrongful death makes a frequent appearance.

The *eraic* was not only payable for bodily injury and death, however; it was also payable in the event of slander and insult. In regard to the latter, Tremayne provides an excellent illustration in *Master of Souls*. There, Fidelma reminds the Venerable Mac Faosma that in insulting her he also insults a representative of the law and, thus, the law itself. The honor price for which Mac Faosma would be liable, therefore, would be due for the affront to the system itself and not solely to the dignity of the individual. In "The Heir Apparent," a short story included in *Whispers of the Dead*, Fidelma alluded to the law text *Bretha Nemed deidenach* on the law of insults when she reproached Augaire for insulting her during a hearing. Augaire's mother expressed concern, since Fidelma's honor price would be greater than her son could pay. His failure to pay would result in the forfeiture of his civil rights, and it would require him to labor until he earned the amount due in order for his rights to be restored. Unstated in this confrontation is the legal principle that an individual's inability to pay an honor price fine may have consequences for his family as well. Under the rule of *cinn comhfhocuis*, the corporate family was responsible for the wrongful acts of each of its members (53). Professor Nicholls observes that the family, or clan, could renounce responsibility for the acts of the accused through a formal and public process, thus making him an outlaw who theoretically could be legally put to death by the family of the decedent if the offense was homicide. Further, Professor Nicholls notes reports of wrongdoers being physically handed over to the injured party in lesser cases if they could not pay the adjudged damages (60).

The Irish system, based as it was on the principle of compensation, stood in stark contrast with the retaliatory system widespread in the rest of Europe at that time. Tremayne uses the plot in *Our Lady of Darkness* to illustrate both the incursion of the European model and the tension, if not open conflict, with the influence of the Church of Rome as the progenitor of the retribution based system. Derived in substantial measure from the legal precepts of the Old Testament, the Roman model drew its authority from Deuteronomy 19.21, which instructs, "Thine eye shall not pity; but life shall go for life, eye for eye, tooth for tooth, hand for hand, foot for foot." On the other hand, some authors suggest that the *eraic* system was repugnant to Roman churchmen because it conflicted with the strictures of Numbers 35.31, which says, "You shall not take money of him that is guilty of blood, but he shall die forthwith" (O'Flanagan 3–4). These and other scriptural references from the Old Testament, curiously to the general exclusion of the more forgiving teachings of the New Testament, were the underpinnings of Roman church support of a punishment-based system. Subsumed into what Tremayne collectively refers to as The Penitentials, this harsher system, prevalent in Europe, had no reference in the ancient Irish law (Ellis 183). Known in legal Latin as Lex Talionis, the retributive system makes no pretense of setting the injured party in a compensated position roughly equivalent to the position occupied before the wrong occurred. Rather, it is intended to visit upon the wrongdoer the same or greater loss as was brought about by the offense itself.

Under Roman criminal law, the restoration of stolen property to its rightful owner was considered almost ancillary to the punishment for the crime. The crime itself was considered an affront to the social order, a disturbance of the peace of the realm. The police power of the state, in a sense, was directed primarily toward the apprehension, conviction, and punishment of the malefactor. Thus, for example, at Roman law, we find the doctrine of lex Hostilia de furtis, a doctrine providing that the state could prosecute a person for theft without the owner's participation, as when the owner was busy on official business. Under the Irish system, Professor Nicholls reports, a thief was to return the stolen property plus its equivalent value, in addition to the cost of recovery. Alternatively, the thief could repay twice the value of the stolen property, plus costs (Nicholls 62). As is readily apparent, the two systems were based on distinctly different rationales. One relied upon the price of compensation as a deterrent, the other upon the fear of harsh punishment. In the Irish system, the wronged individual or his family occupied the center of importance; under the Roman system, the state itself was the aggrieved party.

As in modern society, awards and judgments were not always paid voluntarily. The Brehon laws recognized, therefore, a collection procedure known as distraint or distress; that is, the property of the judgment debtor could be seized after the expiration of a stay period, called an "*anad.*" This interval, though usually a fairly short time, allowed the debtor the opportunity to consider his chances before a judge who would be called upon to confirm the underlying judgment. At the end of the lawful stay, absent further response from the debtor, the creditor could proceed at law and take physical possession of the goods and sell them. The cost of sequestering the goods or cattle would be deducted from the sale price.

In some instances, the plaintiff preceded distraint by "fasting on" the debtor. After serving due notice, the plaintiff went to the house of the debtor and fasted at his door. As long as he remained there, the defendant was obliged likewise to fast. It was considered utterly disgraceful to refuse to submit to the fasting process thus initiated by the plaintiff, though the resolution might take the form of a pledge to pay the debt or an agreement to try the matter before the local brehon. A refusal to take cognizance of the custom meant the forfeiture of all character and resulted in something quite like a universal shunning or boycott (MacManus 136).

Not surprisingly, Fidelma has been called upon from time to time to draw upon her knowledge of the Irish laws of heirship and inheritance. Unlike the system of primogeniture common in parts of Europe, the office of chieftain was decided by a vote of the "*derbfine*," an aggregation of family or clan members consisting of at least three generations of adults. The chieftain himself was not elected at the assembly but, rather, his successor, called the "*tanaiste*," who would assume the mantle of chieftain upon the demise of the serving chieftain. An instructive description of this process appears in the short story "The Heir Apparent" which is contained in *Whispers of the Dead*. Though relatively rare, a female leader might be chosen in the absence of a suitable male. Tremayne discusses the phenomenon of "*banchomarbae*," or a female heir, in *Master of Souls*. This electoral process, called Tanistry, prevailed in Ireland until the reign of James I, when it was abolished and made illegal.

Though durable and popular in its application, the Brehon Code cannot be said to have been simple. The textual language often was arcane in that it was written in one of the oldest dialects of Gaelic. Specific forms were to be used; nuances from related law were to be considered, and a variety of complicated technical terms were employed. The Brehon Code would not have been considered user friendly, and achieving mastery was an arduous process. Tremayne reminds his readers periodically that Fidelma not only completed the rigorous training required to be a lawyer; she was also qualified to the level of "*anruth*," which was one step below the highest level of qualification. Thus, she would have completed more than eight years of legal training. Upon completion of the basic but extensive course of study, the individual was qualified as a "*dalaigh*," or lawyer/advocate. The system itself was administered by brehons who were lawyers of advanced training and experience. The present Irish court system's website describes the brehons as officers similar to but not the same as our modern concept of a judge; their role was analogous to that of an arbitrator whose task it was to preserve and interpret the law rather than to expand it (O'Flanagan 5). The Courts Service essay entitled "Brehon Law" remarks that the absence of a ubiquitous formal court system or a police force suggests that the ancient Irish had a remarkable respect for the law.

Some readers may wonder how brehons made a living. Fidelma, of course, was from the noble class, so one may suppose that she had inherited sources of income. Most brehons were hereditary; some families had been brehons for many generations, as was the case with some of the most important of the hereditary jurist families such as the Mac Egans and the Mac Clancys (Nicholls 52). In Fidelma's case, however, there is no suggestion of an antecedent brehon. Rather, her father was King Failbe Fland, who died the year after her birth, which occurred in 636. Thus, it may be supposed, Fidelma was not dependent upon her income as a *dalaigh*. Her vocation as a religieuse likewise clouds the question. The ordinary lawyer, however, like today, depended upon fees for his living, though some were attached to noble households and were granted land of their own. Not unlike his modern counterpart in Ireland, the seventh-century Irish lawyer was paid by his client, but in contested matters the losing party paid both the fees of his own lawyer and the fees of the winner's lawyer.

As their fee for acting as arbitrators, the brehons received an amount called "*oiledheag*," which was one-eleventh of the sum demanded or awarded as damages, which is to say one-twelfth of the total sum in dispute, plus itself (Nicholls 58). The role of brehon was not without financial risk, however. The arbitrating brehon was obliged to post a substantial sum as security against a false, or incorrect, judgment. In the instance of a reversal of judgment on review, the brehon lost not only his fee but the security as well. Tremayne illustrates this point obliquely but clearly in the short story "A Scream from the Sepulcher" contained in *Hemlock at Vespers* where Fidelma learned that the local brehon, Fiacc, had been reversed on eleven occasions during a short period of time and was reduced to a state of penury, thus establishing the motive for his part in the crime. It seems reasonable to posit that the jurist surety arrangement in ancient Irish law described above vouchsafed that not only was the brehon exceedingly learned in the law but sedulously fair in his decision.

Contemporary lawyers will be familiar with the tenet of the law to the effect that justice must not only be done; it must be perceived to be done. That is to say, not only must the decision at law be fair; it must also be seen to be fairly arrived upon. For brehons sitting in something similar to an arbitration proceeding, it must have been critically important that the proceedings be open and that procedural safeguards be carefully observed. The parties were entitled to be represented by counsel, and rules pertaining to the admissibility of evidence had to be observed. The ancient Irish had a passion for condign justice and had an enormous respect for a well-reasoned, finely balanced judgment (MacManus, 348–49). Reference to the legend of Cormac MacArt illustrates the point. A young prince whose father lost a decisive battle, Cormac MacArt was supplanted as High King by the usurper, MacCon, and went into hiding. His friends and allies continued to press his claim to the throne and in time he made his way to Tara where MacCon held court. Upon his arrival he found MacCon presiding over an important trial. A flock of sheep had strayed from their pasture and grazed on a valuable crop of "*glaisin*," or woadplant, used to produce blue dye. The queen, who owned the crop, instituted proceedings to recover her damages. Upon hearing the undisputed evidence, MacCon declared the sheep forfeited in payment for the lost crop. MacArt stepped forward and challenged the judgment, saying that inasmuch as the sheep had only eaten the fleece of the land, only the fleece of the sheep should be forfeited. Legend has it that his decision was seen to be so just that MacCon was deposed and Cormac MacArt was made High King (O'Flanagan 2). Perhaps it is simply the stuff of which legends are made, but the story demonstrates the Irish delight in recourse to appropriate legal analogy as the basis for judgment. A brehon who could support his reasoning in such fashion was considered endowed with great judicial wisdom.

A career in law in ancient Ireland was no easy undertaking. The training was long and demanding; the subject was abstruse and recondite. The practice of law was exacting and required both an encyclopedic command of the entire field of law and a sound, thoughtful sense of justice. Tremayne's character, Fidelma of Cashel, vividly embodies these characteristics and presents us with a portal through which we may enter the Golden Age of Brehon Law.

WORKS CITED

"Brehon Law." An tSeirbhis Chuirteanna. *Courts Service*. Web. 27 Sept. 2011. <http://www.courts.ie>.
Cahill, Thomas. *How the Irish Saved Civilization*. London: Hodder & Stoughton, 1995.
Ellis, Peter B. *The Celtic Empire*. London: Constable, 1990.
MacManus, Seamus. *The Story of the Irish Race*. New York: Devlin-Adair, 1971.
Nicholls, Kenneth W. *Gaelic and Gaelicized Ireland in the Middle Ages*. Dublin: Lilliput, 2003.
O'Flanagan, Roderick J. *The Lives of the Lord Chancellors and Keepers of the Great Seal of Ireland*. New York: Kelley, 1870. Vol. 1.
Tremayne, Peter. *Hemlock at Vespers*. 2000. New York: St. Martin's Minotaur, 2000.
_____. *Master of Souls*. 2005. New York: St. Martin's Minotaur, 2006.
_____. *Our Lady of Darkness*. 2000. New York: St. Martin's, 2002.
_____. *The Spider's Web*. 1997. New York: St. Martin's, 1999.
_____. *Whispers of the Dead*. 2000. New York: St. Martin's Minotaur, 2000.

Druids and Brehons: Fidelma and the Druidic Tradition

Anita M. Vickers

To the modern world, the term "Druid" evokes mixed images. Some, perhaps knowing of Julius Caesar's account, equate the Druids with bloodthirsty barbarians who had their victims burned alive in a "Wicker Man" (a large wicker effigy where those to be offered to the gods were caged). Caesar (100 B.C.—44 B.C.) did leave the longest account of the Druids (Hutton 43), and much of what historians know of the Druids does come from Caesar. His accuracy, in some cases, and his intent, always, are questionable. Ronald Hutton conjectures that Caesar misrepresented the Druids, depicting them as more powerful, complicated, and threatening than they were—and similar to Roman priests (43–44). By and large, all accounts of ancient Druid life were made by their Roman enemies and their Greek collaborators (Hutton 2), not the Druids themselves. Thus Roman and Greek accounts must be viewed with some skepticism.

For others, Druids hold a mystical attraction as venerators of nature. According to the prominent Celtic scholar, Peter Berresford Ellis, much of common perception of who the Druids were has devolved into figures of soothsayers and wizards; he offers as example the Arthurian figure of Merlin relegated to an archetypal Druid (12). There appears to be no middle ground. In the 21st century Druids are primarily associated with the romantic, the mysterious, the inscrutable, and the ruthless.

As many mystery aficionados know, Peter Berresford Ellis also writes the Sister Fidelma mysteries under the nom de plume of Peter Tremayne. In an early interview, Tremayne addressed his dual role of scholar/mystery novelist, affirming that Fidelma serves as his fictional illustration of what he, as a Celtic historian, sees as the role of women in ancient Irish society, one that differs greatly from other European societies ("Fascination"). He elaborated further, maintaining that his scholarship provides him with the background for writing the series—thus the amount of additional research for him was negligible ("Fascination").

Certainly, Ellis the Celtic historian has produced a prodigious body of work on the ancient Celts and the Druids. He theorizes that the Druids were not barbaric priests and priestesses; instead they formed the intellectual class of society; as the descendents of ancient Indo-European culture, the Celtic Druids paralleled the Hindu Brahmin caste (14). He goes on to say that the Druid caste consisted of people of all the learned professions: religious leaders, philosophers, judges, teachers, political advisors, historians, poets, astronomers, and so forth (14). (Caesar's account does support this historical interpretation.) When the Celtic lands were Christianized, the Druids merged into the new culture with many becoming priests, monks, and nuns (18). It is this theory that, in part, becomes the background for the Fidelma series. Just as in his role as novelist Ellis/Tremayne has used the character of Fidelma to elucidate the true roles women played in ancient Irish society, so he uses the series as a whole to instruct modern audiences as to who the Druids were, what were their beliefs and practices, and, most importantly, how the Christian Brehons[1] were the natural descendents of the Druids.

Duality of purpose is not unusual in crime fiction. The detective or crime novel, by its very nature, is protean, allowing practitioners to explore multiple concerns (Westlake 5). The Fidelma series fulfills the primary purpose of the genre of crime fiction: to tell an entertaining story filled with suspense and to challenge intellectually the reader's powers of deduction. Mystery and detective novels (crime fiction) are the bestselling genre of fiction today in Great Britain and the United States (Winks, Preface ix). Perhaps the combination of entertainment and intellectual challenge is the reason for such popularity. Moreover, the subgenre historical crime fiction is the fastest growing branch of crime fiction (Winks, Introduction ix). While exercising their reasoning powers and being entertained, readers of historical crime fiction have the additional advantage of exploring the past through their reading. Thus often the most ardent fans and proficient writers of historical crime fiction are members of the professoriate (Winks, Introduction xiii). Or, in Tremayne's case, a respected journalist and historian draws upon his life's work to create an intriguing mystery series with an unlikely detective, a seventh-century Irish religieuse.[2] As Browne and Kreiser maintain, successful crime fiction writers authenticate their work by details, for often they reveal events and cultures that are omitted in traditional history books (Introduction 4). The Fidelma series is a prime example of how an historian/novelist provides an enlightening picture of time and people of which most reading audiences have little or no prior knowledge, specifically Irish Druidism.

Within the series Tremayne uses Druids — or references to Druidic practices — to misdirect the narrative, offer up plausible suspects (always found innocent), serve as red herrings, and provide an ominous atmosphere. That is the mark of a good mystery writer. Moreover, as a skilled practitioner of the historical detective subgenre and a Celtic historian, Tremayne has the perfect vehicle to contest and negate popular misperceptions of Druidism. The overarching mystery in the series is who the Druids were. Tremayne offers his readers the solution to this great historical conundrum by incorporating Druids and Druidism into the mysteries. They serve as fictional illustrations of his scholarly theories.

Druid Characters in the Fidelma Series

When Tremayne introduces a Druid in a story, the character invariably becomes an early suspect. Clearly, he anticipates that readers have bought into the negative view of Druids: filthy, ruthless practitioners of human sacrifice. Often these barbaric characters vehemently and vociferously oppose Christianity. In a series where the main detective is a religieuse, this would make them likely crime suspects. But they are never the murderers.[3] At least those who practice the old ways do not murder out of religious fanaticism — unlike the Christians who do murder frequently in the name of religion or theology.

In the short story "Murder in Repose," Erca, the local Druid, acts suspiciously. (A young monk has been falsely accused of murdering a local girl. Fidelma has set out to prove his innocence.) Erca is hostile, dirty, and verbally abusive, very misanthropic in his ideas and behavior. He also is a hermit. Fidelma has met others like him before, so she is not surprised at his appearance or demeanor ("Murder in Repose" 9). Erca hates all Christians and invokes the gods of the De Danann[4] to rid Eireann (Ireland) of their presence. He has no sympathy for the accused monk, Brother Fergal. Worse, when Fidelma finds him, Erca is brewing a deadly concoction of nightshade and hemlock. Later the Brehon adjudicating the case posits that if Fergal did not kill the girl, perhaps Erca did, based on the Druid's hatred of Christians, his knowledge of deadly herbs, and conceivably a desire to harm Fergal ("Murder in Repose" 20).

But Erca (as with all Druids and pagans introduced in the series as suspicious characters) is innocent. Fidelma, we learn, wanted to interrogate Erca not as a possible suspect, but to confirm her suspicion that two drugs were used in the crime that could be found in the area. Erca, then, is not a suspect. He serves as a consultant (albeit unwillingly) in Fidelma's case for the defense.

The Druids, although their numbers are small at this time, are still the keepers of the knowledge of herbs and their medicinal and poisonous usages. Erca proudly proclaims that Patrick may have turned the Irish from the De Danann to Christ, but Ireland's patron saint could not eradicate Druidic knowledge ("Murder in Repose" 10). Erca's expertise is fundamental in aiding Fidelma in solving the case and successfully defending Brother Fergal.

In "Death of an Icon," a distinguished convert to Christianity is the murder victim. The Venerable Connla, a frail 90-year-old monk, has had a remarkable life. His portraits hang in many great Irish ecclesiastical centers (211). The Irish Christians' respect for him borders on adoration. He is the "icon" of the title for Connla was, first and foremost, renowned for his piety and his wisdom. His scholarly output was prodigious. However, this icon of the faith has been found in the early morning hours hanging from a beam in his cell. The Father Superior insists that he was murdered by a band of itinerant mercenaries who stole Connla's rosary and a silver crucifix and two golden chalices from the chapel. But Fidelma is immediately suspicious of such a theory.

During her investigation, Fidelma learns that Connla was the son of a Druid and seer. The young Connla had intended to become a Druid himself. Instead (and we are not given the details), he converts to Christianity, adopts the Christian name Connla, and enters the monastery. He devotes his life to studying the faith and becomes one of its staunchest defenders. When Fidelma rummages around his manuscripts and books, she discovers not just the expected Hebrew, Latin, and Greek works, but works written in Ogham, on wooden wands.[5] Fidelma (who can read Ogham) learns that these wands contain the ancient legends of the Tuatha De Danann. A pious monk should not have need of such tales in his possession.

Motive in this story plays a greater part in this mystery than who murdered Connla. (This story is closer to being a whydunit than a whodunit.) Clearly, the tale of the itinerant mercenaries is a ruse. Only one of Connla's brothers could be the murderer, but which one of them is of small consequence. The real story here is why. Why had this elderly, revered philosopher been brutally murdered? The answer lies in his Druidic heritage.

Fidelma happens across a small piece of parchment in Connla's cell, written in Ogham, that she translates. The Venerable Connla, in his old age, has been reflecting on his life and deeply regrets his youthful zeal in destroying Ireland's ancient lore. He has realized that he, as did St. Patrick, destroyed the cultural wealth of Irish Druidism.[6] For his fellow monks such a belief is sacrilege. They attribute Connla's regrets to senility — but one monk sees Connla's new view of Druidism as dangerous and resorts to murder in his misguided defense of Christian faith.. Sadly, the Father Superior destroys

Connla's writings on the subject in an effort to "save" the Venerable Connla's reputation.

Another Druid, Gadra in *The Spider's Web*, is also limned sympathetically. In fact, Gadra (a peripheral character) is one of the most exemplary people in the series. In contrast to the Christians in the novel, Gadra is far wiser, more compassionate, and spiritually centered. (In *The Spider's Web* once again key Christian characters are depicted as mean, small-minded, and preoccupied with points of theology rather than practicing their faith.) Fidelma praises him as having "the same virtues we all have" (*Spider's Web* 172). Furthermore, Gadra is closer in philosophy to Fidelma than her fellow religieux (Luehrs and Luehrs 49). Both believe that there are many paths to God, in contrast to the Christians who see only one path. This becomes more evident especially in the later novels where, disillusioned, she has left the abbey of Cill Dara (Kildare), and eventually rejects her life as a religieuse completely in *The Chalice of Blood*.

However, the most well-developed (and intriguing) Druid character is Murgal, Brehon and Druid to King Laisre, the pagan chieftain of Gleann Gleis, in *Valley of the Shadow*. To misdirect the reader, early in the novel Tremayne employs serpentine imagery when describing Murgal. His black eyes are "unblinking like a serpent" (57) and "become hooded as he regarded her, assessing her [Fidelma's] qualities as his opponent" (58). Murgal, like other Druids Fidelma has encountered, is immediately on the offensive. He greets her with open hostility and is quick to have her imprisoned (on trumped up charges). This is understandable when considering that in this novel Fidelma is acting as the emissary of her brother Colgú, King of Cashel, to negotiate the establishment of a Christian church and school in Gleann Gleis. For the greater part of the narrative, he seems to function as Fidelma's chief adversary, constantly sparring verbally with her and surreptitiously plotting against her.

And unlike the Venerable Connla and Gadra, Murgal is not above reproach. He drinks too much and takes liberties with women. He appears to be small-minded and capricious in his judgments. His appearance borders on the comic: scrawny and birdlike with a large bobbing Adam's apple, and his richly embroidered vestments do nothing to offset his unattractiveness. But Fidelma soon recognizes that he is a formidable adversary. Murgal is "a spiritual man of deep thought" (*Valley of the Shadow* 66).

Like Fidelma, Murgal's quest for the truth and love of the law overcomes any prejudices he may have. As Brehon, he makes sure Fidelma's hearing is fair and impartial, even offering to guide Fidelma's defender (Eadulf) through the Brehon laws. Though his chieftain undoubtedly wishes Murgal to find against Fidelma, he does not. Murgal is biased against all Christians (echoing

Erca) because he sees them as a petty people, intolerant of the views of others (*Valley of the Shadow* 267), but he overcomes his bias. He hears the evidence and then exercises impartial judgment. Before they part, Fidelma and Murgal commend each other: Murgal praises Fidelma as a moral advocate of Brehon law; Fidelma responds that Murgal is one as well, and also brave and honest (*Valley of the Shadow* 301).

Druidism Motifs

The seventh-century Ireland of the Fidelma series is largely Christian, but the tension between the practitioners of the new faith and the old is palpable. *Badger's Moon* employs Celtic cosmology as the backdrop for the series of murders of three young women who have been studying magic under the tutelage of Liag, an apothecary who has extensive knowledge of "star lore" and worships the moon goddess. The three young women have been slaughtered at the full moon. (The badger's moon of the title is the October full moon, a time sacred to the pagan Irish.) At first it may appear that the murders were somehow associated with ritual worship of the moon goddess, but once again, the motive for the murders has nothing to do with pagan or Druid ritual. Liag is not a killer. He sees himself as having the responsibility to hand down the legends to the next generation because these are the cultural birthright of the Irish (62). He is soon eliminated as a suspect.

Even the Christianized Irish retain beliefs originating in Druidism. In *The Monk Who Vanished*, the yew tree of the Eóghanacht (the royal house of Cashel, of which Fidelma is a member) serves as a sacred totem to the people of Cashel. It is an immense and venerable tree. Eadulf declares it to be "a tree worthy of respect" (66). Fidelma explains to him that each clan has a Tree of Life and when a new king is installed in office, he must take his royal oath under his clan's tree. The people believe that as long as the tree lives and flourishes, so will the people it represents. The tree's life, then, is intertwined with the fate of the people. Thus the destruction of such a tree would herald their destruction. The tree is savagely cut down by the enemies of the Eóghanacht in an attempt to demoralize the kingdom of Cashel (120). Eadulf the Saxon outsider is puzzled by the people's reaction (particularly Fidelma's) to this act. He usually perceives the Irish as more Christian than his Saxon countrymen, but in this case, deems them as illogically and emotionally fixated on the tree — and thus more pagan.

Tremayne's most detailed use of Druidic ritual and tradition is central to *Valley of the Shadow*. What first appears (the operative word here) to be the crime, the ritualistic killing of thirty-three men whose naked bodies are laid out in a circle, is really part of a scheme to start a war between Cashel and Gleann Geis. In pagan times, this ritual was known as the Threefold Death (victims were killed by three different means as part of the sacrifice to the terrible god Cromm, a fertility deity). Fidelma immediately sees this horrific act for what it is and not as representative of the rituals of Gleann Gleis. According to Fidelma (and later reinforced by Murgal), the Threefold Death was anathema to Druids (26). This incident allows Tremayne to subtly repudiate Caesar's account of Druids sacrificing human beings to their bloodthirsty gods.

Fidelma as Druid

In *The Leper's Bell*, Fidelma reasons that the religious are the Druids of their time (147). Tremayne has acknowledged that he had to make Fidelma a religieuse because in early Christian Ireland, the majority of professionals were members of religious orders; this is a holdover from the Druidic caste system where the intelligentsia were Druids ("Fascination" 3). She would have made her decision to enter the religious life at a young age (the Irish "age of choice" for young women was fourteen). As a religieuse she then had the opportunity to pursue her true calling: the law. For Fidelma, the religious life is the means to her study and practice of law. Her calling is the law, not the faith for she never saw herself as a religieuse (*Leper's Bell* 99).

So it is no accident that Fidelma, as a religieuse, is an odd fit (Luehrs and Luehrs 49). She rebels against the monastic life in many ways, seems to chafe under authority, and constantly argues points of theology. Rarely is she described at prayer with other members of her religious community, hearing mass, or saying the rosary — the latter in particular would have been the prescribed form of meditation for a religieuse. In fact, in an early novel, *Shroud for the Archbishop*, Fidelma practices the art of dercad, the ancient meditative practice that Druids used to achieve a state of sitcháin. (Sitcháin is Gaelic for stillness or peace of mind.) Dercad was still practiced by the Druid mystics — limited as their number might have been — in Fidelma's time (*Shroud for the Archbishop* 214). Dercad is what allows her to clear her mind when she has a mental block when trying to unravel a mystery. It also gives her a sense of peace and well-being. Dercad was strongly discouraged among Christians since most followed St. Patrick's strictures against meditative practices as a means of enlightenment. That does not deter Fidelma. She continues to practice dercad throughout the series. Furthermore, she laments the disappearing practice of the ancient rituals just because they had been practiced in pre–Christian Ireland (*Shroud for the Archbishop* 215).

Though she is reverential when airing her opinions of St. Patrick (usually referring to him with the honorific "Blessed Patrick"), Fidelma is hardly a disciple. She decries not only his ban on following Druidic rituals, but also his harsh endeavors to rid Ireland of paganism. Her commentary in *Suffer Little Children* on Patrick's book burning is particularly reproachful, and she hopes "that the treasures of our people are not incinerated and lost because of fashionable practices [book burning]" (27). The historical assessment is that this was a senseless destruction, borne out of over-zealousness (Ellis 165). Patrick's conversion of the Irish, for Fidelma, may have brought them the new faith but at a terrible cost: the irrevocable loss of their ancient culture and knowledge.

Fidelma is also a Pelagian.[7] As a member of the Celtic Church, she is upfront and vocal about her commitment to a theology that had been declared heretical by the Roman Church.[8] The Roman Church had condemned specifically six points of Pelagian doctrine: Adam would have died whether or not he sinned; Adam's sin did not affect the human race; children are born without original sin; the human race neither spiritually dies through Adam's sin nor rises again through Christ's resurrection; Mosaic Law and the Gospel are equal guides to heaven; and before Christ, good men and women could be without sin (Pohle 3). Some Roman church fathers claimed that by denying the existence of original sin and Christian grace, and arguing for free will over fate, Pelagius was attempting to bring back Druid forms of worship (Tremayne, "Fascination"). She is most vocal about the issue of free will over fate. For Fidelma, the individual makes the choice whether or not to sin. God has nothing to do with it.

Fidelma is frequently sympathetic to the old faith. She has a genuine understanding and extensive knowledge of the traditions and legends of pagan Ireland — often shocking her partner and husband Eadulf. (Eadulf is almost fearful of pagan references, having been a follower of Woden and other Saxon gods as a child.) Unlike her fellow Christians, she never shies away from pagan references. She knows the Celtic pantheon and delights in retelling the old stories of deities Lugh, Danu, and Dagda, and feats of the legendary heroes, Cuchulainn and Fionn Mac Cumhail.[9] For Fidelma, to discount these stories is paramount to rejecting one's Irish heritage. These tales hold great cultural truths.

Even when others reject Christianity, Fidelma, the consummate dálaigh, judiciously weighs the argument. The new chieftain of Gleann Geis instructs her to tell her brother the king and the bishop that his community is unwilling to establish a Christian church and school because they have "seen too much of Christian concerns for [their] welfare" (*Valley of the Shadow* 301). Based on the behaviors of the various Christians in this mystery, Fidelma agrees and adds that she "yearns for the old morality of the beliefs of our people" (301).

The Fidelma series deftly illustrates historical theory while telling lively crime stories, filled with all the too human passions of lust, jealousy, greed, and hunger for political power. Tremayne's unusual detective, though garbed and aligned as a Christian religious, has more in common with the Druids, who are shown to be spiritual, intellectual, and honorable upholders of the law. Druids, people who have historically been vilified by their conquerors and romanticized by popular culture, were the learned class of pagan Ireland. By Fidelma's time, Druidism was dying out, replaced by the religious who, like herself, had a professional calling and a love and reverence for the Brehon laws and Irish culture. Fidelma is a worthy successor of the Druids for, in the words of her own-time adversary, the Druid Murgal, she is "a moral advocate of the five kingdoms. It is something to aspire to" (*Valley of the Shadow* 301). She who yearns for the old morality of the Druids exemplifies it. In Tremayne's seventh-century Ireland, the Druids still hold the wisdom, the culture, and the honor of the Irish people.

Notes

1. Brehons were judges in ancient Ireland. Fidelma, trained at the bardic school of the Brehon Morann of Tara, is an advocate of the courts (*dálaigh*). In the series, her mastery of Brehonic laws is extraordinary. She is well versed in the criminal code, *Senchus Mór* (Grand Old Law) and the civil code, *Leabhar Acaill*, having reached the second highest degree of learning in ancient Ireland, that of *anruth*.

2. To avoid confusion from this point on I refer to the writer as Tremayne (with the exception of parenthetical citations of his scholarly works).

3. At this writing, twenty novels in the series have been published. In none of the works thus far has a Druid been the murderer. In one novel, the pagan chieftain Laisre does murder, but his motive comes from his mad desire for more political power, not because he wishes to promote the old faith. Murgal, his Brehon and Druid, condemns his actions.

4. De Danann of ancient Celtic lore are the Tuatha De Danaan, literally translated as "the people of Danu." The Celts, like many ancient peoples, based their beliefs on the concept of a mother goddess, in this case, Danu whose name means "Water from Heaven" (Ellis 42). The ancient Irish traced their high kings' lineage to Tuatha De Danann, an etiological mythology.

5. Ogham, also known as the Celtic Tree alphabet, was an early medieval alphabet. Letters were formed by using one to five angled or perpendicular strokes that met or crossed a center line. Ogham was easily carved into wood and stone and read from bottom to top. The names of the letters correspond to the trees held sacred by the Druids. The appearance of an Ogham wand in Connla's cell would have been considered most unusual, since the alphabet and language it represented was considered to be pagan.

6. Tremayne frequently references St. Patrick's burning of one hundred eighty Druidic books and has characters, often Fidelma, mourn the great loss of such knowledge to civilization. In this story, Connla has come to the same realization: fanatical adherence to a creed is a crime against culture and learning ("Death of an Icon" 225).

7. Pelagius (c. 354–420/440) was monk/ascetic born in the British Isles whose writings were condemned as heresy in 418 by the Council of Carthage.

8. Tremayne frequently references the tensions between Roman Christianity and Celtic Christianity. Though the Celtic Church was part of the Catholic Church and held its ulti-

mate allegiance to the Pope, it differed greatly on many points, primarily the dating of Easter and celibacy of priests, monks, and nuns (Fidelma and Eadulf, for example, are members of a *conhospitae* (mixed) monastery where monks and nuns could marry and raise their families within the monastery while pursuing their vocations), liturgy, and even tonsure. The "Celtic" tonsure was a version of Druidic tonsure (hair was shaved from ear to ear), whereas the "Roman" tonsure, sometimes referred to as "St. Peter's," shaved the head leaving an outer fringe of hair. The Roman Church also accused the Celtic Church of Pelagianism (Tremayne, "Fascination").

9. Lugh was the god of artisans and craftsmen, leading the Romans to associate him with the Roman trickster god Mercury. In addition, Lugh was associated with light and the sun. Danu was the mother-goddess. Dagda was the wisest of the Celtic gods and was worshipped as the Lord of Perfect Knowledge. Cuchulainn was the son of Lugh and is the greatest of the heroes. Fionn Mac Cumahaill (Anglicized today as Finn McCool) was the great mythical hunter.

Works Cited

Browne, Ray B., and Lawrence A. Kreiser, Jr., eds. *The Detective as Historian: History and Art in Historical Crime Fiction*. Bowling Green, OH: Bowling Green, OH: Bowling Green State University Popular Press, 2000.

_____. Introduction. Browne and Kreiser 1–10.

Ellis, Peter Berresford. *A Brief History of the Druids*. Philadelphia: Running Press, 2002.

Hutton, Ronald. *The Druids*. London: Continuum, 2007.

Luehrs, Christiane W., and Robert B. Luehrs. "Peter Tremayne: Sister Fidelma and the Triumph of Truth." Browne and Kreiser 45–59.

Pohle, Joseph. "Pelagius and Pelagianism." *The Catholic Encyclopedia*. Vol. 11. New York: Robert Appleton Company, 1911. 20 Sept. 2011 <http://www.newadvent.org/cathen/11604a.htm>.

Tremayne, Peter [Peter Berresford Ellis]. *Badger's Moon*. 2003. New York: St. Martin's Minotaur, 2006.

_____. *The Chalice of Blood*. London: Headline, 2010.

_____. "Death of an Icon." *Whispers of the Dead: Fifteen Sister Fidelma Mysteries*. New York: St. Martin's Minotaur, 2004. 211–27.

_____. "The Fascination for Sister Fidelma." Interview by Sarah Cuthbertson. *Historical Novel Society*. 2004. Web. 24 May 2011.

_____. *The Leper's Bell*. 2004. New York: St. Martin's Minotaur, 2006.

_____. "Murder in Repose." *Hemlock at Vespers: Fifteen Sister Fidelma Mysteries*. New York: Minotaur-St. Martin's, 2000. 1–23.

_____. *The Monk Who Vanished*. 1999. New York: St. Martin's Minotaur, 2001.

_____. *Shroud for the Archbishop*. 1995. New York: St. Martin's Minotaur, 1998.

_____. *The Spider's Web*. 1997. New York: St. Martin's Minotaur, 2000.

_____. *Suffer Little Children*. 1995. New York: Signet, 1999.

_____. *Valley of the Shadow*. 1998. New York: Signet, 2000.

Westlake, Donald. Introduction. *Murderous Schemes: An Anthology of Classic Detective Stories*. New York: Oxford University Press, 1996. 1–8.

Winks, Robin. Introduction. *The Historian as Detective: Essays on Evidence*. New York: Harper & Row, 1968.

_____. Preface. Browne and Kreiser ix–x.

A Druid in New Guise

Christiane W. Luehrs *and* Robert B. Luehrs

At one point in *The Leper's Bell* Fidelma becomes convinced, erroneously, that the often treacherous Uí Fidgente dynasty is responsible for kidnapping her child. Seething in rage, she threatens one of the clan's chieftains, Cuirgí, with a horrifying Druid curse, an incantation supposedly powerful enough to visit disaster and humiliation on its victim in both this life and the Otherworld. Cuirgí, taken aback, protests that such magic is forbidden by Christianity. Fidelma responds by asserting the durability of cultural traditions regardless of the "New Faith" and then adds "who are we religious but the druids in new guise?" (199).

Such is certainly the case with Fidelma. The Druids were the social and intellectual elite of the ancient Celtic world, and she has much more in common with their outlook than with the authoritarian, restrictive, life-denying innovations being injected into Christianity by Rome in her era. To be sure, she does not practice the religious elements of Druidism. An advocate of rational explanations for all phenomena, she exhibits no particular affinity for the old gods and the old rites, although she is knowledgeable in the mythology of the one and the significance of the other. Despite her momentary and uncharacteristic surrender to mythic thinking in her confrontation with Cuirgí, she rejects the supernatural, even in Christianity. For example, she believes the wine and bread at communion perform only symbolic roles and do not actually transform into the blood and body of Christ as the concept of transubstantiation proclaims (*Hemlock at Vespers* 262, 276).[1] At the Synod of Whitby in 664 when a solar eclipse has the Saxon delegates warning of a divine omen, Fidelma speaks of a natural, astronomical occurrence resulting from the movement of the moon between the earth and the sun (*Absolution by Murder* 70–72). In her crime-solving work she always dismisses claims of demonic atrocities or witchcraft in favor of purely human motivations, frequently greed, for criminal acts. In *The Chalice of Blood* she remarks: "I have never come across a murder committed by a wraith or any other spirit" (66).

What Fidelma does believe in fervently is Truth, and for her Truth can be reached by logic, collection of testimony, careful analysis of evidence, and avoidance of premature hypotheses (*Spider's Web* 231). In his excellent 1994 study *The Druids*, Peter Tremayne, writing under his real name of Peter Berresford Ellis, points out Truth was the essence of the Druid outlook, to them the guiding principle of the universe. "Truth against the world" was their motto, a motto Fidelma herself asserts (Ellis, *Druids* 168; *Absolution by Murder* 82; *Spider's Web* 128). Included within the perimeters of Truth is justice, which Fidelma honors even above the law she is sworn to uphold as a *dálaigh* or advocate in the Irish court system (Ellis, *Druids* 169; *Hemlock at Vespers* 149–51; *Haunted Abbot* 269; *Whispers of the Dead* 341). If Tremayne is correct in seeing the Druid concept of Truth equivalent to the idea of Logos as expounded by the ancient Greek philosopher Heraclitus, then Truth is the blueprint for cosmic harmony, the ultimate guide for human behavior, and the personification of God (Ellis, *Druids* 170). Fidelma would seem to have a religious passion after all (cf. *Behold a Pale Horse* 96).

Although she does not indulge in the rituals and other priestly activities of the Druids, Fidelma does embrace many of their traditional intellectual, social, and administrative functions as Tremayne discusses them in his *Druids*. This is appropriate since she emphasizes the need for a people to maintain continuity with the past if it is to retain a sense of identity and purpose (*Absolution by Murder* 49; *Monk Who Vanished* 343). "You cannot build the future by ignoring the past or trying to destroy past knowledge," she observes in *Badger's Moon* (213).

Instead of being convent educated, Fidelma receives the seventh-century version of Druidic education at the bardic school of Brehon Morann of Tara; she completes eight years, achieving the advanced rank of *anruth* ("noble stream") (Ellis, *Druids* 161). Since she wants to have a professional career based on her merits rather than her royal blood, she follows the advice of her cousin, Abbot Laisran, and becomes a religieuse, a Christian equivalent of a Druidess. For a time she is attached to the abbey of St. Brigid (or Brigit) at Kildare, founded by the daughter of a Druid on the site of a Druid shrine featuring a sacred oak and an eternal flame. The Christian sisters managed to keep this fire burning until the thirteenth century. Little is known for certain about Brigid the saint, and her legends are entwined with those of an ancient, triune mother goddess of the same name, patroness of healing, poetic inspiration, fire, crafts, and the fertility of nature in the spring. Some stories have the goddess Brigid as the originator of the Irish legal system defended by Fidelma, especially the rights enjoyed by women (Condren 48–78, 107; Jones and Pennick 101–02).

Drawing on such ancient sources as Julius Caesar (100–44 B.C.) and the Greek geographer Strabo (c. 64 B.C.–c. A.D. 24), Tremayne says the administration of justice was one of the most important functions of the Druids, and so it is for Fidelma (*Druids* 189–99). In *The Dove of Death*, she remarks, "My first commitment is to serve the law and my people" (31), a proclamation she makes repeatedly throughout the mystery series. The law, she observes in *Badger's Moon*, exists "for the obedience of fools and the guidance of the wise" (251).

Historically, the Druids derived their unquestioned authority to judge civil and criminal cases from veneration for their arcane knowledge, magic powers, and relationship with the gods. So great was this respect for them as arbitrators of disputes, that they sometimes even prevented wars (Aldhouse-Green 44–46). Fidelma commands her jurisdiction in legal matters from her position as a designated advocate for the courts, her status as the daughter of one king and the sister of another, and support from dignitaries who need her help in investigating crimes or suspicious events. Like those of her pagan predecessors, her efforts often enough keep rival princes from engaging in armed hostilities, for example in *Dancing with Demons* and *A Prayer for the Damned*. All in all, she enjoys a reasonable, secular equivalent of the situation the Druids once had.

As protectors of the law, the Druids were also guardians of their people's heritage. Part of their extensive and rigorous schooling involved committing to memory prodigious quantities of esoterica, epic poetry, lore, and chronicles, the oral tradition being preferred to written records as a vehicle of Truth (*Druids* 162, 179; *Badger's Moon* 21; Ross 87; Chadwick 43–44). Likewise, Fidelma often thinks had she not studied law with Morann of Tara, she would have become a historian (*Absolution by Murder* 49). In her view, an understanding of the past shapes both the present and the future; the past must not be forgotten and cannot be distorted if we are to be other than naive children or wild beasts (*Whispers of the Dead* 79, *Monk who Vanished* 343). Hence her unrelenting efforts to preserve pagan books and even whole libraries containing ancient manuscripts and records from being destroyed by Christian fanatics who consider such things evil (*Suffer Little Children* 14).

The mythology of Celtic gods and goddesses along with the supernatural lore surrounding that mythology intrigues her; she is not bothered by the survival of pre–Christian beliefs, ceremonies, or festivals, such as the autumnal New Year's celebration of Samhain, when spirits are supposed to exact revenge on those who had wronged them and fortunes are told (*Smoke in the Wind* 258, 305–06, 358; *Leper's Bell* 89–90). Entering the valley of Gleann Geis, Fidelma and her colleague and future husband, Eadulf, encounter a giant effigy of the luminescent solar deity Lugh, antlers on his head and a snake in his hand. Eadulf is horrified. Fidelma reassures him that Lugh is a "good god," something perhaps no other Christian figure of the time would have said about a horned entity (*Valley of the Shadow* 54–55, 250–51). Fidelma does not approach pagan folk belief with Christian glosses or condemnations (*Whispers of the Dead* 78–79).

Druids were time lords, keepers of the wisdom of the past and interpreters of the omens of the future (Ellis, *Druids* 220–27). Ancient Greek and Roman authors said the most notorious method of Druid divination and even general communication with the gods involved human sacrifice; both Caesar in his *Gallic War* and Strabo in his *Geography* reported the Celts imprisoning captives in a huge wicker cage shaped like a man and setting the colossus on fire as a burnt offering (Caesar bk. 6, chap. 16; Strabo bk. 4, chap. 4). The Fidelma books deny such accusations, and, to be sure, the evidence on Druidic human sacrifice is rather ambiguous (*Spider's Web* 154; *Valley of the Shadow* 69–70; Ellis, *Druids* 143–56). The only exception was the aberrant cult of Cromm Cróich (or Cromm Cruach); in the style of her Druid forebears, Fidelma crushes a resurgence of this bloody sect (*Valley of the Shadow* 30–31; *Dancing with Demons* 194–96, 201–02, 249–50).

Fidelma believes in free will, not fate, destiny, or predestination (*Monk who Vanished* 71). She gives no credence to auguries read in entrails, in the flight of birds, or in the casting of "omen sticks." She prefers astronomy to astrology, but does admit that astrology is part of the Celtic way of life and that many astrologers have become wise through their studies, sometimes in an uncanny fashion (70–72; *Whispers of the Dead* 52–53). Gaimredán, the blacksmith's assistant in *Master of Souls*, accurately deduces her fiery, restless, impatient personality on the basis of her birth at a time when the constellation of Danu, the mother goddess, was rising to ascendancy (204). Conchobhar, the old apothecary at the palace in Cashel, warns Fidelma that the positions of the stars make Imbolc (February 1, Brigid's Day) an inauspicious time for scheduling her marriage to Eadulf; he turns out to be correct (*Prayer for the Damned* 15, 29). Even so, the best Fidelma is willing to grant is the admission fate is inevitable only if we refuse to act to change it (*Whispers of the Dead* 56).

The word "Druid" probably means "immersed in or drenched with knowledge," but the Druids supposedly shared that knowledge cryptically through obscure utterances or riddles (*Dancing with Demons* 22; Ellis, *Druids* 180). Fidelma certainly loves epigrams, preferring those of her teacher, Morran of Tara, or of pagan authors to quotations from the Bible, as would be more seemly for a religieuse. In particular, she likes the pithy maxims of Publilius Syrus, Julius Caesar's favorite comic playwright; one of his sayings is "The judge is condemned when the guilty is acquitted (*Smoke in the Wind* 131;

Publilius vii-x, 41)," adopted as the motto of *The Edinburg Review* quarterly literary journal in the nineteenth century.

As for riddles, Fidelma solves rather than poses them, the more convoluted the better. She finds being merely a royal princess, a wife, and a mother tedious. She is never as alive, as excited, and as focused as when a baffling conundrum, complete with victims murdered for mysterious reasons, presents itself (*Badger's Moon* 31). It is an attitude she shares with another detective, who lives more than a millennium later in the British Isles, Sherlock Holmes. At the start of *The Sign of the Four* Holmes complains of ennui to Watson in terms Fidelma would appreciate:

> My mind rebels at stagnation. Give me problems, give me work, give me the most abstruse cryptogram, or the most intricate analysis, and I am in my own proper atmosphere.... I abhor the dull routine of existence. I crave for mental exaltation [Conan Doyle 1: 611].[2]

Fidelma does not perform all of the functions of a Druid. She is no physician, unless one wants to count her as a psychologist. She is no bard, although on one occasion she does sing of her dynasty's heritage, in a "lilting soprano," during a banquet at Gleann Geis (*Valley of the Shadow* 91–92). Still, despite the Church's disapproval, she practices the calming art of Druidic meditation (*dercad*) more than she prays, and she employs the Druidic technique of unarmed self-defense (*troid-sciathagid*) when necessary (*Shroud for the Archbishop* 214–15, 249–1; *Suffer the Children* 3, 25; *Our Lady of Darkness* 78–79; *Smoke in the Wind* 124–25, 139; *Leper's Bell* 209–10). She also sometimes experiences the mystical union with nature felt by Druids, particularly when she goes horseback riding (*Spider's Web* 224). In many respects she is indeed a Druid in new guise. In her day Druidism is fading as a viable alternative to the New Faith. Even so, true Druids continue to exist, pushed to the wilderness or compelled to deal with social conditions shaped by the New Faith. Most of them see in Fidelma something of a kindred spirit, their reception of her largely depending on their adaptation to Ireland's emergent religious environment.

Erca, the Druid recluse of "Murder in Repose," rejects that environment and shuns his fellow human beings. Having withdrawn from society, he lives in and from nature, gathering and distilling herbal medicines; this skill, he says, is the one thing Christianity cannot take from him. Erca's unkempt appearance belies his inner landscape, one of profound hatred for all Christians and their "foreign god." He wishes the agents of the New Faith driven from the land and so rejects Fidelma at first sight. He refuses to accept her greeting of "Peace to you, brother" because he rejects her idea of the brotherhood of all under a single divine force of many forms. He cannot see beyond

Fidelma's nun's habit to her quest for Truth and justice. He represents one Druid response to the New Faith, that of total abhorrence (*Hemlock at Vespers* 9–10).

In *Valley of the Shadow*, Murgal is a different sort of Druid. He serves as Brehon, the chief religious and legal advisor, for his chieftain in the pagan enclave of Gleann Geis. Spurning the New Faith and its culture, he consciously chooses to live with others of like mind in an isolated community. He knows that Christianity is creeping in — many Christians already live in his valley — but wishes to see it kept at bay as long as possible; he allows Fidelma to see he opposes allowing the building of a Christian church and school in Gleann Geis (116–17). A tall but unprepossessing man, readily sarcastic, and a womanizer, Murgal is nevertheless a powerful figure at court, and a champion of the Old Faith who does not give way easily.

However, as the story evolves into a saga of political turmoil, instigated by his own chieftain, Murgal reveals that he is a consummate upholder of Irish law. He comes to admire Fidelma and her work as a *dálaigh*. He supports her efforts to exonerate herself when she is accused of murder and again when she unravels the plot to overthrow her brother, the King of Muman. In the end, Murgal and Fidelma are in agreement that the law is based upon morality and not religious views (333–34). Even more, Murgal recognizes Druidic qualities in Fidelma. "If I did not see that you carry the symbols of the new Faith, Fidelma of Cashel, I would swear that you were of the old Faith," he says. "Perhaps you are wearing the wrong cloak?" (183).

Liag in *Badger's Moon* is "an old soul," "a repository of knowledge of the ancient beliefs and legends (51, 320). He manages to live in both the Druid world and that of the New Faith. His secluded home is on the edge of his Christian chieftain's village, in a forest on the Hill of the Sacred Tree. Although suspicious of strangers and attuned to nature, he regularly teaches groups of old and young alike Druid lore and astrology, especially that having to do with the moon goddess (63–64, 215–16). Liag is also the area's apothecary and physician, "no mere herb doctor" but fully trained in the medicine of his contemporary, Christian Ireland (60). He comes without question to aid people when requested to do so. He is not a Christian, and he considers them small-minded. When Fidelma and Eadulf come to question him about the three dead young women, he tells them he has "no need of religious here in my sanctuary" (60). However, he receives them on the basis of their being representatives of his king and of the law of Ireland and even strikes a working relationship with Fidelma as she works to solve the murders (322–27, 377–78).

The philosophic Gadra of *The Spider's Web* is a revered, elderly Druid who knows that the old culture and religion are dead and that the ways of the New Faith have taken hold; such is the way of things. He is not bitter. He lives as a recluse, but not because he feels hatred for the Christians; rather, he cannot change his ways and beliefs. He welcomes Fidelma because he sees in her one who appreciates the traditions of the past and is actually a Druid in new guise. To confirm his judgment about her, he asks her three of the thirty riddles the mythological hero Fionn Mac Cumhail asked his prospective bride in the tale "The Wooing of Ailbe;" Fidelma, of course, answers each one correctly. "Then we understand one another well," he remarks (168; Deane 209–10). In turn, Fidelma admires his "sincerity and wisdom" (*Spider's Web* 172).

Gadra is a healer and a devotee of Truth. He demonstrates more compassion than most of the Christians in the story because he sees in Móen, the blind and deaf mute, a perceptive, intelligent fellow human being. The followers of Christ treat the lad brutally, calling him an animal and a monster (81, 169–71, 252–53, 300). Gadra communicates with Móen using the Druid Ogam alphabet of short lines traced onto the boy's hand and willingly helps Fidelma prove him innocent of murder (183–84). The old Druid recognizes a morality and unity of mankind which supersedes all barriers of religion, class, or politics. For him every spiritual path leads to the same Truth, the "same great centre" (336).

The generally lugubrious Brother Conchobar is a Christian who embodies many of the qualities of a Druid. He is physician and apothecary at the royal court at Cashel, serving Fidelma's brother as loyally as he had the previous four kings. Conchobar devotes himself to studying the charts that plot the movements of the planets and stars and issues prognostications based on them; he thinks Fidelma has the potential to make a fine astrologer, although she does not put much trust in portents revealed by horoscopes (*Monk Who Vanished* 9–11; *Whispers of the Dead* 52; *Leper's Bell* 167–68). He seems to have boundless admiration for the Druids. "There were none wiser nor better informed," he tells Fidelma (*Dancing with Demons* 20). Like Fidelma, Conchobar dislikes religious fanaticism and conversions encouraged by force and fear (21). Throughout the series he is Fidelma's confidant, mentor, and guide. He assisted when she was born and understands her better than she understands herself. He knows, for instance, that her decision to enter a religious life, with all of its restrictions, was unsuited to her temperament (20; *Leper's Bell* 178–80).

Fidelma's sympathies for the Old Faith are part of her affinity for Irish tradition. Although she does genuflect, say prayers for the dead, and even attend mass, Fidelma evinces little interest in church rites and rituals (*Shroud for the Archbishop* 323; *Suffer Little Children* 264; *Subtle Serpent* 179; *Monk who Vanished* 13, 146, 213; *Hemlock at Vespers* 132; *Dancing with Demons* 180).

As befits a defender of the law, her main concern is justice in this world, not redemption in the next one. A realist who deals with murderers, deviants, and sociopaths on a regular basis, Fidelma is quite aware of the potential for enormous evil which lies in the human soul (*Hemlock at Vespers* 64; *Smoke in the Wind* 48; *Haunted Abbot* 295; *Leper's Bell* 76). Yet she does not discuss Christ's sacrifice as securing forgiveness for sinners. She accepts the concept of the Trinity, probably because Druids customarily think in terms of triadic deities (Ellis, *Celtic Mythology* 208; Green 214–16; *Master of Souls* 75–76).

For Fidelma, the New Faith urges charity, toleration, forbearance, and moderation, all good Druidic traits according to Tremayne. It does not teach blind obedience to institutional superiors and rigid doctrines such as those propagated by Rome (*Dancing with Demons* 15; *Suffer the Children* 79; *Act of Mercy* 127). Christians stand in moral equality under the protection of a compassionate god who has given them the ability to think rationally and expects them to do so (*Whispers of the Dead* 309; *Shroud for the Archbishop* 171–72; *Hemlock at Vespers* 112). The true Christian is an enemy to none (*Smoke in the Wind* 257; *Prayer for the Damned* 113–15).

In *The Leper's Bell* Tremayne writes, "What Fidelma desired most of all was personal freedom" (258). She does not accept restrictions, and here is one reason why she left the convent (258–59; *Council of the Cursed* 90). For the sake of freedom she is willing to quarrel with no less a luminary than St. Paul, who admonished wives to submit to their husbands and who endorsed celibacy, a pernicious condition Fidelma denounces as "unnatural" (*Shroud for the Archbishop* 174–75; *Leper's Bell* 48).

Further, she rejects the ideas on original sin advanced by Roman Catholicism's foremost theologian, St. Augustine (354–430). Augustine said that Adam's abuse of free will tainted the entire human race with original sin and its vile consequences, including death and damnation; we now cannot do what is good without God's active intervention in our lives through grace, cleansing us. Fidelma's reply is that this view makes God essentially the author of sin. He both ordained and foresaw Adam would be disobedient, did not intervene, and then cursed all of humanity because of this transgression, rescuing only a few arbitrarily chosen souls and leaving the others to suffer. If we have no choice but to submit to the fate God imposed on us at the beginning of time, then morality and law, which are based on our responsibility for our choices, are overturned (*Spider's Web* 126–28; *Whispers of the Dead* 58–9).

Fidelma's favorite theologian is Augustine's contemporary and adversary, Pelagius (c. 354 — after 418). Since Pelagius had the misfortune to be condemned by the Church, we know little about his life, and his writings exist now largely in edited and sometimes inaccurate fragments embedded in the diatribes issued by his opponents. He was a peripatetic layman who lived humbly and simply in the style of the early Christians. He was Celtic, perhaps from Ireland (Pelagius, *Commentary* 10; Ellis, *Druids* 181). Fidelma certainly thinks so. In the preface to the first book of his *Commentary on Jeremiah*, St. Jerome, another of Pelagius' contemporaries and critics, speaks of Pelagius as being "weighed down with Irish porridge," Fidelma's riposte is "Better Irish porridge than blind prejudice" (*Whispers of the Dead* 73).

Some scholars, including Tremayne, see the influence of Druidism in Pelagius' gentle, humanistic insistence we must take responsibility for our decisions; in other words, he rejected Augustinian predestination (Ellis, *Druids* 184–86, 189). Fidelma advocates the Pelagian concept of free will; "Fate is the fool's excuse for failure," she declares (*Whispers of the Dead* 58).

According to Pelagius, we are all endowed from birth with the God-given capacity to choose between good and sinful behavior and so are held accountable for those choices. Our inheritance from Adam is not original sin but an example of how to misuse free will and create misery. By combining reason with baptismal rebirth of the spirit, God's grace, and Christ's lessons we break our habit of doing wrong and nurture a habit of doing what is virtuous (Pelagius, *Letters* 3–7; Pelagius, *Commentary* 17–24, 103–04, 107, 117).

Pelagius considered women quite capable of understanding difficult theological issues and of holding office in the church. He wrote about revering divinity in nature and its creatures. He contended pagans could, using reason and their inborn moral compass, become good persons, just not "perfect" ones (Pelagius, *Letters* 1–35, 64–73; Pelagius, *Commentary* 151). It is no wonder Fidelma praises Pelagius; to her he represents an acceptable blend of the Druidic past and her Christian present along with a vindication of reason. After a few years of debate, the church disagreed. Pelagianism was condemned by several councils and two popes, although Pope Zosimus originally judged Pelagius' ideas quite orthodox (Ellis, *Druids* 183–84). With some justice, Fidelma claims Zosimus ignored the philosophical merits of the case and simply caved in to political pressure put on him by St. Augustine, the North African bishops, and the Roman Emperor Honorius (*Whispers of the Dead* 59).

In Fidelma's day Christianity was compelling the cultural inheritance of real Druidism to fragment and mutate into fading folklore. This situation, with some obvious regrets, she accepts. However, her Pelagian Christianity is also under siege. It is being smothered by a harsher brand of the New Faith, one that rejects the past and, according to Tremayne, is puritanical, misogynic, intolerant, imperious, and power-hungry. For Fidelma, a Druid in new guise, this circumstance is tragic.[i]

Notes

1. All parenthetical references to Peter Tremayne's Fidelma books include only title and page numbers.

2. In "The Adventure of the Beryl Coronet" Holmes says, "When you have excluded the impossible, whatever remains, however improbable, must be the truth" (Conan Doyle 2: 299). Curiously, Fidelma essentially quotes this comment in *The Monk Who Vanished*, attributing it to her mentor, Brehon Morann (324).

3. Miranda Aldhouse-Green discusses the significance of the moon for Celtic culture in *Caesar's Druids* (4–6). Gaius Pliny's *Natural History* described Druids harvesting the holy mistletoe, which supposedly healed, cured infertility, and counteracted any poison, in an elaborate ceremony taking place on the sixth day after the new moon (bk. 16, chap. 95).

4. As Medb (Maeve), the devious and ambitious Queen of Connacht, launches a war against Ulster in the great Irish epic *Táin Bó Cuailnge* (*The Cattle Raid of Cooley*), she asks an attractive young Druidess to predict the outcome of the venture. The girl is named Fidelma, and she correctly foretells disaster for the Queen's army. "I am Fidelma," says the seer. "I hide nothing" (Kinsella 60–62). In that she is much like her namesake in Tremayne's mysteries.

Works Cited

Aldhouse-Green, Miranda. *Caesar's Druids: Story of an Ancient Priesthood*. New Haven: Yale University Press, 2010.
Caesar, Gaius Julius. *Gallic War*. Trans. W. A. McDevitte and W. S. Bohn. Perseus Digital Library. Ed. Gregory R. Crane. Tufts University. Web. 20 July 2011.
Chadwick, Nora K. *The Druids*. Cardiff: University of Wales Press, 1997.
Conan Doyle, Arthur. *The Annotated Sherlock Holmes*. Ed. William S. Baring-Gould. 2 vols. New York: Clarkson N. Potter, 1967.
Condren, Mary. *The Serpent and the Goddess: Women, Religion, and Power in Celtic Ireland*. San Francisco: Harper and Row, 1989.
Deane, Seamus, Angela Bourke, Andrew Carpenter, and Jonathan Williams, eds. *The Field Day Anthology of Irish Writing: Irish Women's Writing and Traditions*. New York: New York University Press, 2002.
Ellis, Peter Berresford. *Dictionary of Celtic Mythology*. New York: Oxford University Press, 1992.
———. *The Druids*. Grand Rapids: William B. Eerdmans, 1994.
Green, Miranda. *Dictionary of Celtic Myth and Legend*. New York: Thames and Hudson, 1992.
Jones, Prudence, and Nigel Pennick. *A History of Pagan Europe*. London: Routledge, 1995.
Kinsella, Thomas, ed. *The Táin*. Oxford: Oxford University Press, 1969.
Pelagius. *The Letters of Pelagius*. Ed. Robert Van de Weyer. Evensham: Arthur James Ltd., 1995.
———. *Pelagius's Commentary on St. Paul's Epistle to the Romans*. Trans. and ed. Theodore De Bruyn. New York: Oxford University Press, 1993.
Pliny the Elder, Gaius. *Natural History*. Ed. John Bostock and H. T. Riley. Perseus Digital Library. Ed. Gregory R. Crane. Tufts University. Web. 20 July 2011.
Publilius Syrus. *The Moral Sayings of Publius* [sic] *Syrus*. Ed. and trans. D. Lyman. Cleveland: L. E. Barnard, 1856.
Ross, Anne. *Druids: Preachers of Immortality*. Stroud, UK: Tempus, 1999.
Strabo. *Geography*. Trans. H. C. Hamilton and W. Falconer. Perseus Digital Library. Ed. Gregory R. Crane. Tufts University. Web. 15 August 2011.

Tremayne, Peter. *Absolution by Murder*. 1994. New York: Signet, 1997.
———. *Act of Mercy*. New York: St. Martin's Minotaur, 1999.
———. *Badger's Moon*. 2003. London: Headline, 2004.
———. *Behold a Pale Horse*. London: Headline, 2011.
———. *The Chalice of Blood*. 2010. London: Headline, 2011. Print
———. *The Council of the Cursed*. 2008. New York: Minotaur Books, 2010.
———. *Dancing with Demons*. New York: St. Martin's Minotaur, 2007.
———. *The Dove of Death*. New York: Minotaur Books, 2009.
———. *The Haunted Abbot*. London: Headline, 2002.
———. *Hemlock at Vespers*. New York: St. Martin's Minotaur, 2000.
———. *The Leper's Bell*. 2004. London: Headline, 2005.
———. *Master of Souls*. New York: St. Martin's Minotaur, 2005.
———. *The Monk who Vanished*. 1999. London: Headline, 1999.
———. *Our Lady of Darkness*. London: Headline, 2000.
———. *A Prayer for the Damned*. 2006. New York: St. Martin's Minotaur, 2008.
———. *Shroud for the Archbishop*. New York: St. Martin's Press, 1995.
———. *Smoke in the Wind*. 2001. London: Headline, 2002.
———. *The Spider's Web*. 1997. London: Headline, 1997.
———. *The Subtle Serpent*. New York: St. Martin's Press, 1998.
———. *Suffer Little Children*. New York: St. Martin's Press, 1997.
———. *Valley of the Shadow*. 1998. London: Headline, 1998.
———. *Whispers of the Dead*. New York: St. Martin's Minotaur, 2004.

Fidelma of Cashel:
The Plight of the Learned Lady

Mitzi M. Brunsdale

Peter Berresford Ellis, a distinguished historian with more than eighty books published under various names, succeeds, as Peter Tremayne, in bringing Celtic Ireland to meticulously researched life. Between the seventh and the twelfth centuries, while much of Europe quaked under successive barbarian invasions, Ireland enjoyed an extraordinary flowering of art, literature, and philosophy rooted in the Celtic love of learning (Scherman 239). To date, in two volumes of short stories and twenty novels, Tremayne has developed a fascinating heroine in Ireland's Golden Age milieu, a gifted woman whose marital situation reflects that of many wives today. Tremayne's insistence that he will write only about sites he knows first hand provides his Fidelma novels with remarkable verisimilitude and sense of place. His conviction that his characters are not modern, placed against a fictional backdrop and events, but convincing figures of their times (Tremayne and Cuthbertson) also allows a fruitful comparison between central concerns of talented, well-educated women then and now.

Fidelma of Cashel first appeared in four short stories originally published in October 1993 and collected in *Hemlock at Vespers* in 2000. Tall, attractive, red-haired, green-eyed, and intellectually brilliant, she had been born in 637 to one seventh-century Irish king and becomes sister to another when her brother, Colgú, becomes King of Muman. In her mid-twenties, she works as a *dálaigh* (advocate) of the Irish courts, qualified to *Anruth*, the second highest level of the Brehon law system (*Hemlock at Vespers* 1, 3), belying her sober religious garb by joyfully relishing all kinds of action as she relentlessly champions "the truth against the world" (*Absolution by Murder* 82). At first, Fidelma also exemplifies a myth for the feminist intellectual which appears in contemporary popular culture, a figure associated with "daring, youth, and successful defiance" (Showalter 137). In "Murder in Repose," one of her first appearances, young Fidelma dares to contradict the chief judge of the ruling Eóghanacht clan of Cashel, when he arrogantly assumes that no girl her age could possibly be qualified in Éireann's law. She solves the case with a canny mixture of "elementary deduction and bluff," forcing him to admit she is "an excellent advocate." She deftly replies that presenting clever and polished arguments is easy; the better gift is perceiving and understanding the truth (*Hemlock at Vespers* 1, 3, 23).

As her cases proceed, however, Fidelma's charming urchin grin and her delight in living occasionally disappear; her eyes more frequently shift ominously from green to blazing blue; and her lips, more often than not compressed with rigidly controlled anger, issue deadly indictments — even to her husband. Fidelma increasingly displays her irritation not only with fools, hypocrites, fanatics, and criminals but with those nearest and dearest to her, and as her legal triumphs burgeon, her inner conflicts mount, too, illustrating a problem bedeviling women and their spouses since the Garden of Eden: does a woman with an unquenchable thirst for learning balance her career with or against her love for her mate?

In ancient Ireland and its Celtic Church at the beginning of the Christian era, relations between the sexes, even between men and women in religious orders, were surprisingly liberal and even uninhibited.[1] Virginity does not seem to have been prized, and trial marriages were acceptable. Women could do the wooing, and frequent changes of partners were usual until fairly late in the Middle Ages (Taylor 53).[2] A man might have both a "primary" wife and a secondary one; a woman might join a nunnery and be considered a "holy virgin" regardless of her previous sexual experience (Harrington 18); priests, monks, and nuns could and did marry; and married couples in religious orders could raise their children in dual religious establishments ("*conhospidae*"), often headed by an abbess rather than an abbot (Harrington 130). From 658, when she qualified as *Anruth* and then took religious vows at St. Brigid's abbey at Kildare, through the late summer of 670, when after many investigations at home and abroad she returned to her brother's capital of Cashel, Fidelma conducted her legal and detective work while struggling with two romantic involvements: her early affair with Cian, a handsome, shallow warrior of the High King's bodyguard she met around 654, and her subsequent relationship with Eadulf, the appealing Saxon monk she met ten years later and married in 668. Both relationships forced Fidelma to make crucial choices that reveal her profound personal conflicts, showing her, like many of today's professional women, torn between career and family. In her 2011 memoir, English professor Mary Clearman Blew voices their anguish: "I've given way to self-pity for my failures in love and marriage, which I blame on being born with a brain and then insisting on educating that brain — 'I'm a freak!' I sob" (quoted in Thomas 8).

Tremayne does not reveal much about Fidelma's childhood and early upbringing. She never knew her parents, since her mother's death preceded her father's and King Failbe Fland of Muman (Munster) died when Fidelma, his youngest daughter, was less than a year old. Her childhood was supervised by her distant cousin, Abbot Laisran of Durrow, not an unusual circumstance, since ancient Irish custom demanded that noble daughters be fostered from age seven until the "Age of Choice," fourteen. Fidelma never forgot that she was a princess of Muman's ruling Eóghanacht, a clan related to Ireland's High Kings, and she often used her position to advantage in solving her cases and achieving justice.

At fourteen, Fidelma began her studies at Brehon Morann's bardic school at Tara, where she excelled, but four years later her passionate affair with Cian, which she reveals in unhappy retrospect in *Act of Mercy* (1999), nearly wrecked her professional aspirations. The Celtic bardic schools dated from pre–Christian times, and certain druidic vestiges, like their oral tradition, lingered in them after the Druids were reinvented as Christian Brehons. Even after Ireland was Christianized by St. Patrick in 457,[3] who drew substantially on druidic customs and even adapted Christian theology to fit Irish rhetoric (Johnson-Sheehan and Lynch 233), bardic schools continued as lay, not monastic, Irish institutions until the mid–17th century. Each head professor (*Ollamh*), usually attached to a local king, *was* the school; it went where he resided ("Law, Literature and Legend"). The bards, highly trained poets, chroniclers, and satirists, drew on a strong perceived bond between magic and rhetoric and used language-based practices to heal, teach, judge and entertain (Johnson-Sheehan and Lynch 242). Their schools required expertise in Irish history, law, language, genealogy, and literature; the bards composed verses for the subjects they taught, because students could memorize poetry more easily than prose. Fidelma often demonstrates her powerful memory, honed in this fashion, by quoting pertinent fragments of Irish and classical legend and literature as well as Brehon law. The ancient Irish facility with eloquent narrative-based language (Johnson-Sheehan and Lynch 234) she perfected under Brehon Morann often proved her path to power over evildoers, who defy the major themes that shaped Fidelma's Irish culture: courage, generosity, loyalty, and beauty.

Ireland's indigenous Brehon law respected women's rights to a degree remarkable even today. In general, paying a fine could atone for almost any crime (Kelly 61). This legal system respected individuals first before property, revering the sanctity of contract, the environment, hospitality and the protection of strangers as accepted duties for all. It gave women equal property rights to men, and enabled them to divorce their husbands under a wide range of circumstances. Professional women had "honor prices" of their own, which had to be paid against any offense ranging from an insult to murder, and indeed they could receive their entire honor price if kissed against their will (Lonigan). Women might also inherit land if they had no brothers (Kelly 60–61). Brehon law needed no enforcement arms like police because the Irish held it in such profound respect ("Law, Literature and Legend"), but to Fidelma's dismay, Brehon Morann's bardic school was disbanded around 670 (*Act of Mercy* 144), a foreshadowing of the protracted demise of Irish law which began with the 1155 Bull of Pope Adrian IV, the only English pope, empowering Henry II to conquer Ireland.

Eighteen-year-old Fidelma was Brehon Morann's most promising student when hormonal lightning struck. Today's psychology names "lovestyles": Eros (physical attraction) and Mania (dependent love), which characterize adolescent relationships, and Storge (friendship), Pragma (practical love), and Agape (altruistic love), usually characterizing more mature attachments (Cramer 411).[4] Literature abounds with examples of ruinous adolescent love (Eros/Mania), when promising and infatuated young women can easily lose their reason over handsome Romeos or unscrupulous Don Juans, and if they don't perish, they may later find themselves Derby winners hitched to coal carts, abandoning their early promise for a prosaic and unchallenging life (Sayers, *Gaudy Night* 45). Blinded by her first lust and love, Fidelma could not see that her brilliance made her a prize that Cian, ruthlessly bent on amatory conquests, would later boast about and abandon. Cian represented everything she detested — arrogance, vanity, and martial pride — but she ignored all that in an illusory rapture that sabotaged her intellect and concentration. When she was nearly failing her studies, Brehon Morann told her that she was risking her ability, mental agility, and intellectual promise that had rewarded him for his many years of frustrating teaching (*Act of Mercy* 42), but swept away by passion (*Act of Mercy* 30) and convinced Cian would marry her, Fidelma defied Morann, stubbornly refusing to realize she had lost her rational judgment. She sacrificed her studies, Morann expelled her, and she became the mistreated mistress Cian only occasionally visited, cruelly accusing her of being too intellectual and demanding she rid herself of her books (*Act of Mercy* 62). Finally after three agonizing months, a friend told Fidelma that Cian had married the daughter of the High King's steward (*Act of Mercy* 83–4). Brehon Morann took a devastated Fidelma back and she did become his finest student, but as he sadly observed, bitterness had replaced what ought to have been Fidelma's joy (*Act of Mercy* 85).

In pre-Christian Ireland, all professionals and intellectuals had belonged to the Druid caste, and after Ireland's conversion, such individuals generally joined Christian religious orders. Counseled by her cousin Abbot Laisran that the religious life would offer her the security to practice her profession (such decisions usually had to be made for women by their male guardians) (Harrington 131), Fidelma entered St. Brigid's mixed abbey at Kildare in 658, only to leave that community some time after 664, because she discovered unacceptable hypocrisy in its administration (*Hemlock at Vespers* 155–156). Even by 666, she had not yet completely recuperated from her disastrous affair with Cian. After the shock of meeting him aboard the *Barnacle Goose* on her way to St. James' Spanish shrine in *Act of Mercy*, she had to admit to herself that she not only had been infatuated (Eros), she had been in love with him (Mania) (*Act of Mercy* 30). After he had abandoned her, she had suppressed her anger, humiliation, grief, and self-disgust, but she had not faced and overcome them. Her subsequent actions suggest that she must at least unconsciously have vowed never to allow herself to fall victim to such a man again,[5] but when just before the synod at Whitby she literally ran into another man who also appeared to be everything she didn't want—a Saxon and a Roman, rather than a Celtic Christian (*Absolution by Murder* 50)—Eadulf became the other significant love of her life. He too collided with Fidelma's ferocious pride in her legal prowess.

Eadulf grew up in the seventh-century pagan warrior Saxon culture, one antithetical to Fidelma's far more civilized Ireland. At twenty he had rejected his hereditary position of *gerifa* (magistrate) of Seaxmund's Ham in East Anglia (*Absolution by Murder* 36) and the fearsome old Germanic gods that demanded death in battle as the price of entering Valhalla. After an Irish missionary had guided him to Christianity, Eadulf became a monk with scholarly credentials no less impressive than Fidelma's. He studied a year at Durrow, the world-renowned Irish monastery, before training for four years at Tuaim Brecain, Ireland's illustrious college of medicine, a profession demanding compassion as well as intellect, thus differing from the chillier rigors of the law. After two subsequent years in Rome studying the growing differences between Ireland's Church and Rome's, Eadulf left off the Irish tonsure and adopted the Roman one, signifying his acceptance of Roman theology.[6] Despite his Saxon background, his medical training, and even his quiet, solid strength, opposites again irresistibly attracted each other, and a moment of "pure chemistry"— Eros (Cramer 411)—flashed between him and Fidelma (*Absolution by Murder* 50).

Working together from *Absolution by Murder* onward, Fidelma and Eadulf grow close in a different kind of love, a combination of "Storge" (friendship), "Agape" (helpfulness), and "Pragma" (practical love) (Cramer 411), so that in their investigations Fidelma's brilliance balances Eadulf's steady thoroughness and compassionate insight.[7] After she finally exorcises Cian from her soul in

Act of Mercy, Fidelma realizes that Eadulf is the only man of her age with whom she can be herself without concealing her rank and her profession (*The Monk Who Vanished* 315). Not he, but she, as a traditional Irish woman, takes the lead in changing their circumstances: in 666 she decided they should undertake a trial marriage of a year and a day, one of nine legal marriage forms under Brehon law (*Badger's Moon* xiv), and in *The Leper's Bell,* after their son was born between June and July 667, she asked Eadulf if he wanted her to be his first contracted wife. Their formal marriage ceremony took place at Cashel in early 668.

Even before that wedding, however, Fidelma's emotional and psychological pressures had begun to threaten their relationship. Though she denies it, she suffers from postpartum depression in October 667, only partially relieved by Eadulf's herbal concoctions, and at the close of *Badger's Moon,* even though she has a reliable and near-constant child-care arrangement, she yearns for her former freedom from maternal responsibility and for the challenges of the legal profession (307). In *Chalice of Blood,* set in the late summer of 670, their marriage reaches its tipping point. When Eadulf's hopes for a peaceful future raising their son together in some quiet dual monastery clash with Fidelma's long-contemplated decision to renounce her religious vows and pursue the position of her brother's Chief Brehon, Fidelma's prideful anger erupts and she drives Eadulf away.

By that time, Eadulf is sick of the hectic travels that Fidelma, like many peripatetic Irish missionaries of her time, thrives upon, especially since he has little experience with or liking for horses and always suffers from seasickness. Since meeting at the Synod of Whitby in 664, they solved the Archbishop of Canterbury's murder in Rome in *A Shroud for the Archbishop*; after Eadulf went missing on a Gaulish merchant ship in *The Subtle Serpent,* they returned to Cashel where Fidelma's brother was named King in 666; in *The Spider's Web, Valley of the Shadow,* and *The Monk Who Vanished,* they probed crimes in other Irish venues, and in *Our Lady of Darkness,* Fidelma saved Eadulf from hanging in Leinster. *Smoke in the Wind* took them to Canterbury, and then they dashed back to Ireland in *The Leper's Bell,* to save their infant son from a kidnapping, and in 668, prior to their formal marriage, they solved more Irish crimes in *Master of Souls,* and *A Prayer for the Damned.* They investigated the High King's murder at Tara in *Dancing With Demons;* in 670, for *Council of the Cursed,* they journeyed to Autun in Burgundy, and returning to Ireland aboard the *Barnacle Goose,* Fidelma and Eadulf narrowly escaped slaughter by pirates. In 670, though she still refers to Eadulf as "my husband" (*Chalice of Blood* 112), they are now by her choice occupying separate bedrooms (93) in the forbidding Irish abbey of Lios Mór. Those years of near-incessant travel and the emotional and physical strains of the homicide investigations and legal battles that have debilitated Eadulf have challenged Fidelma's intellect, fueling her pride and wreaking havoc on their marriage.

Further, though Eadulf had accepted her decision that they should settle in her brother's kingdom, he is chafing at its ramifications. They both know all too well that under Irish law, as an outsider he is considered inferior to Fidelma (*Chalice of Blood* 45); he dislikes the Irish custom that requires their son to be fostered from seven to seventeen; his male ego resents his forced financial dependence on his wife; and when she demands, "Use your senses!" (172) over an investigational detail in *Chalice of Blood,* he explodes. He tells Fidelma that he had fallen in love with her humorous and sensitive nature, but lately he has had to endure her arrogance, criticism, and dismissal of his views, all voiced with her pitilessly sharp tongue (*Chalice of Blood* 172–3). At this point, Eadulf probably would agree with Lord Byron, whose wife was a talented mathematician:

> Oh! Ye lords of ladies intellectual,
> Inform us truly, have they not hen-peck'd you all?
> [*Don Juan,* Canto I, xxii].

Eadulf's outburst shocks and saddens Fidelma into reevaluating their situation (*Chalice of Blood* 173), a predicament facing many women of intellect through the ages. Having painfully survived the early onslaught of "Eros" and "Mania" and having promised themselves never to make such mistakes again, they seek fulfillment with men who offer "Storge" (friendship), "Pragma" (practical love) and even "Agape" (helpfulness or altruistic love)—though sooner or later their talents and ambitions may drive such women to marginalize their mates and children in pursuit of their professional goals. If on the other hand gifted women try to abandon those goals, they risk condemning themselves to live out regret-ridden lives that sour them and their husbands into oblivion. Tremayne tantalizingly leaves Fidelma at the close of *The Chalice of Blood* with a decision made but unrevealed, while she tells Eadulf he will have to make a choice of his own when they return to Cashel (428). Though a hint at their future appears in the epilogue to *The Council of the Cursed* (305), in *Behold a Pale Horse,* 2011, Tremayne returns to the year 664, with Fidelma in the seaport of Genua on her way back from Rome to Cashel—alone. If thirty-something Fidelma and her spiritual daughters have learned, as the modern Irish bard William Butler Yeats suggested, "Romantic Ireland's dead and gone," for many gifted women his disturbing question in "No Second Troy" still may linger:

> Why, what could she have done, being what she is?
> Was there another Troy for her to burn?

Notes

1. The legendary Queen Medb is supposed to have boasted to her husband that she had had a secret lover as well as an official one before she was married (Taylor 54).

2. Before the Great Famine of 1845–1851, Irish attitudes to sex earthily celebrated women's sexuality as well as men's. A legend even related how St. Brigid met a young woman distressed over her pregnancy, prayed, laid her hands on the woman's womb, and the fetus disappeared. Under the stringent Roman Catholic "Penitential" orientation Fidelma so disparaged, however, Ireland between the 1850s and the late 1990s was considered the most sexually repressed country in Europe. (In the 1940s and 1950s, Ireland, heavily governed by the Roman Catholic Church, passed a series of laws which contributed to isolating women in the home as second-class citizens [Mary Ryan 109].) This situation has rapidly changed, however. The current Irish *taoiseach* (prime minister) Bertie Ahearn lives openly with his unwed partner, who attends state visits as his "first lady" (Horgan).

3. St. Patrick was a slave in Ireland from the age of 15 to 21, and according to his earliest (7th century) biographer, Muirchu, Patrick's master, Miliucc, was reputed to have been a Druid high priest. After his return to Ireland as a missionary, Patrick adopted a druidic guise and employed preliterate non–Roman Irish rhetorical usages to survive and carry out his work of conversion (Johnson-Sheehan and Lynch 244).

4. See J.A. Lee, *Lovestyles* (London: Dent, 1976). Lee's five "lovestyles" resemble components of "love" earlier described by Z. Rubin as dependence (Mania), helpfulness (Agape), absorption (Eros), respect (Pragma), and similarity (Storge) (Cramer 411–412).

5. Contemporary psychologist Alex Benzer (*The Tao of Dating*) contends that the smarter a person is, the more clueless about dating he or she will be, and the more problems such a person will have in his or her dating life. Benzer believes "smart people," have an exceptional talent for obstructing their own romantic success.

6. Tremayne has noted that the Roman Catholic Church was centralized, while the Celtic Church was not, developing from early Christian ideas that meshed with the Celtic cultural ethos. The Celtic Church did not completely dissolve after the Synod of Whitby and was not absorbed by Rome until the Synod of Cashel, 1172 (Tremayne and Cuthbertson).

7. Commentators often liken the relationship between Fidelma and Eadulf to the one between Sherlock Holmes and Dr. Watson, but Tremayne's pair of investigators shares a far more complex comradeship, involving powerful emotional, sexual, and cultural elements.

Works Cited

Benzer, Alex. "Why the Smartest People Have the Toughest Time Dating." *The Huffington Post.* http://www.Huffingtonpost.com, 2 March 2009. Web. 15 July 2011.

Byron, George Gordon. *Byron: Complete Poetical Works.* Ed. Frederick Page and John Jump. Oxford: Oxford University Press, 1970.

Cramer, Duncan. "Dimensions of Romantic Love in British Female Adolescents." *The Journal of Social Psychology* 133 (2001): 411–13. Print.

Harrington, Christina. *Women in a Celtic Church.* Oxford: Oxford University Press, 2002. Print.

Horgan, Goretti. "Changing Women's Lives in Ireland." *International Socialism Journal* 91 (2001). http://pubs.socialreviewindex.org. Web. 8 August 2011.

Johnson-Sheehan, Richard, and Paul Lynch. "Rhetoric of Myth, Magic, and Conversion: A Prolegomena to Ancient Irish Rhetoric." *Rhetoric Review* 26 (2007): 233–52.

Kelly, Fergus. "The Brehon Laws." *World of Hibernia* 6 (Winter 2000): 60. Print.

"Law, Literature, and Legend." http://ua_tuathal.tripod.com/lllaw.htm. Web. 8 August 2011.

Lonigan, Paul R. "Women and the Celts in the Middle Ages." http://www.aislingmagazine.com. Web. 8 August 2011.
McNamara, JoAnn, and John E. Halborg, eds. *Sainted Women of the Dark Ages*. Durham: Duke University Press, 1992. Print.
O'Connor, Pat. "Understanding Continuities and Changes in Irish Marriage: Putting Women Centre Stage." *Irish Journal of Sociology* 5 (1995): 135–163. Print.
Ryan, Mary. "What's Love Got to Do with It? Family, Sex, and Domestic Violence in Contemporary Irish Women's Fiction." *disClosure* 20 (2011): 106–31. Print.
Sayers, Dorothy L. *Gaudy Night*. New York: Harcourt, Brace, 1936.
Scherman, Katharine. *The Flowering of Ireland*. Boston: Little, Brown, 1985. Print.
Showalter, Elaine. "Laughing Medusa: Feminist Intellectuals at the Millennium." *Women's Cultural Review* 11 (2000): 131–138. Print.
Taylor, G. Rattray. *Sex in History*. New York: Vanguard Press, 1954. Print.
Thomas, Louisa. "Look Back in Anger," rev. of *This is not the Ivy League*, by Mary Clearman Blew. *New York Times Book Review* 4 September 2011: 8. Print.
Tremayne, Peter. *Absolution by Murder*. New York: Signet, 1997.
_____. *Act of Mercy*. New York: Signet, 1999.
_____. *Badger's Moon*. New York: Signet, 2006.
_____. *Behold a Pale Horse*. London: Headline, 2011.
_____. *The Chalice of Blood*. London: Headline, 2010.
_____. *Council of the Cursed*. New York: St. Martin's Minotaur, 2010.
_____. *Dancing with Demons*. New York: St. Martin's Minotaur, 2009.
_____. *Hemlock at Vespers*. New York: St. Martin's Minotaur, 2000.
_____. *The Leper's Bell*. New York: St. Martin's Minotaur, 2006.
_____. *Master of Souls*. New York: St. Martin's Minotaur, 2007.
_____. *The Monk Who Vanished*. New York: St. Martin's Minotaur, 1999.
_____. *Our Lady of Darkness*. New York: Signet, 2004.
_____. *A Prayer for the Damned*. New York: St. Martin's Minotaur, 2008.
_____. *Shroud for the Archbishop*. New York: Signet, 1998.
_____. *Smoke in the Wind*. New York: Signet, 2005.
_____. *The Spider's Web*. New York: Signet, 2000.
_____. *The Subtle Serpent*. New York: Signet, 1999.
_____. *Valley of the Shadow*. New York: Signet, 2001.
Tremayne, Peter, with Sarah Cuthbertson. "The Fascination for Sister Fidelma": Interview with Peter Tremayne. *Salander: The Magazine of the Historical Novel Society* 8 (May 2004): 2–6.
Yeats, William Butler. *The Collected Poems of William Butler Yeats*. New York: Charles Scribner's Sons, 1996.

Pursuing the Mystery of Religious Life

Patricia C. Flynn

Detective fiction and religion seem to have a special affinity and have often been presented as mirror images of the same passion for truth and justice. In his famous commentary on the appeal of detective literature, W.H. Auden characterized the genre as concerned with the great religious themes of death, retribution and punishment and noted that it provided an opportunity for the reader to experience the expiation of the pervasive sense of human guilt. Contemporary mystery writer P.D. James makes this claim even more explicit when she describes the hero detective as "a secular priest expert in the extraction of confession whose final revelation of the truth confers a vicarious absolution on all but the guilty" (James 180).

If detective fiction can take on religious attributes, religion can also be seen as possessing the passion of a relentless detective. In his essay "The Divine Detective," Christian apologist and mystery writer G.K. Chesterton defined the Christian Church as "an enormous private detective" whose role was to correct the injustices of the official detective — the State. While both Church and State search out wrongdoers, for Chesterton, the Church's goal was not punishment but pardon. "The Church is the only thing that ever attempted by system to pursue and discover crimes, not in order to avenge, but in order to forgive them ... the unrelenting sleuthhound who seeks to save and not to slay" (Chesterton 156).

It is not surprising, then, that detective fiction in which religion provides not only the setting for the plot but also the characterization of the protagonist and the motivation for the crime as well, has a potent appeal. This combination also can suggest that there may be more at stake in such novels than mere entertainment. Such is the case with the mystery series authored by Peter Tremayne. Set in seventh-century Celtic Ireland, the novels feature Tremayne's heroine sleuth, Sister Fidelma, and use the tensions between the Celtic Church and the Roman Church over matters of church authority and the control of liturgical and religious life to provide a fertile field for intrigue, malice and murder.

Like Auden, I confess to an addiction to murder mysteries and I find Tremayne's Sister Fidelma series particularly interesting on several levels. There are, of course, the carefully constructed plots, embellished with rich historical detail that offer the opportunity to experience another time and culture. For me, however, there is something more. While the novels are not meant as theological treatises, they deal with issues of deep religious significance. As a member of a community of women religious for over forty years I find myself engaging with Tremayne's portrayal of religious life and its place in the life of the Church from my own perspective and experience of religious community after the renewal initiated by the Second Vatican Council. Some of the questions raised by Tremayne in his description of the religious struggles between the Celtic and Roman Churches still resonate today.

The purpose of this essay is to examine Tremayne's characterization of religious life as lived in Celtic Ireland, and especially as experienced by his heroine, Sister Fidelma. There is a mystery here that goes beyond the familiar whodunit: the mystery of the identity of a particular lifestyle within the Church and the mystery of an individual's discernment of that lifestyle. I will begin by summarizing Tremayne's description of Celtic religious life and challenge some of his assumptions regarding important elements of that lifestyle. I will then examine those aspects which, despite the separation of time and culture, still continue to trouble the relationship between religious life and the Church. Finally, I will examine Sister Fidelma's own struggles with religious life. Tremayne has created a complex character who must solve the ultimate mystery of her own vocation in life.

Religious Life: Past and Present

Two themes emerge in Tremayne's account of Celtic religious life. One is the role of celibacy as a requirement for religious life and the other is the right of the Roman Church to stand as the sole authority regarding the practice and interpretation of religion in general and of religious life in particular. Both of these themes appear in almost every novel, sometimes as part of an on-going background conflict among the characters and sometimes holding center stage as an integral element in the plot of the mystery itself. The two themes intertwine as the issue of religious celibacy becomes identified with allegiance to Rome.

Tremayne's choice to characterize his protagonist, Sister Fidelma, as a married religious allows Tremayne the opportunity to explore a form of early Celtic religious life that, while historically based, seems alien to the rules of contemporary religious communities. When Tremayne introduces Sister Fidelma, she is a member of a monastic community founded at Kildare by St. Brigid. The Abbey of Kildare was a *conhospitae* or double house where "men and women lived raising their children in Christ's service" (*Absolution by Murder* ix). While Tremayne's novels also include descriptions of other forms of religious life present at the time in Celtic Ireland such as the harsh penitential community of monks on the remote island of Sceilig Mhichil in *Suffer Little Children* (1997) and the single monasteries of men in *The Haunted Abbot* (2003) and of women in *The Subtle Serpent* (1998), it is clear that Tremayne's sympathies are with the tradition of the *conhospitae* and it is this tradition that he uses his characters to defend.

The discussion of the Roman imposition of celibacy begins in Tremayne's first novel, *Absolution by Murder* (1997), set at the Council of Whitby. Here Sister Fidelma admits that she had never really given the question of celibacy much thought, taking her life at the double monastery of Kildare as an unchallenged norm. She is, however, not swayed by the arguments of the Roman delegation to the Council and recognizes that Northumbria's acceptance of Rome's demands is motivated by political pragmatism, not Scriptural or theological mandate.

As the novels progress and the relationship between Sister Fidelma and Brother Eadulf deepens and becomes formalized in marriage, the antagonism between Celtic married religious life and Rome's requirement of celibacy grows. The arguments for each position are starkly stated. The proponents of celibacy support their demand by appealing to an Augustinian perspective of fallen human nature that denigrates the body, sees sexuality as evil, and bases its hope for salvation on physical purity (*A Prayer for the Damned* 45). Fidelma and Eadulf, on the other hand, see their life together and the married religious life in general, as a natural response to one of life's greatest sources of happiness, and one of God's most important gifts. While they admit that some few ascetics might choose to renounce sexual relations, they continually express their confidence that religious celibacy will never become popular as an accepted practice in religious life (*Valley of the Shadow* 107).

Tremayne is able to use the dynamics of the murder mystery itself to support his own views on this issue. Since several of his villains uphold the requirement of celibacy, and some are even willing to kill in its name, the reader can have the impression that celibacy is the root of all evil — or at least a motive for murder! Tremayne wants us to feel repelled by the sinister pair of Bishop Leodegar and Abbess Audofleda (*The Council of the Cursed*) and the deceitful and manipulative Abbot Ultan (*A Prayer for the Damned*) in whom fanatical adherence to celibacy co-exists with explicit malice. Conversely, since Fildelma and Eadulf emerge at the end of each novel as the defenders of truth and justice, it seems very credible that they must be right about the rejection of celibacy as well.

The confrontation between the Celtic and Roman churches over the issue of celibacy and Roman control reaches its climax at the Council of Autun, the setting for Tremayne's *The Council of the Cursed*. Like the Council of Whitby, the Council of Autun was an historical event called to establish the Roman Church's primacy in regulating elements of the creed and religious rule. As Bishop Leodagar informs Sister Fidelma, the goal is to agree that there should be "one set of laws as to how each community should conduct themselves" (*The Council of the Cursed* 43). Fidelma's response describes the diversity that characterized Celtic religious life: "But all our religious houses draw up their own Rule according to their individual needs and purposes" (*The Council of the Cursed* 43). Some of these Rules might include celibacy but many did not.

Ultimately, this universal religious rule would be the Rule of St. Benedict with its requirement of a vow of celibacy. The novel, however, is set in a monastery that had already adopted the Roman rule and the results are meant as a tragic prediction of what the imposition of this vow would mean. Monks had been forced to publicly renounce their marriage vows and send their wives and children away. This cruel disruption of marriage and family life provided the opportunity for a sinister plot to emerge—the selling of the now abandoned women and children as slaves.

While Fidelma can put an end to the abuse of the former wives and their children she cannot stop the march of Roman control, though she sees the mandated standardization of religious life as "leading to great suffering rather than a universal brotherhood and sisterhood among the religious" (*The Council of the Cursed* 302). Safely back in Ireland, Fidelma hears from a couple that decided to continue their lives as married religious in spite of the new requirement in a form of underground religious life: "We maintain our Faith in the Christ Jesus but not in men who would try to claim dominion over us and regulate our lives with petty rules that are unnatural to human life. We deny those disciplines for we are human, no more but certainly no less. We are as the Creator made us, and, if there is truth in religion, we are as we were meant to be" (*The Council of the Cursed* 307). While it will take centuries before Rome's domination of the Celtic Church and Celtic religious life is complete, it is inevitable, and Tremayne's words here and in his novels in general mourn the passing of a lifestyle that was marked by equality between men and women, mutual respect and natural happiness based on sexual freedom.

One cannot argue with the historical accuracy of Tremayne's account of Celtic religious life. After all, he is a noted Celtic historian in his own right and has published widely regarding the role of women in Celtic Ireland (Ellis). I do think, however, that some questions can be raised regarding his defense of Celtic religious life and his criticism of the role that celibacy should play in that lifestyle.

Tremayne's description of Celtic religious life takes the mixed houses of the *conhospitae* as the norm and describes their members as ordinary married couples, living together and raising their children in the Lord's service. While this was certainly one form that religious life took in Celtic Ireland, it was not the only form. Indeed, the history of Irish monasticism is rich and varied, and Tremayne's fascination with the role of mixed monasteries may have limited his appreciation of the positive aspects of celibacy within religious communities. As another historian of the period states, "[T]he inevitable historical debate over the nature and endurance of 'double' communities loses relevance; rather groups of male and female religious lived and labored in a whole range of situations of varying integration, some more formal than others, just as men and women lived in varying arrangements in secular life" (Bitel 174). There were women's monasteries, men's monasteries, and monasteries where both sexes interacted either temporarily or permanently, and no consensus seems to have existed regarding the superiority of one type over another.

Tremayne, in his historical writings, seems particularly unwilling to recognize the possibility that some of these mixed houses might have been examples of a syneisastic approach to religious life—men and women living in some sense together but separately, as "soul friends" rather than married couples (Ellis 144). For Tremayne, such a lifestyle could only be motivated by an unnatural desire for self-mortification. Other scholars, however, describe this approach in more positive terms as a relationship that freed both men and women from the limitations of the traditionally defining roles of kinship and marriage (McNamara 74; Bitel 181ff). Fidelma herself seems caught between those two roles—sister to the King and companion to Eadulf. One wonders if Tremayne's desire to portray a strong Celtic woman of the period might have been better served by a fuller exploration of this syneisastic option.

Tremayne's enthusiastic embrace of the married religious life as the norm for Celtic religious life suffers from the thinness of his description of how this lifestyle might actually have been lived. While his standard description of the *conhospitae* is that they live together and raise their children in the service of the Lord, there are few other details provided. Happily married religious couples are hard to find in the novels and accounts of how families might be raised are absent as well. Little time is spent describing any intimate relations, even between Fidelma and Eadulf. The reader might be actually surprised when Fidelma announces that she is pregnant since there have been few indications of any interest in or time for the requisite intimacy, and the pregnancy and birth seem strangely missing from any consideration in the novels.

Alchu, the infant son of Fidelma and Eadulf, is the only small child that plays a role as the offspring of a religious couple and his future upbringing seems problematic (*The Leper's Bell*). Other children appear only as adults whose complicated relationships with their parents and other members of the religious community form the background for intrigue and even murder (*The Subtle Serpent*). The particularity reflected in the natural affection of parents for their children and the special obligations that family members have to each other are at odds with the more impartial and generalized concern that religious owe to all the members of their communities. When the welfare of the child is threatened by the needs or demands of the community, which should take priority? Tremayne's characters make their choices with often disastrous results. While the reader might sympathize with the maternal favoritism shown by Abbess Draigen in appointing her own daughter to the influential position of *rechtaire*, the ensuing mayhem in the community had near fatal consequences (*The Subtle Serpent*).

The tension that married religious couples must have faced between their natural love for each other and their children and the love and obedience they owed to the community leads to my final criticism of Tremayne's description of Celtic religious life. The only argument that Tremayne offers for the vow of celibacy is a negative one — the rejection of sexuality as evil. Studies of the history of religious life suggest that a fuller story needs to be told, one that can account for the enduring and pervasive role that celibacy has played in defining a particular lifestyle within the Catholic Church.

In a recent analysis of religious life, noted Catholic theologian Sandra Schneiders, I.H.M. begins with an anthropological consideration of monasticism as a human phenomenon in which Catholic religious life is a relative newcomer. While temporary or permanent celibacy characterizes all forms of monasticism, Schneiders points out three different motivations for this celibacy. Non-Christian forms of monasticism are often motivated by an ascetic desire to control bodily urges and passions. Related to this motivation is a desire for a freedom from marital or family obligations that would interfere with religious duties. While Schneiders admits that both of these rationales have been used in the past to justify Catholic religious celibacy, she suggests that "neither of them have been fully convincing, even in times past" (Schneiders, *Religious Life* 14).

For Schneiders, the only viable motivation for a life of permanent celibacy is a personal and total commitment to a relationship with Jesus Christ characterized by a psychological-spiritual exclusivity that makes marital relationships impossible. This vowed commitment "implies no negative judgment on human sexuality or pejorative comparison with marriage. It is a personal response to a personal call that is specific but neither superior nor normative" (Schneiders 14). This motivation is what distinguishes a clerical celibacy mandated by Church discipline still problematic in the Catholic Church today from the freely chosen vow of celibacy that is at the heart of consecrated religious life. It is this radical celibacy, not where one lives or what ministry one does, or even whether one is ordained, that distinguishes religious life from other forms of commitment within the Church.

The tradition of married religious life that Tremayne describes is more indebted to historical circumstances than to theological arguments (Ryan 96–104). The enthusiasm of the monks who proselytized Ireland for their own vocation failed to separate the call to Christianity from the more specific call to religious life, leaving the new Irish Christians to adopt monastic structures as an essential part of their practice of their new religion. The newly converted were not presented with other options for the lay practice of their faith. Such an approach ignored the special call that religious life has always been. As Schneiders notes, "Monasticism is, like art, a particular and specialized vocation, and it is probably not meant to supplant ordinary life within a religious tradition" (*Religious Life* 11). It is the realization of this special call and response that accounts for the primacy of celibate religious life over the short-lived experiment with mixed religious communities that was part of the Celtic experience.

While I can take issue with Tremayne's description of the prominence of married religious life, I can sympathize with his account of the struggle between the Celtic and Roman Churches over issues of authority and control regarding the elements of religious life. Such tension is inherent in the nature of religious life and in the hierarchical structure of the Church. While religious communities exist within the Church and are officially recognized as part of the Church by its leaders, religious communities are not created by the Church. They are given to the Church as gifts by the Spirit to highlight specific Gospel responses to the needs of the world (Flannery 611). Such gifts take the form of a particular founder's vision, and like all gifts, are always beyond the total control of the recipient.

The Church has always struggled to embrace the prophetic creativity that religious communities have brought to the interpretation of the Gospel message, whether that was the radical poverty of the Franciscan mendicant movement in the thirteenth century or the active embrace of apostolic life outside the cloister walls by the foundresses of women's communities in the nineteenth century. While the mid-twentieth century witnessed a call from the Church for the renewal of religious life by a return to these founding charisms, the last thirty years of hierarchical pronouncements have tried to curb the changes that the subsequent period of experimentation unleashed. Thus in 1980 Pope Paul VI attempted to promulgate some Essential Elements of Religious Life in order to standardize traditional aspects of religious life such as religious garb and formal communal housing that had been discarded as contemporary religious communities responded to what they saw as the "signs of the times." Most recently, the Vatican's concerns about American women religious motivated an Apostolic Visitation to investigate the fidelity of apostolic communities of women in the United States to Rome's more conservative view of religious life. While no murders occurred during the investigation, the anxiety, anger and fear surrounding a process that was both secretive and divisive could have rivaled the tensions that Tremayne describes between Ireland and Rome!

Discerning a Call

Tremayne's novels provide not merely a description of Celtic religious life in general but also an account of one person's experience of that life and her discernment of her vocation as a religious. Here the conflict is not between ecclesial powers and traditions but rather between the desires of Sister Fidelma's heart and the expectations of religious life. This tension between Sister Fidelma and her vocation is obvious in Tremayne's standard physical description of his heroine: an attractive and vigorous young woman whose confident demeanor is plainly at odds with the expected somber dignity of the average religious. The rebellious strands of red hair that are always escaping from her head-dress symbolize an internal rebellion that will gradually become a focal point in the later novels ("Murder in Repose" 1).

Tremayne traces the origin of Sister Fidelma's vocation to the advice of her cousin Abbot Laisran who saw religious life as an appropriate vehicle for the professional legal career that Sister Fidelma had been trained to pursue. As a religious she would automatically achieve the same revered status and protection that had been granted to the pre–Christian Druids who had exercised similar roles of advocates, doctors and teachers. Thus she enters the Abbey of Kildare for cultural, not religious, reasons and it is not long before she becomes disenchanted with religious life and resentful of its demands.

The complicity of her own religious superior, the Abbess of Kildare, in a murder causes Sister Fidelma to leave the Abbey and return to her brother's castle at Cashel ("Hemlock at Vespers"). While Sister Fidelma ceases to identify herself with Kildare, she maintains her title as a religious, but it is as a religious without a community and thus without a rule of life. Lacking the support that these elements of religious life might have provided, it is not surprising that her discernment of her call to continue as a religious now begins in earnest. Her participation in the pilgrimage that forms the setting for *Act of Mercy* allows her time to not only solve multiple murders but to ponder her life's direction. She discovers that "her one abiding interest and passion had been the law, not religion in the sense of sublimating herself to a life of devotion within some monastery away from the rest of her fellow beings" (*Act of Mercy* 12), and while she would remain a religious in name, her role as *dalaigh* would always come before any contemplative life.

This same period sees her growing attachment to Eadulf and the formalization of their relationship in marriage. The protest by Abbot Ultan over married religious life that disrupts her wedding ceremony causes Sister Fidelma to consider whether it would be better for all involved if she just left religious life, since she admits that "she has never been a religious in the strict sense" (*A Prayer for the Damned* 43) but she stubbornly refuses to give the Roman faction the satisfaction of her withdrawal. Being a married religious had less to do with being a religious than it had to do with taking a stand against the authority of a foreign Church.

Marriage and motherhood bring further challenges as the demands of being a wife, mother and a religious continue to restrict Sister Fidelma's freedom to follow her legal profession. She is torn between the affection that she feels for Eadulf and her son Alchu, and the exhilaration that she experiences as she exercises her power of analysis and her skill at detection. When Eadulf suggests that it is time to put an end to their traveling and pursue a true religious vocation of prayer and reflection together in a small mixed community, Sister Fidelma counters with her own plan — leaving the religious life altogether and becoming the official legal advisor to her brother the King of Cashel (*The Dove of Death* 369). As of this writing, Tremayne has yet to reveal what this decision will mean for the relationship between Sister Fidelma and Eadulf, but it is clear that for Fidelma, the religious life is not part of their future together (*The Chalice of Blood* 428).

Fidelma is perhaps not so different from the young women who entered American religious communities between 1940 and 1960, attracted to a cadre of educated professional women at a time when few women had careers outside the home. Many of these same women were part of the exodus from religious life that followed the Second Vatican Council in the 1960s and 1970s when they realized that they could pursue ministries of service, even within the Church, without being a member of a religious community. As Sandra Schneiders reminds us, the more interesting question for twenty-first century religious life is why women continue to enter and to stay in religious life. Contemporary women religious must "find the taproot of their vocation, not in peer group euphoria, social status or preferential treatment by the hierarchy, but in the core of their spirituality, face to face with the One to whom they had given their lives in celibate love..." (Schneiders "Why they stay[ed]").

Sister Fidelma concludes that she no longer needs the status and protection that her cousin thought that religious life would provide, but the reader might question whether she ever really needed it at all. A consideration of the novels would indicate that it is actually her position as sister to the King and her degree of *Anruth* that provide all the support that she needs to solve her cases. Granted that her position as the sister of the King is only established in Tremayne's third novel, and that her own status as a distinguished *dalaigh* may have needed a comparable amount of time to be recognized, it often seems that little is gained, at least in the later novels, by her vocation as a religious. Indeed, she struggles to have people even acknowledge her religious title in preference to her royal status (*Act of Mercy*). Perhaps her discernment to leave religious life is Tremayne's recognition that he has said all that he wants to (or that can be said) about Celtic religious life and that there is more historical detail and malicious intrigue to be mined from Sister Fidelma's membership in a royal clan and a secular professional class.

Conclusion

I began this essay by noting some similarities between detective fiction and religion. Both pursue mysteries, and their pursuits captivate the human mind and heart. In detective fiction, the mystery is short-lived and the reader has the ultimate satisfaction of the denouement offered by the successful sleuth in the final chapter where the culprit's identity is revealed and the tangle of clues unraveled. For the detective writer and reader, mysteries are problems to be solved, and there should be no loose ends, no unanswered questions. The escape provided by detective literature lets us experience a world where evil is always punished, goodness is always rewarded and logic reigns supreme — unlike our everyday experience.

Religion, however, presents us with another approach to mystery, one in which there are few definitive answers and where the questions themselves are more valuable than any solution, since any solution, in the face of eternity, is bound to be temporary at best. Here the lines between good and evil may be less clear, the possibility for both fall from grace and redemption stands available for all, and the ultimate judgment must wait until the end of time itself. In religious mystery, logical deduction, and even the ability to concretize one's ideas in words can fail and the only response available is trust in what cannot be understood. The transcendent always outruns the human attempt to comprehend and structure the religious experience, whether in the form of a particular religious community or an institutional church.

Peter Tremayne's Sister Fidelma series certainly provides an excellent example of historical detective fiction that allows readers to immerse themselves in the culture of another time and place and experience the satisfaction of a good murder mystery solved. The portrayal of Tremayne's characters and the themes that he pursues, however, go beyond simple entertainment. I have suggested that there are serious religious questions that deserve to be considered in their own right. Religious life, both as a lifestyle in the Church and as an option for a particular individual, is a mystery — not one that can be solved by logical reasoning, but one that must be lived in trusting relationship with the Divine. While Tremayne's attempts to solve this deeper mystery may fall short, they at least raise questions that might move the reader to another level of reflection and even, perhaps, into a dialogue with the Source of all Mystery.

WORKS CITED

Auden, W.H. "The Guilty Vicarage: Notes on the Detective Story by an Addict." *Harper's Magazine* May 1948. Web. 12 July 2011. <http://www.harpers.org/archive/1948/0033 206>.
Bitel, Lisa M. *Land of Women: Tales of Sex and Gender from Early Ireland*. Ithaca: Cornell University Press, 1996.
Chesterton, G.K. "The Divine Detective." In *A Miscellany of Men*. Philadelphia: Dufour Editions, 1969.
Ellis, Peter Berresford. *Celtic Women: Women in Celtic Society and Literature*. Grand Rapids: William B. Eerdmans, 1995.
Flannery, Austin O.P., ed. *The Second Vatican Council: The Conciliar and Post Conciliar Documents*. Northport, NY: Costello, 1996.
James, P.D. *Talking About Detective Fiction*. New York: Alfred A. Knopf, 2009.
McNamara, JoAnn Kay. *Sisters in Arms: Catholic Nuns through Two Millennia*. Cambridge: Harvard University Press. 1996.
Ryan, John. *Irish Monasticism*. Ithaca: Cornell University Press, 1972.
Schneiders, Sandra M., I.H.M. *Religious Life in a New Millennium: Finding the Treasure*. New York: Paulist Press, 2000.
_____. "Why they stay(ed)." *National Catholic Reporter* 2009. Web. 5 Aug. 2011. <www.ncr online.org/new/women/why-they-stayed>.
Tremayne, Peter. *Absolution by Murder*. 1994. New York: Signet, 1997.
_____. *Act of Mercy*. 1999. New York: St. Martin's Minotaur, 2001.
_____. *The Chalice of Blood*. London: Headline, 2010.
_____. *The Council of the Cursed*. 2008. New York: St. Martin's Minotaur, 2009.
_____. *The Dove of Death*. 2009. New York: St. Martin's Minotaur, 2010.
_____. "Fidelma's World." *The International Sister Fidelma Society*, 2001 Web. 26 July 2011. <www.sisterfidelma.com/fidelma.html>.
_____. "Hemlock at Vespers." *Hemlock at Vespers*. New York: St. Martin's Minotaur, 2000: 127-56.
_____. *The Leper's Bell*. 2004. New York: St. Martin's Minotaur, 2006.
_____. *Master of Souls*. 2005. New York: St. Martin's Minotaur, 2007.

_____. "Murder in Repose." *Hemlock at Vespers.* New York: St. Martin's Minotaur, 2000. 1–23.
_____. *A Prayer for the Damned.* 2006. New York: St. Martin's Minotaur, 2008.
_____. *The Subtle Serpent* 1996. New York: St. Martin's Press, 1998.
_____. *Suffer Little Children.* 1995. New York: St. Martin's Press, 1997.
_____. *Valley of the Shadow.* 1998.. New York: St. Martin's Minotaur. 2000.

The Sister Is a Mother: Sister Fidelma and the Celtic Church

Frank A. Salamone

Although the author has stated his purpose was to write his stories as "mystery entertainments" against a historical background that he knew well as a historian, the Sister Fidelma series has become connected, consciously or not, by some readers with the modern religious obsession to find a relevant Christianity with something to offer our age. There can be little doubt that old forms no longer fit the needs of many people. Attempts to reform Catholicism, for example, met with vigorous opposition and a general feeling that the reforms were a failure. Some argued that the reforms had gone too far. Others that they had not gone far or fast enough. Both sides invoked the shibboleth of "early Christianity," as if it were a unitary holistic thing. Father Gregory Tillett in the *Glastonbury Review* notes:

> The desire to rediscover a Christian spirituality relevant to contemporary Western society led some to look to the origins of Christianity in the West and, since for many of these people "the West" was defined as the British Isles, and as English-speaking nations with some, at least, British association, the quest became one for early Christianity in Celtic Britain. It should be noted that amongst those who still spoke Celtic languages the desire to preserve and maintain their ancient cultural inheritance, however much it may have been oppressed and suppressed, can never have been said to have died out....

Tillett indicates that Peter Berressford Ellis is deeply involved in this movement and quotes Ellis enthusiastically. Ellis is, of course, Peter Tremayne:

> The Celtic Church — I shall use that popular term for this entity because any other term would be too cumbersome — could be designated as a singular cultural entity within the greater Christian movement, delineated by its practices, philosophies, social concepts and art forms. These individualistic practices — and its observances and customs in respect of Easter — its asceticism, monastic extremism and, indeed, fanaticism, its attitudes to social order, views on land

tenure, contrary philosophies towards feudal and hereditary rights, brought it into early conflict with Rome. Absorption was inevitable; inevitable because of its very individualism, its lack of cohesion and centralism. But that absorption took many centuries. Even as late as the 14th century A.D. in Scotland there were still bodies of Celtic monks (Culdees) clinging to the old ways.

I am concerned with one major aspect of the Celtic Church; namely, its views on clerical and monastic celibacy. Contrary to some current stereotypes of Celtic puritanical sexual attitudes (Messenger, for example), the Roman Church viewed the Celtic Church as too free with sex and the independence of women. Indeed, it appears rather strange today to note that nuns and monks were allowed to marry and live in the same communities. Moreover, there was not the same obsession with "the body" as prevailed in the Roman Church under the influence of St. Augustine of Hippo. The body-soul dichotomy which obsessed him and many philosophers and theologians of the Roman Church did not serve to poison the Celtic Church about which Peter Tremayne writes in his Sister Fidelma novels.

The Celtic Church and Women

There is no need to go into great length about the manner in which Catholicism and later forms of Christianity oppressed women, while professing to elevate them. There is ample documentation on the subject. Still, a few examples may be warranted to offer contrast with Sister Fidelma's situation and that of women in Ireland at her time.

Here are three quotes from "The Status of Women in the Bible and in Early Christianity" on *Religious Tolerance.Org*:

> As regards the individual nature, woman is defective and misbegotten, for the active power of the male seed tends to the production of a perfect likeness in the masculine sex; while the production of a woman comes from defect in the active power..."—Thomas Aquinas, Summa Theologica, Q92, art. 1, Reply Obj. 1.

> And a man will choose ... any wickedness, but the wickedness of a woman.... Sin began with a woman and thanks to her we all must die"—*Ecclesiasticus, 25:18, 19 & 33*.

> And I find more bitter than death the woman, whose heart is snares and nets, and her hands as bands: whoso pleaseth God shall escape from her; but the sinner shall be taken by her"—Ecclesiastes 7:26, from the Hebrew Scriptures (Old Testament).

The site continues to give examples of Church leaders who considered women the source of sin and inferior to men in all ways. Martin Luther has a statement which sums it all up rather well in Part Three of *The Estate of Marriage* (1522):

> If they [women] become tired or even die, that does not matter. Let them die in childbirth, that's why they are there.

The evidence that women should and could not be equal with men and were to be mothers and wives, in the mode of the Virgin Mary, is a bit daunting. There is, however, strong evidence that Jesus had different views and that women in the early Church had greater positions of power than later. A reflection of how that worked is found clearly in the historical writings of Ellis and, more popularly, in his Sister Fidelma novels.

Fidelma

Fidelma is an Irish woman who lives in the mid seventh century. She is a member of the religious community of St. Brigid. However, she is more than that; she is also a dalaigh. That makes her a person of prominence, for a dalaigh was a sort of lawyer in the courts of Ireland, who could argue either side. The dalaigh's job was to ensure that justice prevailed. The Laws of the Fenecus (land-tillers) formed a sophisticated law code going back to ancient times. St. Patrick is said to have helped translate these laws into Latin.

The Irish laws differed from many others of the time in giving women numerous rights and guarantees, strikingly modern in their tenor. Indeed, women were not barred from many professions and offices typically reserved to men at the time in other lands. These positions included all fields, including warriors and political heads. Indeed, there were women judges, doctors, poets, and, yes, lawyers like Fidelma.

Moreover, there were modern sounding protections against sexual crimes, including harassment and rapes. In contrast with other societies of the time, women had a right to divorce and to compensation in divorce. These feminist rights included medical rights as well. In sum, Fidelma lived in a society far advanced in rights for women compared with its contemporaries. It is important to understand that fact in appreciating the novels and the contrast between the Celtic and Latin Churches.

She was orphaned early and raised by a relative. She studied law and reached high ranks in both criminal and civil law, As befitted a professional, Fidelma joined a religious house, initially that of St. Brigid. However, she left soon after in disillusionment as recounted in "Hemlock at Vespers" in which the mother superior of the house prods a simple-minded servant into murdering a guest. The guest was a mine expert sent by a nearby king to find gold. Unfortunately, the gold is under the convent, and finding the gold would have meant tearing down St. Brigid's religious house. Fidelma chooses to keep the murder quiet and save the house but goes off on a pilgrimage to atone for her own guilt in covering up a murder.

During the period of the Fidelma stories, Ireland was experiencing a Golden Age of Learning. Students came to Ireland from all over Europe, including royal sons. In turn, Irish men and women missionaries went to Europe to convert those who had either lost their Christianity or had never been Christians. Irish missionaries reached Kiev in the east, the Faroe Islands in the North, and Taranto in Italy in the south. Despite these missionary endeavors, the Celtic Church was in constant dispute with Rome on a number of matters, not the least of which was the independence and equality with men of its women. These issues loom large in the Fidelma series.

However, to a modern reader, it is surprising that the issue of celibacy was not one of the issues of dispute between Rome and the Celtic Church. Even though some communities in both churches promoted celibacy, it took at least four more centuries for Rome to ban priestly marriage for those below the rank of Bishop or Abbot in the Latin Church and even more centuries to enforce the ban effectively. Celibacy was enforced by the Latin Church through such means as forced separation of children and wives from their priestly husbands, labeling the children as illegitimate, forbidding people to feed or care for the women and children, disinheriting the children ("Clerical Celibacy"). The Celtic Church resisted banning clerical marriage longer than Rome, even when absorbed by Rome.

In Fidelma's time the issue of clerical celibacy was a nonissue. When one understands that fact then the issue of her becoming a wife and mother also becomes a nonissue. Moreover, her joining a religious community is no surprise, even for such an independent woman, when one realizes that religious communities were intellectual centers and did not cut her off from the secular world and the practice of law. She remained a princess, a legal expert and scholar, and a devoted wife and mother.

Love in a Religious Community

The Celtic church followed the spirituality of St. John, the evangelist. This was a spirituality rooted in the omnipresence of God and the sacredness of all he made. It viewed both grace and nature as treasured gifts of God. Its love of mysticism and poetry is still found deeply embedded in Irish life. There was also a love and respect for women, as noted in the equality of women before the law and in clerical marriage. Moreover, the Celtic Church was grounded in a rural and tribal tradition. Interestingly, male abbots provided leadership in this Church.

There is a Celtic tradition which notes that when St. John leaned upon the breast of Jesus at the Last Supper, he heard the heartbeat of God. Therefore, all humans are to listen for God's heartbeat in all creation, including themselves. It is a mystical view of creation and life, and a view that sees all creation as inherently good because it comes from God and is part of God. That includes sexuality as well (Newell).

Thus when Irish monks spread Christianity to the farthest reaches of Europe one has to understand the word "monks" as including women as well as men. There is clear evidence, according to Roger E. Reynolds, of approved sexual relations between men and women on these missionary trips. Indeed, the Latin Church found it necessary to condemn the taking of a "virgin" along with monks. The repeated issuing of these warnings makes it obvious that the warnings were ignored and the Latin Church, increasingly male dominated and misogynous, was becoming obsessed with sexuality.

Celtic religious communities, then, could house married couples, one or both of whom were religious who had taken vows as such. There was not the obsession with celibacy which came to mark the Latin Church along with its misogyny. In modern terms, there was a healthy attitude toward sexuality, seeing it as a gift from God and something holy and necessary to life. Procreation was part of God's plan for the world, something good in its proper place, not something to be hated and feared.

Fidelma displays her intelligence and humanity in this regard as in many others. In *Absolution by Murder*, the first novel in the series but not the first story, Fidelma meets her future husband, Brother Eadulf, an Anglo-Saxon monk with a Roman-style tonsure instead of a Celtic one. Both are in Whitby at a Synod in 664 to debate the merits of the Celtic and Roman churches. To be precise they are at the Abbey of St. Hilda's. While there, someone kills a Celtic participant, Abbess Étain, There are many plots and subplots, including one to kill King Oswy of Northumbria. Initially, suspicion falls on the supporters of Rome.

Fidelma, a supporter of the Celtic cause, is paired with Eadulf, a Roman advocate. Both are trained in the law but very different in temperament and loyalties. Of course, there is some friction between the two, most if not all coming from Fidelma. Inevitably, they become close friends, destined to wed in a later novel. First, however, they must solve the murder of the Abbess and then travel to Rome where they solve the murder of the Archbishop of Canterbury.

Synod of Whitby — A.D. 664

It is appropriate for Treymayne to set his first novel in the Fidelma series at the Synod of Whitby. It came at the apex of Celtic Christianity as well as at the time when it had begun its descent, although it would take centuries for that descent to become complete. The Irish resisted Latin influence and managed to hang on to their traditions long after the victory of the Latin Church ("Brief Introduction to Celtic Spirituality"). Fidelma is a living embodiment of that stubborn resistance and of the will to preserve the independence of women.

In real life, as well as fiction, the Celts guarded their traditions by oral means, passing down the richness of their spiritual beliefs and practices. They recited their prayers at the rising and setting of the sun, during work, and at times marking various states of life, such as birth and death. These prayers and rituals shared the mysticism that came with the belief in the sacredness of creation and the omnipresence of God in his creation. Moreover, Celtic creativity continued at a high level for centuries after the Synod of Whitby, as the *Book of Kells* and the Celtic Crosses that dotted the land affirm. Fidelma represents that joy in creation and the continued creativity of the Celtic spirit.

It is significant that she meets her future husband at the Synod of Whitby. It is also significant that he is an adherent of the Latin Church. It is not reading too much into the event to note that it symbolizes a marriage of the Celtic and Latin traditions with each maintaining its dignity and remaining equal partners, providing a model that was not carried out in real life. It also emphasizes the acceptance of clerical marriage, even in monasteries, at the time, an acceptance that was to end in a few centuries. The equality of men and women is also part of the lesson driven home in the series. It was an equality that disappeared in the Latin Church and has yet to fully reappear.

The Sister Is a Mother

Perhaps the most surprising focus in the Fidelma series is that on human love in religious life. Coupled with the independence and equality of women in Ireland, it becomes even more formidable. Add the element of trial marriage, as elaborated in *Badger's Moon*, and the modern reader may think Treymayne is playing an elaborate joke. However, all this is no joke. Treymayne is putting historical facts into his narrative to make a strong plea for feminine equality and the humanization of religion. He is talking about a loss in Ireland. There is indeed a touch of Pelagian ideas in his narrative as there was in Celtic Christianity. Nature is mystical and sacred. It was not destroyed or tainted by original sin. Pelagius was a Fifth Century "heretic" who taught that human nature is not inherently corrupt, among other things, which upset St. Augustine.

Certainly, the Celtic Church did not view sex as something rather dirty which was a necessity to propagate the race. It rather saw sex as something good, part of nature and a gift from God. The entire thrust of the thinking is rather more positive than that of medieval Latin Christianity. However good sex may be, Fidelma does go through a bout of post-partum depression.

In *Badger's Moon* she seeks adventure in solving yet another case to shake off those blues, taking with her Eadulf, her husband. She leaves their child with a nurse while she pursues her legal career to solve a triple murder. There are hints of Fidelma's difficulty in juggling her religious life, legal career, and being a mother. While Eadulf appears the perfect liberated father and husband, she is still facing a dilemma modern liberated women face; namely, how is it possible to have it all and not collapse? In addition, when Fidelma begins to have concerns regarding her religious commitment, their marriage undergoes a crisis.

Conclusion

The Fidelma series is an honest attempt to set a character in a carefully depicted historical setting. It is also an honest attempt to display a society with remarkably pro-women attitudes regarding equality with men and independence of life. Moreover, it depicts a period in which Christian Churches were still independent and allowed great freedom from Rome. The Celtic Church was one such Church, but its time of independence had reached its peak in the series and was going to end in a few centuries.

Thus, while the series depicts a Golden Age of Celtic Christianity, it does not present a merely unverifiable set of cultural beliefs. It depicts a character who is put into unusual situations but who acts in a manner consistent with her times. Real historical events make up a good part of the series. While the modern reader may be surprised at many of these events and at Fidelma's behavior, they are not implausible. Thus, Fidelma could have been a religious woman in a religious community and a mother as well. Granted, she was no model of motherhood, leaving her child in a nurse's care to go off on an adventure, but even that event has the ring of truth. Would a man's actions in that situation even raise a doubt about his ability to parent?

The series is aimed at modern issues. Tremayne is obviously upset with the modern Church, especially Catholicism; he is for the full equality and independence of women; he is opposed to Puritanism and in favor of a mysticism and even a whimsical element in religion. Moreover, he is tired of the body/soul dichotomy and the too frequent condemnation of the "world" as inherently evil. These are traits he finds in Celtic Christianity and he mourns their loss—and so should we all.

Works Cited

"A Brief Introduction to Celtic Spirituality." *Patmos Abbey—The Order of St. Columba* <http://www.patmosabbey.org/celtic-spirituality.html>.
"Clerical Celibacy." <http://www.badnewsaboutchristianity.com/gfa_celibacy.htm>.
Ellis, Peter Berresford. *Celtic Inheritance.* London: Constable, 1992.
The Estate of Marriage (1522). <http://pages.uoregon.edu/dluebke/Reformations441/LutherMarriage.htm#PartIII.
Messenger, John C. *Inis Beag: Isle of Ireland.* New York: Holt, Rinehart & Winston, 1969.
Newell, J. Philip. *Listening for the Heartbeat of God: A Celtic Spirituality.* New York: Paulist Press, 1997.
Religious Tolerance.Org. <http://www.religioustolerance.org/fem_bibl.htm>.
Reynolds, Roger E. "Virgines Subintroductae in Celtic Christianity." *The Harvard Theological Review* 61.4 (1968): 547–66.
Tillett, Gregory. "Reconstructing Celtic Spirituality: Searching for a Western Early Church." *Glastonbury Review.* Reprinted on the site *The British Orthodox Church within the Coptic Orthodox Patriarchate* <http://britishorthodox.org/miscellaneous/reconstructing-celtic-spirituality-searching-for-a-western-early-church/>.
Tremayne, Peter. *Absolution by Murder.* 1994. New York: Signet, 1997.
_____. *Badger's Moon.* New York: St. Martin's Minotaur, 2005.

Nothing Hidden That Shall Not Be Known: Mystery and Detection in the Sister Fidelma Novels

John Scaggs

In his introduction to *Hemlock at Vespers*, which is invaluable to anybody interested in the genesis of the Sister Fidelma mysteries, Peter Tremayne describes Brother Eadulf, Fidelma's companion in investigation, as her "Doctor Watson"' (xi), and the comparison is an interesting one for a number of different reasons. The most significant point to be made is that Tremayne's comment reminds us that the Sister Fidelma novels draw on two different kinds of "history." The first is history as most of us know it, the history of the chronicles and annals detailing dates of birth, marriage, and death of historical figures; describing the wars, marriages of state, and political maneuvering that have shaped the world. This sort of stale political, military, and economic history is given life by the consideration of social history, which is more interested in how "normal" people lived and died, and this is the kind of history that most readers of the Sister Fidelma novels would be consciously more familiar with as Tremayne, of course, uses this history to form the fabric of the novels. This aspect of the novels is more normally the focus of reviews and analysis, but there is another kind of history that also importantly informs the novels, and this is literary history.

As Tremayne's comparison of Brother Eadulf to Sir Arthur Conan Doyle's Dr. Watson clearly indicates, Tremayne is working with, and within, a literary history that runs at least from the various mystery short stories of Edgar Allan Poe, such as "The Murders in the Rue Morgue" and "The Purloined Letter," through the Sherlock Holmes stories and novels of Conan Doyle, and on through what has been termed the "Golden Age" fiction of writers such as Agatha Christie, Margery Allingham, and Dorothy L. Sayers. It even encompasses, as will be discussed later, the more recent "legal thrillers" of John Grisham and Scott Turow. Within the broader history of literature, it is the history of the genre of what is termed "crime fiction" which is significant here. Clearly, therefore, a consideration of this literary history, and Tremayne's use of it, can offer valuable insights into the Sister Fidelma mysteries, and in particular into the types of crimes she investigates and the methods she employs to do so. As a final point here, in my discussion of how mysteries are unraveled in the Sister Fidelma series it will be necessary for me to reveal certain plot elements that might spoil the novels in question for first-time readers. Since it is impossible to discuss the mystery and detective aspect of the novels without some reference to plot details, this is unavoidable.

Readers familiar with the Sister Fidelma novels will know that Brother Eadulf's role in the series is a central one. In addition to providing a love-interest in the series, Tremayne makes clear in his reference to Conan Doyle's Dr. Watson that Eadulf has other, perhaps more important, duties to perform which parallel those performed by Watson in the Sherlock Holmes stories. There are four main duties performed by what is commonly termed the "Watson figure" in the mystery story. First, he is a friend and colleague, and in the case of Eadulf and Fidelma, eventually a husband. I use the pronoun "he" with a reason, as the Watson figure, for reasons discussed below, is normally a man. Second, he is a foil for the detective's genius, and in this regard normally represents the educated intelligence of the average middle-class reader. Watson, for example, while educated and clearly intelligent, is not in the same league as Sherlock Holmes, although he does embody, in his intellect and attitude, various characteristics of the middle-class reading audience of the Sherlock Holmes stories, and this leads to the third duty he performs in the narrative. Watson is an embodiment of the positive qualities of Victorian middle-class masculinity, such as honesty, loyalty, and bravery (Scaggs 48). The same thing can be seen in Agatha Christie's narrators, who are all embodiments of middle-class respectability: pastors, doctors, and retired military officers. Christiane and Robert Luehrs, in this respect, identify Eadulf as "earthbound and plodding, a meat-and-potatoes Englishman much like Poirot's Hastings" (53). Significantly, Watson is a doctor, and it is intriguing to note that Eadulf is also a medical man, having studied at the medical college of Tuaim Brecain. He is also a former heir to the post of Saxon magistrate, or *gerefa*, and he is, of course, a religieuse, all of which makes him the perfect embodiment of trustworthiness and respectability in the novels.

However, there is a fourth duty of the Watson figure, associated with this respectability, which Eadulf significantly does not share. Normally, the Watson figure is the narrator, functioning as the eyes and ears of the reader, and it is interesting, therefore, that the Sister Fidelma novels employ not a first-person narrator who embodies trustworthiness and respectability, but an impersonal third-person omniscient narrator. This omniscient narration is more normally associated with historical fiction, as it facilitates the inclusion of period detail and description in a way that a first-person narrative cannot. Significantly, Eadulf has a role to play even in this regard. As an outsider, that is, a Saxon in Ireland, Eadulf's presence in the narrative allows Fidelma to explain aspects of ancient Irish culture through him to the reader. In *The Spider's Web*, for example, Fidelma's explanation of the difference between what was termed in the Brehon system the "unfree class" and what Eadulf, from his Saxon point of view, calls "slaves," is made to the reader through Eadulf (31).

If Eadulf is to Fidelma, then, as Watson is to Holmes, the obvious conclusion to be drawn is that as Eadulf parallels Watson in various ways, so too does Fidelma parallel Sherlock Holmes. The most obvious point of comparison is that they are both genius detectives, whose skills and intellect are far superior to the majority of the population. Holmes's feats of deduction, for example, lead Watson to describe him in "A Scandal in Bohemia" as "the most perfect reasoning and observing machine that the world has seen" (161), while in *The Monk Who Vanished*, Eadulf describes Fidelma as "the most rational and analytical of people" (162), an admiring observation that is frequently repeated throughout the series. Fidelma's methods, furthermore, closely parallel Holmes's methods, and are based on careful observation and rational and logical deduction. The foundational importance in Fidelma's method of close observation and analysis, particularly of the scene of the crime, is made clear in her favourite axiom: "Speculation without knowledge is dangerous" (*Monk Who Vanished* 236). To this template she adds a tendency to verbally bully and browbeat suspects and witnesses into revealing any information they might be withholding from her, a tendency which leads Eadulf to admonish her in *The Spider's Web* when he tells her: "My mother once told me that you cannot unpick a piece of embroidery with an axe" (133).

This analogy, which describes a mystery as a piece of embroidery, is an interesting one, and almost every novel in the series provides some sort of similar analogy. In *The Monk Who Vanished*, for example, Fidelma uses the metaphor of a jigsaw puzzle, or what she calls "*tomus*" (299), in order to explain her investigative method to Eadulf. The word "*tomus*," according to Fidelma, means "seeking out" or "weighing matters," and she explains the analogy, and the progress of her investigation in the novel, as follows:

> It's just that I feel that I have all the pieces spread out on a table before me. Some of them have already fitted themselves into a pattern. Some are more intriguing and seemed to fit here or to fit there. But what it needs is one more single piece which would suddenly make all the pieces fit and thus the picture will be clearly revealed [300].

The analogy is not the only one that Fidelma uses in the series to explain her methods to her companion Eadulf. In *Suffer Little Children*, she likens the process of gathering information to that of gathering the ingredients to cook a particular dish (85), while in *The Spider's Web*, as the title indicates, the analogy she employs suggests that a number of separate incidents are connected by a central figure, in the manner of a spider at the centre of a web (203). In *Shroud for the Archbishop*, she uses the analogy of painting a picture that echoes that of the jigsaw puzzle in *The Monk Who Vanished*, but there are two important points about the latter of the two analogies that are significant here. The first of these is evident in the parallels between Fidelma's investigative methods and the reading process, which is a process of filling in the gaps in a broader pattern of cause and effect. The second is the idea that as a game, of sorts, between the mystery writer and the mystery reader, there are certain rules involved in the process of both writing and reading mysteries.

The first of these points, concerning both Fidelma's investigative method and the reading process as attempts to "make sense" of things by filling in narrative gaps, is neatly demonstrated by yet another role played by Eadulf in the series. Before considering this role, however, it is necessary to explain what a "narrative gap" is, and how one is created. A "narrative gap" is any gap in the narrative chain of cause-and-effect which prevents the immediate solution of a mystery or puzzle, and which the detective attempts to "fill in" through the process of investigation. In other words, narrative gaps correspond to the gaps in a jigsaw puzzle, or *tomus*, which Fidelma uses as an analogy to describe her investigative methods. These "gaps," therefore, are a deferral device, as they defer the ultimate solution of the mystery, or the completion of the picture in the *tomus* analogy, and are also essential in creating and maintaining tension in the mystery story. Denis Porter identifies how a mystery novel "prefigures at the outset the form of its denouement by virtue of the highly visible question mark hung over its opening" (86). Typically, this question mark consists of the question that describes an entire genre: *whodunnit?* It is for this reason that the effect of the crime to be investigated must be presented early in the story, and since murder is the most common crime investigated in mystery fiction, a corpse normally makes an early appearance in the narrative. Although not so quick off the mark as Christie to introduce a corpse and the mystery surrounding it, Tremayne nevertheless normally does so by the end of the first chapter, as in *The Subtle Serpent*.

However, there are other kinds of "question mark" that can be hung over a narrative, such as the "will they, won't they" question concerning Fidelma and Eadulf. Fidelma's feelings for Eadulf, and his for her, provide the means for a protracted narrative deferral across the series, specifically, the deferral of the consummation of their relationship. This deferral across the series parallels the sort of narrative deferral in each novel which is characteristic of crime fiction, in which a crime is committed, and the crime is not solved until the end of the novel. It is the deferral of the solution to the crime, but also, paradoxically, the certainty of its ultimate solution, that is central to the entertainment that the crime novel, and particularly the mystery novel, provides. It is significant, therefore, that in interviews, Peter Tremayne insists that the Sister Fidelma novels are written to entertain, and it is important to note that the participation of the reader in the process of detection is central to its success in this regard. In *Bloody Murder: From the Detective Story to the Crime Novel*, Julian Symons, the mystery writer and critic, identifies how by the end of the 1920s there was already a view of the detective story "as something having *rules* which could be strictly formulated" (104). While for most readers the rich historical detail of the novels is as much a part of the entertainment that they provide as the reader's participation in the solving of the mystery is, Tremayne's plotting and narration clearly, and sportingly, conform to certain ideas concerning the notion of "Fair Play" set down as early as 1929 by an organization of British mystery and detective writers called The Detection Club, whose members included, among others, Agatha Christie, whose novels the Sister Fidelma mysteries parallel in various ways.

In essence, "fair play" is the assumption that, in principle at least, a careful and observant reader should be able to solve the mystery at the heart of the story. So central to the mystery genre was this assumption that the reader should be able to participate in the solving of the mystery that in 1929, Father Ronald Knox, a Catholic priest and mystery writer, established ten basic rules for the genre. The parts of Knox's "Detective Story Decalogue" relevant to this study are summarized below:

I. The criminal must be someone mentioned in the early part of the story [....]
II. All supernatural or preternatural agencies are ruled out as a matter of course [....]
III. Not more than one secret room or passage is allowable [....]
VI. No accident must ever help the detective, nor must he ever have an unaccountable intuition which proves to be right [....]
VII. The detective himself must not commit the crime [....]
VIII. The detective must not light on any clues which are not instantly produced for the inspection of the reader [....]
IX. The stupid friend of the detective, the Watson, must not conceal any thoughts which pass through his mind [....]
X. Twin brothers, and doubles generally, must not appear unless we have been duly prepared for them [....] [194–6].

The stipulation that the criminal must be somebody "mentioned in the early part of the story" is essential for the participation and enjoyment of the reader, who will generally feel shortchanged if the criminal is a character who is introduced only in the final chapters. Tremayne is scrupulous in this regard, providing the reader with a broad cast of suspects early on in the novel. As a rule of thumb, characters introduced after Chapter Three in a Sister Fidelma mystery can generally be discounted as a viable suspect, even if the finger of suspicion is pointed at them at some point in the novel. Often, the murderer is a character who is mentioned early on, but not introduced or described until later in the novel, such as Laisre, the Chieftain of Gleann Geis in *Valley of the Shadow*, Father Gormán in *The Spider's Web*, Brother Febal in *The Subtle Serpent*, and Donndubháin, the *tánaiste*, or heir-elect, of Muman in *The Monk Who Vanished*. Tremayne also makes frequent use of the device of the "least likely suspect," which will be discussed later, and which was, and still is, a staple of the genre as a whole.

Ruling out "supernatural or preternatural agencies" in mysteries featuring not just one religieuse, but two, creates its own problems and tensions. It is interesting to note that central to Fidelma's character is the fact that, as Luehrs and Luehrs point out, "She is no adherent of Christian orthodoxy" (49). She is rarely, for example, seen at worship, unless she is shamed into it by the more religiously orthodox Eadulf who sourly notes in *Valley of the Shadow* "that Fidelma took the religious part of her life less seriously than she took her duties as an advocate of the law" (36). Importantly, she "evinces skepticism about the possibility of miracles or other supernatural intrusions into everyday life" (Luehrs and Luehrs 49), which means that supernatural intervention is considered as an explanation by all *except* Fidelma, and this includes Eadulf, who in many respects is a superstitious man. Fidelma's insistence on logic and rationality directs her investigations appropriately, and she believes in scientific or rational explanations even for apparently supernatural events, such as the solar eclipse during the Synod of Whitby (Luehrs and Luehrs 52) in the first Fidelma novel, *Absolution by Murder*.

The third rule of the Decalogue, that not more than one secret room or passage is permissible in a mystery novel, might at first seem an unusual prohibition, but is directed more at the use of such secret rooms or passages as a *deus ex machina*, or a lazy means to explain away the inexplicable and tie up loose ends. So while mines, caves, and underground chambers feature frequently in the Sister Fidelma series, they are not used to free Tremayne from the rigors of the mystery plot. Rather, these secret, subterranean locations form a motif in the series that symbolizes dark and hidden knowledge which it is Fidelma's task to bring to light. Significantly, Fidelma often finds valuable clues in these locations, which are many. They include the Roman catacombs in *Shroud for the Archbishop*, an underground chamber on a farmstead in *The Spider's Web*, mines for precious metals in *The Subtle Serpent* and, again, *The Spider's Web*, and a secret passage whose entrance is hidden under the altar of a chapel in *The Monk Who Vanished*, while in *The Subtle Serpent*, the original resting place for the golden calf, the desire for which precipitates the series of murders that Fidelma investigates, is in a cavern under the chapel of the community of The Salmon of the Three Wells. The labyrinth motif is, of course, symbolic of the labyrinthine mysteries and riddles that Fidelma investigates throughout the series, and can be equated more broadly with narrative in general, which as described above is often defined more by its detours and deferrals than it is by its conclusion.

The sixth rule in Knox's Decalogue concerning "unaccountable intuitions" clearly indicates that well-structured and plotted mysteries should have no need of "hunches" on the part of the detective in order to solve the crime. What is interesting about this objection to intuitive hunches in relation to the Sister Fidelma mysteries is that Eadulf is often praised by Fidelma as being "brilliant and intuitive" (*Monk Who Vanished* 293), in contrast to Fidelma's own remorseless logic and analytic rationality. However, on closer inspection his intuitive brilliance is clearly more of the order of common sense than inexplicable intuition. In *The Monk Who Vanished*, for example, Fidelma observes how "[n]ow and again Eadulf had the ability of stating the obvious when others had overlooked it" (90), and while the obvious inference is that Fidelma numbers herself among the "others" that she refers to, it is also clear that this ability of Eadulf's also serves an important narrative purpose, reminding the reader of key facts and details that, in their mundane or quotidian nature, may have been overlooked or forgotten by even an attentive reader. In a way, this point prefigures Knox's ninth rule, that the "stupid" Watson figure should not conceal any thought "which passes through his mind." Since Eadulf, unlike most Watson figures, is not a first-person narrator, he must risk Fidelma's disdain by stating the obvious aloud, rather than thinking it to himself. For this reason, as a general rule of thumb, even Eadulf's apparently innocuous statements should be considered carefully by an attentive reader, as they will often set Fidelma in a new direction in her investigations.

While Tremayne adheres to the seventh of Knox's rules — that the detective him- or herself must not commit the crime — suspicion can fall on Fidelma in order to heighten tension, defer the solution of the mystery, or alert her to the possibility that a previously unsuspected individual might in fact be the criminal. In *Valley of the Shadow*, for example, Fidelma is falsely accused of murder in order to put a stop to her investigations, and it is only Eadulf's intervention and own investigations which exonerate her and allow her to apprehend the real murderer. In *Our Lady of Darkness*, the situation is reversed, and Fidelma must fight to clear Eadulf of a similarly false accusation of murder, and here there are certain parallels with Christie's *The Murder of Roger Ackroyd*, in which the novel's narrator, Dr. Sheppard, uses his position of trust as both a doctor and Poirot's narrator to hide the truth of the murder of Roger Ackroyd.

The eighth rule in Knox's Decalogue, that the detective must not discover any clues that are not immediately presented to the reader, is perhaps the most important one in relation to the idea of fair play. Furthermore, Tremayne is scrupulous in this regard, as Fidelma analyses crime scenes with the trained eye of a Brehon and turns up clues that are essential for the "filling in" of the gaps in the chain of cause-and-effect which she attempts to reconstruct in order to solve the crime. For reasons which will be discussed later, the victims of violent crime in the Fidelma novels are often discovered in their beds. In fact, bedchambers are a dangerous place to be in Fidelma's world. In *Absolution by Murder*, Fidelma's friend Étain is found dead in her cot (75). In *Shroud for the Archbishop*, the murdered body of Wighard of Canterbury is found sprawled across his bed in his chambers in the Lateran Palace in Rome (64). In *Suffer Little Children* the Venerable Dacán, a respected scholar, is found dead in his cot in the abbey of Ros Ailithir (59). In *The Spider's Web*, Eber, the chieftain of Araglin, is stabbed to death in his bed (73), while at the end of the first chapter of *Act of Mercy*, a young religieuse is found hacked to death in her bed in the room of a tavern (9).

As a result, many of the clues that Fidelma discovers are often found under beds, and are frequently, although not always, of a domestic nature. Some clues are physical items, such as the *ogham* rod which Fidelma finds under the bed of the Venerable Dacán in *Suffer Little Children* (83). Others are marks or items left by the murderer or during the act of murder, such as the brooch of the murderer clutched at by his victim in *The Monk Who Vanished* (319), or the strands of coarse woolen fiber snagged on a splinter of wood in *Absolution by Murder* (203). Other clues are contextual ones, such as finding a lamp burning in the bedchamber of Eber, the chieftain of Araglin, in *The Spider's Web*, despite the fact that the accused murderer is blind, as well as deaf and dumb, and would therefore not have needed the light that the lamp offered. The list, of course, goes on, but what is important to note is that every clue that is connected to the central mystery, and many that are not, are presented by Tremayne to the reader the moment they are discovered. The art, of course, is to present clues to the reader without drawing attention to them, and this is as much a part of the game governed by the idea of fair play as the clues themselves are. For example, while Tremayne uses twins as the central plot device for two of his novels, *Valley of the Shadow* and *The Monk Who Vanished*, he manages to avoid breaking Knox's tenth rule by preparing the reader adequately for the revelation of their importance to the plot. *The Monk Who Vanished*, in particular, employs twins but distinguishes between them by using a clue that Tremayne often favors, that of the tonsure. Specifically, it is the difference between the two types of tonsure, the tonsure of Columba (that is, of the Celtic Church), and the Roman tonsure (sported by Eadulf), that distinguishes the twin monks apart to the attentive reader.

The notion of fair play informs the structures and devices of most Golden Age detective fiction, and for this reason it might not come as any surprise to learn that the Fidelma mysteries have much in common with Golden Age detective fiction, such as that of Christie. Golden Age detective fiction is the fiction produced in Britain in the years between the First and Second World Wars by authors such as Christie, Margery Allingham, Dorothy L. Sayers, and Ngaio Marsh, and its defining characteristics are also clear to see in the Sister Fidelma mysteries, although often in a slightly different form. These characteristics, important also in the Fidelma novels, include a restricted setting, a closed circle of suspects, the convention of the "least likely suspect," the corpse-as-signifier, and the restoration of the social order.

The restricted setting of Golden Age detective fiction is the one most neatly appropriated by Tremayne in the Sister Fidelma novels, where the small, idyllic rural community typical of Christie's novels, for example, which set the template for what has become known as the "country house murder," becomes the culturally and historically specific setting of either the *rath*, or fortified settlement, or, more normally, an abbey or monastery. Religious communities, particularly isolated ones, are the ideal setting for mysteries. Despite the shock of violent murder in an apparently peaceful environment, restricted settings are enormously reassuring for the average reader, reducing the world, as they do, to self-contained, enclosed, and, therefore, manageable proportions. Furthermore, in addition to limiting the number of suspects to the members of the community, they provide a restricted setting from which the various suspects cannot leave (at least not without being noticed) and into which new suspects cannot enter. Tremayne makes use of the restricted setting from the first novel in the series, *Absolution by Murder*, in which the delegates at the Synod of Whitby are confined to the Abbey of St. Hilda until the identity of Étain's murderer, confined in the abbey along with the entire Synod, has been discovered.

The *rath*, or fortified settlement, is similar in many ways to the restricted setting of the abbey or monastery. It is literally restricted, in that normally it is a community protected by a fortified curtain wall, which makes unseen entrance and egress almost impossible. This setting can be even further restricted by locating the *rath*, as Tremayne does more than once, in a remote area. The best example of this is the community of Gleann Geis — the "forbidden valley" — in *Valley of the Shadow*, but what is more important about such communities is that they are restricted in other socially and historically specific ways as well. In general, these communities are composed of a small number of families, which means that the closed circle of suspects that the restricted setting creates is made even more tightly knit by the simple fact of familial relationships. The surrogate families of religious communities, suggested by the terms "brother" and "sister" that are used to refer to their members, suggest that these settings are similar in this regard, and it is therefore not surprising, perhaps, that many of the Sister Fidelma mysteries hinge crucially on some sort of concealed familial relationship. The largely domestic setting explains why bedchambers are such a dangerous place in Fidelma's world. Furthermore, the discovery of violent murder at the most intimate heart of the domestic environment heightens the disruption of the social order that the crime of murder inevitably causes.

An extreme form of restricted setting which developed in the Golden Age novel is termed "murder afloat," in which a murder occurs on a ship, effectively cut off from the outside world until it reaches port. The most famous example is Christie's *Death on the Nile*, which Tremayne appropriates in *Act of Mercy*, in which Fidelma joins a group of pilgrims on their way to the shrine of St. James, in Santiago de Compostela in Galicia. The setting of a ship at sea provides numerous possibilities that earthbound settings must work harder to provide, including the various opportunities for accidents that can complicate the plot and action, and the potential for atmosphere offered by the cramped, claustrophobic setting. Ships and the sea, of course, are also a rich repository for superstitious beliefs, allowing Fidelma's rationality and logic to conflict with the beliefs of the crew and of her fellow travelers and add to the paranoia created by virtue of the simple device of placing a murderer in such a restricted and claustrophobic setting.

Whatever the setting, or however its restrictions are contrived (and Golden Age writers occasionally went to absurd lengths to contrive such settings), the prevalent use of the device of the least likely suspect is one that clearly depends on certain assumptions on the part of the reader, and as such, can be identified as part of the "game" of the mystery or detective novel. The least likely suspect is that character who seems to have the least motive, means, or opportunity to have committed the crime, but is revealed by the detective at the end of the novel as the murderer. Once the device of the least likely suspect had been introduced, however, and was known to the attentive reader, a process of double-guessing on the part of both the reader and the writer has resulted in narratives where even the most likely suspect — that is, the character who seems to have the most motive, means, and opportunity to commit the crime — is in fact the least likely. It is clear that Tremayne tremendously enjoys playing with this device, as with the character of Móen in *The Spider's Web*, who, as he is blind, deaf, and dumb, is clearly the least likely suspect, but since he is discovered sitting astride the murdered body of Eber, the chieftain of Araglin, blood-soaked and with a blood-stained knife in his hand, he is also clearly identified as the *most* likely suspect.

It is Fidelma's task, and the reader's, to sift through the clues that are discovered, sort most likely suspects from least likely suspects, reveal the concealed familial relationships that are central to the mystery, and identify the criminal. The criminal in Fidelma's world is normally a murderer, of course, and the corpse of the murdered victim is often the richest repository of clues in a Sister Fidelma novel. The central importance of the device of the "corpse-as-signifier," central to Golden Age fiction, is made clear in Tremayne's novels by the presence of Eadulf in the narrative. Eadulf, who has trained at the medical college of Tuaim Brecain, has the medical knowledge to read the corpses of the recently deceased as a repository of clues. He understands the workings of various poisons, for example, and knows enough about bodily processes to make relatively accurate estimations about time of death. This, combined with Fidelma's ability to observe and interpret various, and often minute, bodily details such as muscle development, calluses, condition of the hands, and ink stains, allows Fidelma and Eadulf, between them, to draw various links between these signifiers and the occupations, activities, and violence that the body, while still alive, was subjected to. Factors such as these allow Fidelma to identify two corpses as those of a professional archer and a monk, respectively, in *The Monk Who Vanished*, and the combined skills of Fidelma and Eadulf are essential throughout the series in allowing them to retrace the stages in the chain of cause and effect that have led to the discovery of the corpse of the victim.

The identification of the corpse, of course, is just one step along the chain of cause and effect that leads, eventually, to the murderer, and this is what the narrative structure of each novel is directed towards. Denis Porter identifies how crime fiction "is a genre committed to an act of recovery, moving forward to move back" (29), and this observation contains two points that are relevant to the Sister Fidelma novels. Fidelma's investigations, as outlined above, consist of a retracing of the chain of cause and effect back in time, even as the narrative moves forward to its denouement. The purpose of this double movement is to solve a crime committed in the past — normally a murder — in order to restore order in the present, and it is this restoration of a social order disrupted by violent crime which is the "act of recovery" referred to by Porter above, in which a "Paradise" in the past, characterized by stability and order, is the "Paradise Lost" that the current "fallen" society longs to return to (Scaggs 46–8).

In this respect, it is significant that Fidelma is both a *dálaigh*, or advocate of the Brehon law system, and a religieuse, as in this way she is a representative of both secular *and* religious authority, and as such it is her duty to restore and maintain the social order. This is reinforced by the fact that her brother, Colgú, later in the series becomes King of Muman, linking her directly to the embodiment of secular law in a monarchical society, and by the fact that on least two occasions Fidelma's successful investigations prevent violent civil war: in *The Valley of the Shadow* and *The Monk Who Vanished*. Civil war, of course, is the ultimate symbol of the disruption of the social order, in which brothers and cousins fight one another, and the very fabric of national, social, and cultural identity is threatened. Furthermore, the damaging effects of civil war have an obvious resonance in Irish culture, allowing the Sister Fidelma novels, although set in the seventh century, to reflect both on conflicts in more recent history and in the contemporary period. The fact that Eadulf, who as a former heir to the post of Saxon magistrate, or *gerefa*, and as a religieuse, like Fidelma, also embodies both secular and religious authority, only adds weight to this analysis.

Fidelma's authority, while it is often questioned by various characters throughout the series, either because of her gender or her position as a religieuse, is typically consolidated at the end of each novel by a denouement that combines elements of both the Golden Age novel and the contemporary legal thriller. Typically, in the Golden Age novel, particularly those of Christie, the restricted setting allows the detective to gather the closed circle of suspects together and reveal the logical and interpretive processes that have led to the identification of the murderer. This is a common device in the Sister Fidelma novels, but often the gathering together of the suspects is carried out within a courtroom setting. Here, Fidelma outlines the chain of cause and effect which leads to the identification of the murderer, but she does so by following the legal procedures necessary to return a verdict of guilty within the parameters of the Brehon law system. In other words, the identification of the murderer is transformed from a personal triumph into a legal verdict, a verdict, furthermore, which carries with it a prescribed punishment backed up by the weight of law. In this way, the reassuring reinstatement of the social order that Fidelma brings about at the end of each novel has behind it the full weight of secular authority. As history has taught us, however, peace and order are transitory, ephemeral things, which means that there will always be new crimes for Fidelma to solve and new ways to put the world right once more.

Works Cited

Christie, Agatha. *Death on the Nile*. 1937. London: HarperCollins, 2001.
———. *The Murder of Roger Ackroyd*. 1926. London: HarperCollins, 2002.

Conan Doyle, Arthur. *The Penguin Complete Sherlock Holmes.* Harmondsworth: Penguin, 1981.
Knox, Ronald A. "Detective Story Decalogue." *The Art of the Mystery Story: A Collection of Critical Essays.* Ed. Howard Haycraft. New York: Carroll & Graf, 1992. 194–6.
Luehrs, Christiane W., and Robert B. Luehrs. "Peter Tremayne: Sister Fidelma and the Triumph of Truth." *The Detective as Historian: History and Art in Historical Crime Fiction.* Ed. Ray B. Browne and Lawrence A. Kreiser, Jr. Bowling Green, OH: Bowling Green University Popular Press, 2000. 45–59.
Porter, Denis. *The Pursuit of Crime: Art and Ideology in Detective Fiction.* New Haven: Yale University Press, 1981.
Scaggs, John. *Crime Fiction.* London: Routledge, 2005.
Symons, Julian. *Bloody Murder: From the Detective Story to the Crime Novel.* 3d rev. ed. New York: The Mysterious Press, 1993.
Tremayne, Peter. *Absolution by Murder.* London: Headline, 1994.
_____. *Act of Mercy.* London: Headline, 1999.
_____. *Hemlock at Vespers.* London: Headline, 2000.
_____. *The Monk Who Vanished.* London: Headline, 1999.
_____. *Our Lady of Darkness.* London: Headline, 2000.
_____. *Shroud for the Archbishop.* London: Headline, 1995.
_____. *The Spider's Web.* London: Headline, 1997.
_____. *The Subtle Serpent.* London: Headline, 1996.
_____. *Suffer Little Children.* London: Headline, 1995.
_____. *Valley of the Shadow.* London: Headline, 1998.

Lady Justice: Social Sleuthing and Sister Fidelma

Jennifer Molidor

"I am in charge of the pilgrims. Who are you to give orders, Sister?"
"I am a *dálaigh*. My name is Fidelma of Cashel."
—"Corpse on a Holy Day," *Whispers of the Dead*

In the best mysteries, a literary detective can restore moral order, even if only imaginatively. We, the reader, derive pleasure from partnering with the detective who repeatedly enters dangerous situations so gripping we can hardly keep from turning the page, even if it means staying up late at night to finish the story in order to see the safe return of a just society and the dastardly criminal outsmarted and punished. We become the *voyeur,* which is a central part of the pleasure in detective fiction. First appearing in 1994, Peter Tremayne's Sister Fidelma series does not disappoint these desires for restored social justice and the vicarious experience of adventure and intrigue.

Tremayne's stories of Sister Fidelma (Fidelma of Cashel), set in seventh-century Ireland, engage an audience seeking a rich medley of history, sexual politics, social crises, and puzzle-crimes. What is unusual about this series, besides Fidelma's character and qualifications, is her focus on both legal and social justice. Throughout the stories, the reader is reminded that Fidelma is not only a member of the religious community, but also a *dálaigh,* an advocate of the Irish courts. She has achieved the rank of *anruth* after eight years of academic training in Brehon Morann's school, a degree granted by the ancient colleges of Ireland, and second only to the rank of *ollamh,* or professor. Fidelma holds counsel with chiefs and kings, and is a Lady, as sister to the King of Cashel. Her formidable reputation precedes her, not only throughout the five kingdoms of Éireann (Ireland) but also abroad. Her legal position as an advocate for the courts serves to gratify the modern reader who may relate to the power struggle between the sexes, and who would wish for greater continuity between the place women enjoyed in seventh-century Irish society and modern Ireland.

Although readers are shown women's remarkable ability to achieve high distinction in seventh-century Irish society, they also read of her frequent conflicts with male authority figures. These conflicts serve to distinguish national characters, as it is usually the men abroad who find most problems with her rank as a woman. But her resolution of these disputes solidifies her audience's sympathy with this respected woman in a world of men. She holds her own against men who attempt to orchestrate her failure, and readers enjoy seeing her triumph.

As a *dálaigh,* Fidelma's sleuthing skills combine intuition and logic with a highly trained mind for the law. Often when she evaluates suspects, she draws upon wisdom from classic works to determine her next step in interrogations. In "Scattered Thorns" from *Whispers of the Dead,* for example, when she meets the reformed warrior-turned-thief Brother Caisín, whose appearance gives her a moment of distrust, she changes her view as "the line from *Juvenal* came to her mind: *fronti nulla fides*—no reliance can be placed on appearance" (252). Seeking truth and justice, Fidelma refuses to automatically assume the blame of those who have suffered social hardships. In the same story Fidelma solves the puzzle by telling Brehon Tuama that "Pubilius Syrus once wrote that the stolen ox sometimes puts his head out of the stall" by way of noting that by observing matters more closely, she sees the character who protested the most is the one hiding his guilt, hinting that crime often comes from greed, not poverty (255).

Fidelma's sleuthing augments that classic trope of detective fiction, Edgar Allan Poe's notion of "ratiocination" or deductive reasoning. In "Death of an Icon" from *Whispers of the Dead,* Fidelma refuses to blame a band of traveling itinerants on a circumstantial class-based suspicion alone. "I deal with facts," Fidelma states; "that is the business in which I am engaged because in so considering the 'why' and 'wherefore,' often one can solve the 'how' and 'who'" (294). This story also presents the locked door mystery: how did an elderly and feeble Connla come to be hung in his room, with the doors and windows locked? The answer is to be understood in the simple facts of "why" and "how," and her skill is revealed in separating social prejudice and religious conspiracy from the facts of the matter at hand.

Unlike modern defense lawyers, Fidelma's loyalty is not to her client but to the legal system. In "The Astrologer Who Predicted His Own Murder" from *Whispers of the Dead,* she tells Father Abbot her task is to "investigate the facts and if the facts show you to be guilty, then my oath as a *dálaigh* forbids me to hide your guilt from the court" (67). One of her main modes of investigation is interrogation, or questioning, and she likes to hear things from people's own mouths, careful to avoid hearsay. In "The Blemish" from *Whispers of the Dead* she notes, "It is merely my duty to ask questions and through the answers to discover the truth" (84). In "The Blemish" she passes her exam interview with sharp-witted answers and knowledge of the law even when thrown off balance by being late for her exam, thus demonstrating her ability to withstand discord in seeking justice.

While her methods of deduction involve logic, she does not hesitate to draw upon her own sense of intuition. In the first novel, *Absolution by Murder*, she feels "a curious pricking at the back of her mind that she was overlooking something" when investigating the scene of a crime (91). This narrative device tells the reader to pay attention to clues, as well as to show that Fidelma is a close observer, in tune with her senses and female intuition. These skills allow her to see beyond immediate impressions and social constructions by delving into deeper layers of human motivation. She intuits that the young maiden couldn't have been killed by the sheepherder in "Whispers of the Dead," for example, as another's greed was a stronger motivation. She correctly interprets social clues and uses these insights to assess the dead maiden's true identity and social rank. Where the men around her see the illusion of the poor countrywoman's garbs, Fidelma notices the uncalloused hands and feet, the neat braid, the fair skin. She reads people as she reads the clues, understanding human motivations, emotions, and desires.

Fidelma is especially adept at intuiting the hidden workings of male and female relationships. Her deductive reason, intuition, and legal training help her to interpret who harbors deep desires for another man's wife, who has been faithful and who not, and the real impulses behind marriages and murders of greed. She also understands jealousy as in "Gold at Night" from *Whispers of the Dead,* in which she solves a case of a man who kills the woman he obsesses over when he thinks she is having an affair with his friend. She is not, but he would rather believe that her rejection of him had to do with her having another lover rather than her being simply uninterested in him. Of this she says, "It is not love that is blind, Rumann, but jealousy" (288). Fidelma does not draw her conclusions on male and female relationships from abstract philosophy, but rather from lived experience.

Much has been made of Fidelma's marital status, both as a religious and as a detective. In this period members of the religious community could marry and live together with their children, dedicating their lives to the service of God in a mixed community of religious known as a "double house." The practice is more common in Ireland, whereas the bishops of Rome favor following the Apostle Paul's model of celibacy for the religious. The matter becomes increasingly controversial and leads to fundamental changes in the church, as well as to violence against those who do not follow the new policy changes, as we see in *Council of the Cursed*. To Fidelma, celibacy is but one choice available to the religious.

She meets Brother Eadulf, a Saxon, at the famous Synod of Whitby, depicted in *Absolution by Murder,* where both are assigned to investigate the murder of the Abbess Étain of Kildare. For practical reasons, his presence as a male companion provides Fidelma the ability to walk through worlds of men otherwise unavailable to her. Many have likened her Eadulf to Sherlock Holmes' companion Dr. Watson; like Watson, Eadulf is possessed of apothecary skills. Similarly, his logical but inaccurate theories in attempting to solve the cases help the reader find the correct solution to the cases. For Fidelma, Eadulf is a world outside her career, a masculine center of calm that contrasts with Fidelma's fiery femininity and aids her as a sleuth and as a human.

The relationship between Fidelma and Eadulf, as Colmán describes it to Abbess Hilda in *Absolution by Murder,* is "like putting a wolf and a fox together to hunt a hare" (85). Fidelma contemplates how "she had never worked with anyone else since she had qualified as a *dálaigh* of the Brehon courts. She had always been the sole arbiter of the truth. Never had she had to rely on a second judgment" (179). As Fidelma gets to know Eadulf and struggles with her attraction to him, she refuses to let him be in charge, insisting "strength, like intelligence, is not solely possessed by man" (89). Eadulf is "unused to being ordered by a woman" but eventually capitulates to a team effort (88). They set up a model of partnership that carries them through the rest of the stories; he begins to intuit her thoughts, and she begins to trust him with her plans.

Unlike other literary mixed-gender partnerships, such as P.D. James's Cordelia Gray to Adam Dagliesh, Fidelma plays the main role, and having a supportive husband allows Tremayne to develop a character who is both an adventurous *dálaigh* in the public sphere, and wife and mother at home. Fidelma rescues Eadulf in *The Subtle Serpent* when he is kidnapped while traveling to Cashel as an emissary of the Archbishop of Canterbury. She also defends him against a murder charge in *Our Lady of Darkness.* They later marry and have a son, Alchú. As Fidelma ages, her career affects their marriage. She becomes more of a political advisor for the courts, and to Eadulf's dismay considers renouncing her religious vows. She vies for a position as Chief Brehon of Muman, her brother's kingdom. Fidelma and Eadulf separate, and although reunited in a murder at the Abbey of Lios Mor, their reunion is fragile.

Like other female detectives before her, Fidelma's insights are sometimes drawn from her relationship with a man in her life, combining physical evidence with a fresh understanding of the psychology of human motivation.

As with Sue Grafton's Kinsey Millhone (who discusses cases with her wise male friend and landlord), Fidelma's profession is inherently part of her personality, allowing us to understand a female view on events. Although her cases are neither the dark world of hard-boiled detectives, nor the modern intricacies of police procedurals, nor the gruesome cadaver based stories of Patricia Cornwell or Tess Gerritsen, Fidelma does share the need to be just a bit tougher, a bit more confident than her male counterparts, and to constantly prove herself in a man's world. Though married, she is not a "housewife" detective, and while youthful, vibrant, and wise beyond her years she is hardly a Nancy Drew or Veronica Mars, who both turn to their fathers for advice in sleuthing and searching for social justice.

Perhaps Fidelma might have more in common with Alexander McCall Smith's Mma Ramotswe from the popular *The No. 1 Ladies Detective Agency* series set in modern day Botswana. Mma Ramotswe, like Fidelma, is married, her cases appeal to an international audience and grapple with history, politics, and a changing traditional culture, as well as domestic themes and female experience. Primarily they are stories about human motivations, relationships, and the complexities of a troubled society. Similarly, Fidelma's cases represent classic aspects of all social classes from princes to paupers, husbands to wives, parents to children, and the vitriolic relationships between religious sects.

Like Agatha Christie's Miss Marple, who solves crimes by closely observing people in social situations, Fidelma's observation skills are crucial in solving cases once the facts have been laid out. Yet Fidelma appeals to the reader because she is not an armchair detective solving small village crimes, but instead travels Ireland and abroad, throwing herself into the lion's den of politics, religious conflicts, and powerful men who resent her. For example, in solving the mystery in the *Council of the Cursed* she wears disguises, sneaks forbidden into the *Domus Femini*, and eventually is kidnapped and almost traded as a slave. In other instances, she is pursued in high-speed chases, almost killed, and takes serious risks to solve her cases if it means restoring social justice. Her adventurous attributes are repeated throughout the stories to develop the genre and the audience expectation: she is an *anruth*, is not easily intimidated, has a "well-proportioned figure" never fully hidden beneath her cloaks, and is attractively "Irish" with intense green eyes and rebellious red hair, a classic Irish appearance that empowers the reader to identify with her mental, emotional, physical, and moral strength.

One of Fidelma's strengths is a refusal to back down in her search for social justice. In *Absolution by Murder* she stands up to King Oswy when he attempts to place a political condition upon her investigation: that she must work with Brother Eadulf to give the appearances of fairness (her first meeting with Eadulf, her future husband). She defies expectations of female behavior and horrifies the Abbess Hilda by responding to Oswy, the king, "I am an advocate of the Brehon courts. I do no work under any condition excepting my duty to uncover the truth" (81). She gives no more than a slight bow to Alhfrith of Deira, to his fury, for in Ireland the practice of someone of her rank overly demonstrating deference is not common, and she refuses to do it to lower her place as a woman in a foreign land. As she states, "My primary aim is to get to the truth of this matter and truth should be served more than princes" (110). She commands with authority and without fear. One senses also that she enjoys the adventure of defiance.

Yet her defiance is always with the aim at establishing what is right, what is just, and what is law. Throughout the series, Fidelma maintains humanist views, despising practices such as slavery, and is outraged by what she sees as the unjust practice of burning and flogging people. She struggles with her horror, for example, when Alhfrith is ready to burn the prophetic astrologist without evidence, and when the street people stone to death an outsider with the yellow plague. In *Whispers of the Dead,* the story "The Fosterer" displays Fidelma's legal and moral distaste for corporal punishment and for mothers who resort to it despite the law against it. In this story, despite her strong views in favor of following the law, Fidelma recognizes that the law does not always represent social justice.

Justice is not an abstract concept for Fidelma. Sometimes, especially in socially important cases, Fidelma gathers everyone involved for the stunning denouement, as she reveals the truth of the crime. As in the *Council of the Cursed,* she does not simply pronounce her verdict but recreates the story of the crime, contextualizing the truth to the victims and the aggressors involved. In demonstrating her logic, and bringing the light of justice to the dark world of corruption, murder, and depravity, at the end, all is right again. As a *dálaigh,* Fidelma understands the darkness of human nature but doesn't become possessed by it, unlike hard-boiled sleuths, whether male or female, who become a part of the noir world they inhabit. Fidelma is instead appalled by the violence, deception, and cruelty she sees. When she is traveling through the dark parts of her world, witnessing stoning, flogging, torture, flagellation, lynching, and burning people alive, Fidelma's horror allows the reader to be horrified as well.

Fidelma is repelled by the social consequences of laws for the lives of women, especially when she encounters misogynistic and antimarriage sentiment in *Council of the Cursed.* In this novel, she must solve a crime in an abbey under the new Rule of Rome in which male brethren have been forced to divorce their wives and renounce their children. Perhaps one of the most disturbing instances of social injustice comes when Fidelma is kidnapped amongst the wives and children of the brethren. Their captor calls them "whores" and snarls that they "made the choice to have liaisons with male clerics and religious. Councils in many lands have ordained that this is an affront to the Faith. All wives of the religious are to be rounded up and sold as slaves for the greater good of the Faith" (262). Of Bishop Leodegar, who has instilled the Rule of Rome and separated the male brethren from their wives, Fidelma explains, "Trying to deny equality, trying to denigrate women or, indeed, denigrating anyone is a sign that you really fear them" (209). Yet it is not only men who violently oppress women in the Fidelma stories.

In *Council of the Cursed* women are largely the culprits of antagonism, and sometimes violence, against other women. For example, the Abbess of the *Domus Femini* despises Fidelma and her investigation and says, "That is not a woman's place, especially one who purports to be a religious" (116). It is important that the character holding these views, the Abbess Audofleda, is despicable to the modern reader. Fidelma then triumphs against Audofleda when she complains to Bishop Leodegar and cleverly preempts Audofleda's complaint. She deftly works his vanity with her own self-confidence and appeal to a higher authority (157). An even more formidable antiwoman sentiment comes from the dangerous Lady Beretrude, who echoes Audofleda's comment that Fidelma's task is "most unsuited for women" (176). In an important showdown between the two women, Beretrude implies that Fidelma is a woman from a land of cannibals and heathens, and denigrates Fidelma. Although furious, Fidelma remains calm and takes the woman down a notch with her superior knowledge of complex literary and historical works and of complex sub-textual layers of politics and nationalisms. More to the point, it is Lady Beretrude who leads Fidelma into the garden with the poisonous adder and orchestrates the selling of the wives as slaves. Yet another woman, Sister Inginde, is the "female conspirator" (297) and sets the events of the novel into motion.

Due to experiences like these, Fidelma feels decreasing kinship with the religious around her. Perhaps because of the politics involved, Fidelma becomes less interested in religion, and eventually considers renouncing her vows. When, for example, she discusses the position of Rome versus the Irish teachings with Abbot Ségdae in the *Council of the Cursed*, she states her opinion bluntly, "If Rome wants to go down that path, why follow them?" (80). And yet, as Eadulf points out with his own social wisdom, the Council meeting in this novel demonstrates stubborn adherence to principles rather than open discussions, and that "where minds are already made up, no discussion and exchange of ideas can thrive." That the separate house ends up being an abbey in which the wives and children are kidnapped into slavery is not just a historical reference but also suggests for the reader the unfortunate treatment of women from the changes in the Christian Church originating from Rome.

This is to say the Irishness, the Celtic uncorrupted Church, would have suited women and Ireland better, and the problems result from a foreign influence.

Although the stories of Sister Fidelma are popular with a widely international audience, the series is a project embedded in modern Irish society. The series grapples with the intersection of nationalism and gender by making a fairly modern appeal to its modern audience. Much in the way nationalist literature gives us pleasure by linking us to an authentic traditional past before colonization, Fidelma gives us a sense of history, authenticity, and something to link us to a time before the place of women was dramatically privatized and monitored by the Irish state.

Where Sherlock Holmes cases, for example, show how British culture viewed people from other lands in Arthur Conan Doyle's period, and the American love of hard-boiled detective genre, such as Raymond Chandler's *The Big Sleep,* may reveal the glorification of the American hero enmeshed in national, masculine values, the Fidelma series also alludes to national sentiment. Tremayne repeatedly depicts the lack of deference to authority as a distinctly Irish quality in this period. In the stories, Irishness includes charitable natures, not possessing slaves (or at least having only temporary slaves who may work their way free), and an inclination toward civility and the open air rather than the stench, muck, and brutality of the civilized towns Eadulf and Fidelma visit abroad.

Similarly, the gender dynamics of the world Fidelma traverses in her homelands are starkly contrasted with the gendered construction of lands abroad. Tremayne makes efforts to note the distinctions in the ways men and women are treated to contrast the kingdoms in Ireland with the lands of the Saxons, the Britons, and others. The story "Gold at Night" from *Whispers of the Dead* discusses the Aenach Caman (or Fair of Carman, held during the Feast of Lugnasadh, what we would now call August) in which nobles, chiefs, Brehons, and professional men and women would gather together. On the first day the sexes met separately and decided on matters pertaining to their sex. On the second day they met as a group and decided on matters pertaining to all people. Unlike other series that feature a female detective as the lead, Tremayne does not attempt to normalize Fidelma into a male world, but rather draws attention to the gender dynamics of the culture and the politics of the time, particularly contrasting a humanistic Celtic culture with a more brutal, barbaric world of the Angles, Saxons, and Britons.

The Sister Fidelma series provides an excellent medium for teaching courses in literature, writing, history, classics, theology, and law. The detective genre provides for an interdisciplinary range of courses because of its emphasis on logic, critical thinking, and solving puzzles. Its formulaic development allows for gender studies as well as cultural and historical studies. One might ask students if they prefer the criminals or the detective in a given story, and thus perform both a psychological investigation of character and vicarious experience in storytelling, as well as a study of law in a legal class. In my course on "Gender and Genre: The Detective in Film and Literature," Fidelma stories are read alongside classic works in the detective genre, like those by Edgar Allan Poe, Arthur Conan Doyle, and Wilkie Collins. As the detective genre was once ridiculed but now is critically acclaimed, students investigate changing categories of reading and readership by finding past reviews of detective fiction to compare with modern reviews. For what was popular then and what is popular now reflect changes in social reading patterns.

Gender-based assignments are particularly relevant. Some students choose to compare the female sleuth with the classic figures of male detectives. Others create mock dialogues between Fidelma and the male figures she encounters to "hear" the negotiation of the gender contract in their own terms. Additional gender based assignments include comparing depictions of Fidelma as detective and women as victim of sexual crimes or homicide. We also compare Fidelma's international popularity and "literary" quality with American trends toward hard-boiled popular fiction and British trends towards the police procedural, alongside other international writers like Alexander McCall Smith. Finally, students are asked to write research papers that perform close readings of Fidelma's search for social justice amidst an ever changing world of sexual politics and religious decree. Studied as a whole, or by individual story, Tremayne's Fidelma series continues to provide learning and entertainment for scholars and popular audiences alike.

Works Cited

Tremayne, Peter. *Absolution by Murder.* 1994. New York: Signet, 1997.
_____. *Council of the Cursed.* 2008. New York: St. Martin's Minotaur, 2010.
_____. *Hemlock at Vespers. Fifteen Sister Fidelma Stories.* 2000. New York: St. Martin's Minotaur, 2000.
_____. *Our Lady of Darkness.* 2000. New York: St. Martin's Press, 2002.
_____. *A Prayer for the Damned. A Mystery of Ancient Ireland.* 2006. New York: St. Martin's Minotaur, 2008.
_____. *The Subtle Serpent.* 1996. New York: St. Martin's Press, 1998.
_____. *Whispers of the Dead. Fifteen Sister Fidelma Stories.* New York: St. Martin's Minotaur, 2004.

Fidelma and the Irish Language

Anna Heussaff

Millions of Fidelma readers around the world are familiar with the Irish language words that pepper her stories, including occupations such as *dálaigh, anruth, rechtaire* and *bó-aire,* and placename terms such as *cnoc, ráth* and *sliabh.* Avid readers of the books and website have also studied explanations on "How to pronounce Irish names and words" and have learned that the language used in the seventh century is described today as Old Irish. Its shapes and patterns are clearly very different from those of English, Spanish and other languages that are dominant today, and help to give the stories their special atmosphere and allure.

Almost fourteen hundred years after Fidelma's era, Irish is still spoken and written in her native country. It has changed in many ways, just as Latin has become today's Italian and English has taken diverse forms on either side of the Atlantic. Irish (sometimes called Gaelic by outsiders, from its name in Irish, "Gaeilge") has also changed from being the daily speech of most people in Ireland, and indeed in Scotland, to being a minority language often considered in danger of dying out. Today's visitors to Ireland see placenames in Irish as well as English on signposts, and they may even come across radio and television programs in Irish. But hearing it spoken naturally in city shops or in rural pubs takes a lot more effort, except perhaps for the growing numbers who attend Irish language courses and conversation groups in the United States and elsewhere, and devote their holidays to further study in places such as Donegal, Connemara, Kerry, or Dublin.

So imagine if Sister Fidelma were to turn up in twenty-first-century Ireland — she would be literally at a loss for words. Her form of Irish would sound unintelligible to today's speakers, her Latin would be understood by only a handful of clerics and scholars, and her ears would fill with English, a language that was still in its early formative stages in Eadulf's Anglo-Saxon world. If she called into a bookshop or was shown the wonders of the Internet, she would discover that stories of her crime detection appear in at least eighteen languages, including Japanese, Argentinean Spanish, and many of continental Europe's languages. But if she wished to read one of them in her own first language, she would be disappointed. She would find only one short story published in booklet form, *Scréach ón Tuama* (2008), and even that would not be available on the shelves of most outlets.

So how can this absence be explained — this dog that has not barked in the night, these novels that have not yet appeared in Irish? In this essay, I would like to describe my pursuit of this intriguing mystery, and the clues and leads encountered in a year of carrying out research and questioning witnesses both in Ireland and other countries. It is a conundrum that has not been fully solved to date, however, and a happy ending cannot be guaranteed. But the story of the quest itself is also the story of what has happened to the Irish language since the days of Fidelma, and I hope it will prove to be a page-turner for her loyal students.

From Strength to Near-Extinction in Twelve Centuries

It is thought that the Irish language in its earliest form had already been in Ireland for at least a thousand years when Cormac's Eoghanacht reigned in Cashel. It is one of the Celtic group of languages that branched out from the common Indo-European rootstock of most language groups in Europe. We have early Irish stone inscriptions in a notched script known as *ogham* from the fifth and sixth centuries, and by the seventh century, Irish was being written in the Roman alphabet, and ecclesiastical terms such as *eaglais* (church) and *ifreann* (hell or inferno) had arrived on the tide of Christianity's Latin. Every century since then has provided us with a wealth of texts, poetry and prose literature in Irish, and it is the oldest written language still being spoken to the north of the Alps.

Invasions by the Vikings of Scandinavia in the ninth and tenth centuries brought many new words into Irish, including *dorú* (fishing line) and *fuinneog* (window). They also brought pillaging attacks on the monasteries that were the guardians of learning, but over time the Viking or Norse newcomers intermarried and settled among local people, and Middle Irish, as we now call it, was the language of their descendants by the time the next wave of invasions started in the late twelfth century. Those invaders were Anglo-Normans, who took control of many towns and fertile areas of the country in the period up to the fifteenth century. They too brought new terms and concepts with them, first in Anglo-French and later in English, including *contae* (county), *oidhre* (heir), *seomra* (room) and *suipéar* (supper). Ireland was a multilingual country, but as time went on, what is now called Early Modern Irish held sway as the spoken language of the majority. There was also a standardized classical form of Irish used in the Gaelic aristocracy's schools of poetry. In the great manuscripts transcribed in the period, we find pagan-era sagas of warrior contests and doomed love, as well as annals recounting the country's history in heroic terms. Meanwhile, continental influences brought new forms of courtly romantic poetry, whose fusion with Irish lyricism eventually produced wonderful love songs that are still sung in Irish today.

But Gaelic Ireland came under sustained assault in the sixteenth and seventeenth centuries. The Tudor rulers of England, Henry VIII and Elizabeth I especially, strengthened their own power against rivals at home, gained great wealth by taking over the ancient monasteries in the name of Protestantism, and triumphed over the power of Catholic Spain. They advanced the military conquest of Ireland at the same time, ruthlessly exploiting the all-too-frequent infighting among Irish *taoisigh*, or chieftains. Wars, upheavals, and expropriations continued throughout the seventeenth century under the Stuart kings and the ruthless parliamentarian Cromwell. Gaelic leaders fled to the continent as their lands and those of their followers were seized for "plantation" by loyalist incomers from England and Scotland. The cultural supports of the learned Irish-speaking classes crumbled; and from then on, the language of law, government, ecclesiastical power, and the printing press was English. The same became true of commerce, business, and formal education.

Literature in Irish did not disappear quickly in the face of these cataclysms. On the contrary, new forms flowered, including bitterly eloquent political poems that lamented the disappearance of the old order. Throughout the eighteenth century, while penal laws denied the majority Catholic population their legal rights, richly descriptive poems were composed, sung, and passed on in the visionary *aisling* genre, in which Ireland appeared as a goddess or muse whose salvation depended on a savior prince from abroad. The stylized language of the trained hereditary poets gradually fused with the speech rhythms of ordinary people, producing great lyrical freshness and verve.

In the eighteenth century too, Irish was replaced by English as the daily language of those who had money and standing in society, or who gained new economic opportunities as the penal laws were relaxed. The power and influence of the Roman Catholic Church grew from the late eighteenth century onwards, but most bishops and priests regarded speaking Irish as a badge of poverty and superstition, and encouraged its abandonment in favor of English. A similar attitude was taken by the hugely popular early nineteenth-century leader, Daniel O'Connell, a native speaker of Irish whose aunt Eibhlín Dhubh Ní Chonaill had composed a famous lament on the death of her husband, *Caoineadh Airt Uí Laoghaire*. By the mid-nineteenth century, half of the rapidly increasing population, four million people, were Irish speakers; but most of them were desperately poor cottier farmers or landless laborers, and during the Great Famine of 1845-49, their numbers were decimated by starvation, disease, eviction, and emigration.

The trauma of that period, followed by huge economic and social changes, further destroyed confidence in speaking Irish; meanwhile, the new national schools had a policy of systematically punishing children heard speaking it. As emigration to America, Britain, and Australia came to be seen as the only beacon of hope, countless families decided to follow the one-way language shift to English, even when that meant that grandparents or even parents could not converse with their children. By the late nineteenth century, all the pressures of society — political, economic, social, and psychological — were working towards the extinction of Irish. If Sister Fidelma had reappeared in Cashel at this time, and helpfully suggested the idea of a bilingual society in which both languages could prosper side by side, most people would have favored locking her up in one of the new lunatic institutions.

From Revival to the Present Day

But as the fictional Fidelma is apt to realize, what seems obvious and predictable may not be the full picture. In spite of every tribulation, a wealth of folklore tales, songs, and knowledge was still being passed on by native Irish speakers, many of them living on the remote windswept islands of Kerry, Galway, and Donegal, and in impoverished areas of the rural mainland. Nationalist ideas were spreading across Europe, inspiring both antiquarian scholars and political activists to urge the value of indigenous culture. By the turn of the twentieth century, a movement for the revival of Irish, *Conradh na Gaeilge*, or the Gaelic League, was sweeping across the country, modern short stories and plays were beginning to emerge, and arguments got underway about how to marry the dispersed spoken dialects with the requirements of a standardized written grammar and spelling.

Political rebellion in 1916 was another outcome of the spread of nationalism, and following the War of Independence, the Irish Free State was established in 1922. Irish became a compulsory school subject, and in the 1937 constitution it became one of the two official languages of the country. Some hoped it would soon replace English in homes all over Ireland; but just as learning mathematics in school does not guarantee an ability to use that knowledge in adult life, passing exams in Irish did not result in most people speaking it among their friends and family. State and other institutions tended to treat Irish like a piece of antique silver to be shown off on special occasions;

but the communities in which it was spoken continued to shrink, especially as further generations followed the emigration trail across the seas.

There have been many positive developments in the past few decades, however: the spread of schools in which pupils learn through Irish; thousands of teenagers attending annual summer camps in the *Gaeltacht* Irish-speaking areas; economic and cultural development and a growth in self-confidence in those same western seaboard areas; the establishment of a small *Gaeltacht* in Belfast city, and stronger community supports for the thousands who speak Irish in Dublin and other urban areas; better official recognition and funding structures; and a far more sophisticated understanding, among language campaigners, academics and government officials, of the processes and challenges of reviving a minority language or even maintaining it on life support.

There is worrying evidence that young native speakers in the *Gaeltacht* areas opt to speak English among themselves, just as teenagers in most places tend to follow the crowd; but at the same time, fluency among second-language learners in the rest of the island has increased over the past few decades. In Northern Ireland in 2001, 10.4 percent of people claimed some knowledge of Irish, and in the 2006 census in the Republic, 1.6 million people, almost a third of the population, said they could speak it to some extent. The numbers actually speaking Irish every day in the Republic is 80,000 people at most, but a government strategy has recently been agreed to try to increase daily use to 250,000 people in the next 20 years, equivalent to perhaps 5 percent of the population. In mid–2012, when detailed results of the Irish language questions in the 2011 census are published, it will be evident whether the gap is closing or widening between that aspiration and the reality in today's Ireland.

It is notable that the leaders of the main political parties in the Republic at present are fluent Irish speakers, and the successes of the Irish language television station, TG4, which was established in the early 1990s, has encouraged politicians and public figures to give interviews and be seen to use Irish more frequently than before. Many surveys have shown that the majority of people want Irish to survive and be supported. It is easy, of course, to pay lip-service to such an aspiration — making it happen is a lot more challenging. By the age of three or four years, most children realize that English is the language of advertising, of most television, of computer and other electronic games, and of all or many of their neighbors. From then on, it is uphill work for parents and schools to convince them that Irish also has its own purpose and value.

The situation in Ireland has parallels around the world, as thousands of languages are now at risk of extinction. Many of them also suffered from colonization, and today, the pressures of globalization are making English, Spanish, Mandarin Chinese, Arabic, and other dominant languages more powerful than ever. On the other hand, easier travel and web communications are encouraging people in many countries to learn Irish and to visit our small island filled with an infectious enthusiasm for it.

Irish-Language Books Today — and Why Fidelma Is Not Among Them

Many people in Ireland are able to read Irish, but only a fraction of them make a habit of doing so. The majority of bookshops do not even stock Irish-language books; and indeed, 80 percent of English-language books come from Britain, the United States and other countries. So even Ireland's English language publishers face a challenging job, and as for those working in Irish, much of the business is not commercially viable, and is reliant on ever-precarious state grants. In order to cover costs, it is necessary to sell 2,000 copies of a book in either language; as for bestsellers, 10,000 copies is the accepted threshold in the English-language market in Ireland, whereas an Irish-language book selling over 1,000 copies can be called a bestseller, and many titles sell a mere 250–500 copies. Sales figures for Irish language books are not readily available to the public, however, and examples given in this essay have been compiled from the author's own research.

The figures vary according to genre as well as quality: for example, Irish-language children's picture books can sell several thousand copies but poetry collections — probably the most published single genre for adults — are usually at the low end of the scale; highly stylized or challenging novels are also unlikely to sell more than a few hundred copies, but a few recent crime novels (including this author's first) have reached and even breached sales of 2000 copies.

State funding subsidies have been available since the 1950s and currently assist the publication of an average 100 new books in Irish each year, excluding textbooks and academic studies. Some grants are given directly to independent publishers, and others are awarded as individual commissions to writers, paid in advance for a particular work. Nobody gets rich on them and indeed many applications are refused; but those who succeed at least get an opportunity to work part-time on their craft. There are four publishers that focus mainly on books for young readers. One of them, An Gúm, is directly state funded, and as such makes its own policies, which include regular use of translations from English for both textbooks and children's fiction. Six or seven publishers, all privately owned, produce fiction for adults as well as other genres. But the largest of them employs a total of five staff, and several small imprints rely on one or two committed individuals working in their spare time. A few of the English language publishers also produce occasional books in Irish.

This is the context, then, in which Peter Tremayne's agent approached publishers in Ireland in 2005. One company told him that there was no market for translations from English, as all readers of Irish were bilingual and would choose to read the originals in English. Another publisher, Mercier Press, expressed initial interest in the project but was rather unsure of the market. One problem was that — for whatever reasons — Sister Fidelma is not a household name in Ireland; and in any case, Mercier found out that a novel translated from English would not qualify for a funding subsidy, and would thus be unviable in commercial terms. After further unsuccessful inquiries, the International Sister Fidelma Society decided to publish a translation of a short mystery, "A Scream from the Sepulcher," from the collection *Hemlock at Vespers*. But distribution problems arose when the society tried to get the resulting booklet, *Scréach ón Tuama*, into bookshops. This was still the situation when Peter Tremayne asked my advice.

I agreed to do some research on the reasoning behind the restrictive funding policy, in preparation for a talk at Féile Fidelma in September 2010. I also decided to write a follow-up for a leading literary magazine in Irish, *Comhar*. The article included comments from several publishers, writers and translators, and it led to Foras na Gaeilge, the main funding and promotion body for the Irish language, inviting me to carry out further research. My brief was to interview some more people involved with books in Ireland; to find out what translation policies operated in the case of comparable minority languages in other countries; and to write a report for Foras na Gaeilge, making recommendations for changes to their policies on both English-Irish and Irish-English fiction translations. The report will be discussed by the policymakers in December 2011 — and in turn, that may eventually open the door to translations of Sister Fidelma and many other novels.

Some Research Findings

I started my inquiries by asking why the door had been closed in the first place. I knew there had been a very different policy in place in the early years of independence, when large numbers of classics, both literary and popular, had been translated from several other languages into Irish. Those from English included Shakespeare's *Macbeth* (Ó Súilleabháin, 1925) Emily Bronte's *Wuthering Heights* (Ó Cíosáin, 1933) and Arthur Conan Doyle's *The Hound of the Baskervilles* (Tóibín, 1934) They were published by the state company, An Gúm, then the sole publisher of fiction in Irish, and some did very well.

But by the 1950s, the policy had fallen into disrepute and a heavy reliance on translations had come to be seen as an obstacle to original new writing. Such writing flourished considerably in the following decades, and translation was used mostly for children's books; in other genres, translation was supported from languages other than English in order to widen the cultural experiences of Irish language readers; but as for English itself, subsidies were available only in exceptional cases, where a book or an author had a very particular connection with Irish or with *Gaeltacht* areas.

In recent years, however, a new policy has been formally adopted, ruling out even those exceptions. I interviewed two publishers who are strong supporters of this current approach, and four others who are strongly opposed to it and wish to reinstate subsidies for a limited number of translations from English. The supporters argue that all scarce resources should be devoted to original writing, and that in any case, there is no point in providing a version in Irish of something that readers can easily access in English. The opponents' view is that there are several categories of books that work well as translations or co-editions (where a book is produced in several languages simultaneously) and that the Irish language market can benefit greatly from the stimulus of outside influences. The categories include children's picture books; popular fiction series for teenagers; classics such as Ken Kesey's *One Flew Over the Cuckoo's Nest* and Yann Martel's *The Life of Pi*; and plays, novels, and other works set in Irish-speaking environments of the past or the present.

With or without funding support, some notable translations have in fact been published in the past decade and a half, and their sales figures have proved to be interesting. J. K. Rowling's *Harry Potter agus an Órchloch*, the first novel in the phenomenally popular series, is reliably believed to have sold 10,000–20,000 copies in Irish, although official figures are never released on Rowling's instructions. Julia Donaldson's *The Gruffalo*, a much-loved rhyming tale of a mouse taking a walk in the woods, became *An Garbhán* in 2000 and sold over 4,000 copies. Bram Stoker's iconic *Dracula* had already been translated into Irish in the 1930s, and two new editions of it were produced in the 1990s, one for adults and an abridged version for teenagers. They have each sold over 900 copies. Several novellas, originally aimed at adults who struggle at reading in English, were translated into Irish and published by New Island in 2007. Their authors are famous Irish writers such as Maeve Binchy, Marian Keyes, and Roddy Doyle, and sales figures in Irish have ranged from 700 to 1,700 copies.

These figures speak for themselves, and are also supported by the views of two bookshop managers, of An Siopa Leabhar in Dublin, which specializes in Irish-language books, and of the flagship store of Ireland's leading book retailer, Eason. Both managers say that customers are very responsive to translations of well-known books in English because of their great brand recognition and the familiarity of their contents. This is true, they say, of customers keen to renew their ability to read in Irish but lacking confidence in their own skills, and of some fluent and habitual readers who also seek out translations. Positive comments came from several writers and translators too, on the potential enrichment of style and language brought about by the task of adapting one language to another. Translation can also encourage writers to try new genres that are still sparsely available in Irish, such as crime, romance, horror, and teenage adventure.

The second part of my research project, investigating the policies in use for other minority languages, proved to be equally interesting. Contact was made by email and phone with people in funding agencies, publishing companies, and scholarly institutes working in eight languages in total: Scottish Gaelic, the closest Celtic language to Irish; Welsh and Breton, both of them "cousin" Celtic languages to Irish; Basque in the north of Spain and southwest of France; Frisian in the northeast of the Netherlands; Friulian in northeastern Italy; Maltese in the Mediterranean island south of Italy; and Faroese in the islands of the North Atlantic. They concurred with the view expressed by all interviewees in Ireland, that new writing has to be fostered and given priority; but while they have a variety of approaches to translation, none has a rigid policy of refusing financial support to translations from the dominant or majority language in their country.

Indeed, the strongest of these endangered languages seem to have the most open policies on translation. In Welsh, spoken by up to half a million people, teenage readers have had access since the 1980s to many highly popular series translated from English, and as a result of this and the excellent original books written for young people, the numbers of regular readers in Welsh has increased in recent years. Translations for adult readers are far less common than they were twenty or thirty years ago, when many crime novels and tearjerker romances were provided from English. One of the difficulties with crime novels, however, was that the work of translating three hundred to four hundred pages was uneconomic in a small market. Most translations today are of shorter works, but exceptions are made from time to time.

Another burgeoning language is Basque: it was harshly suppressed under the Spanish dictator, General Franco, but its half a million speakers in the semi-autonomous areas of Spain enjoy status and financial supports today; in France, however, where minority languages get short shrift from the government, its use is in decline among its 50,000 native speakers. A policy of translating classics — from English, Spanish, French, and other languages — has been pursued by Basque publishers for many years with financial assistance from the regional government; and children's books are widely co-produced or translated from Spanish, Catalan (spoken by six million people in the Barcelona region) and other Iberian languages in particular.

In the Basque region, translation is widely seen as an enriching and stimulating part of their literary culture, and a similar attitude seems common in the province of Fryslan in the Netherlands. Translating plays from Dutch is particularly popular, for performance by the hundreds of amateur drama groups; but novels and other genres are translated too, not only from Dutch, but also from English and German, which many Frisians also speak fluently. A point made by many interviewees, however, was that only translations of a high standard are welcomed by readers; it was also said that simplifying or adapting the language of the original can be appropriate for some books and genres.

In the case of several of the languages investigated, translations from the dominant language are mostly confined to children's books; but there is a desire to publish in Scottish Gaelic new adaptations of popular classics such as the Sherlock Holmes stories in the near future. Peter Tremayne's novel *The Dove of Death* (2009) and several shorter stories have been translated into Breton, in spite of being widely available in French; but while adults as well as teenagers read the Breton versions of comic series such as *Tintin*, *Astérix*, and *Peanuts,* other fiction translations from French are uncommon. In Maltese, no public subsidies are provided for publishers or writers, and as a result, only 6 percent of the books in the shops are in the language spoken daily by 75 percent of the people; the shelves are full of cheap books in English, the second language learned by everyone at school. Co-productions and translations from other Nordic languages are popular in the Faroes, especially for children and teenagers. According to one publisher, these publications have "contributed to the fact that we set higher requirements for our own writers and that our literature will be of a higher quality" (Jacobsen).

Conclusion

Sister Fidelma's sleuthing adventures have brought enjoyment to millions of readers, and in the process, they have brought to life the cultural, religious, and political milieu of Irish society in the seventh century. The Irish language so elegantly blended into the stories contributes greatly to them; and so it seems obvious that they should be available in translation to today's readers of Irish. But where human activity is concerned, little is as simple as it may appear. The shape and sounds of the language itself have changed in fourteen centuries; its use, status, and literary possibilities have undergone profound traumas in that time, too; and Irish people today have quite complex and even confused attitudes to "the first official language," as it is known, somewhat ironically. As for Fidelma, the funding door may open in the next year or two to the possibility of a translation to Irish — but readers will have to await a sequel to this article to find out whether or not she is finally invited in.

Works Cited

Bronte, Emily. *Arda Wuthering*. Trans. Seán Ó Cíosáin. Dublin: An Gúm, 1933.
Conan Doyle, Arthur. *Cú na mBaskerville*. Trans. Nioclás Tóibín. Dublin: An Gúm, 1934.
Donaldson, Julia. *The Gruffalo*. New York: Dial Books for Young Readers, 1999.
Heussaff, Anna. "Béarla na Leabhar." *Comhar*, Deireadh Fómhair 2010, Imleabhar 70, Uimhir 10.
Jacobsen, Marna. "Development of Faroese Children's Literature: Challenges in a Minority Society." Web. <www.ibbycompostela2010.org/descarregas/11/11_IBBY2010_14.pdf>.
Kesey, Ken. *One Flew Over the Cuckoo's Nest*. New York: Signet Books, 1962.
Martel, Yann. *Life of Pi*. New York: Harcourt, 2001.
Ní Chonaill, Eibhlín Dhubh. *Caoineadh Airt Uí Laoghaire*. Ed. Seán Ó Tuama. Dublin: An Clóchomhar, 1999.
Rowling, J. K. *Harry Potter agus an Órchloch*. Trans. Máire Nic Mhaoláin. London: Bloomsbury, 2004.
Shakespeare, William. *Traigéide Mhic Bheatha*. Trans. S. Labhrás Ó Súilleabháub. Dublin: An Gúm, 1925.
Tremayne, Peter. *The Dove of Death*. London: Headline, 2009.
_____. *Hemlock at Vespers*. London: Headline, 2000.
_____. *Scréach ón Tuama*. Trans. Gearoid Ó Laoi. Charleston, SC: International Sister Fidelma Society, 2008.

Additional Works of Interest

There are many books and websites in English that can provide further information on general topics raised in this essay, including the literary, political and socio-linguistic history of the Irish language; the challenges to be overcome if the living language is to survive in the future; analysis of census population and other data on the numbers of speakers of Irish today and in the past; and the opportunities for adults living outside Ireland to participate in Irish-language courses and conversation groups. The following is a guide rather than a comprehensive list. In addition, a list of Irish-language publishers in Ireland is given below.

Books

Cronin, Michael, and Cormac Ó Cuilleanáin, eds. *The Languages of Ireland*. Dublin: Four Courts Press, 2003.
Mac Murchaidh, Ciarán, ed. *Who Needs Irish? Reflections on the Importance of the Irish Language Today*. Dublin: Veritas, 2004. (This book includes an essay by Anna Heussaff, "The Irish for Multicultural.")
Ní Chartúir, Darerca *The Irish Language: an overview and guide*. New York: Avena Press, 2002. Print.
Nic Pháidín, Caoilfhionn, and Seán Ó Cearnaigh, eds. *A New View of the Irish Language*. Dublin: Cois Life, 2008.
Ó Murchú, Helen. *More Facts about Irish*. European Bureau for Lesser Used Languages. Dublin: Irish Committee, 2008.
Titley, Alan. *A Pocket History of Gaelic Culture*. Dublin: O'Brien Press, 2002.

Online Sources

www.cso.ie: The Central Statistics Office of Ireland publishes a volume of data on the numbers of Irish speakers recorded at each census of population, with detailed breakdowns available according to area, age groups, gender, and other factors, as well as a summary of the most significant findings. Data for 2011 will be available in June 2012; those for 2006 are at: http://www.cso.ie/en/census/census2006reports/census2006-volume9-irishlanguage/

www.daltai.com: Daltaí na Gaeilge has been promoting and teaching the Irish language in many locations in the United States since 1981, and provides an online discussion forum as well as much practical information on classes, resources, and activities.

www.gaeilge.ie: The website of Foras na Gaeilge provides pages both in English and in Irish on the history of the language, its position today, the Irish language abroad, and other topics.

http://irishlanguage.nd.edu/: The University of Notre Dame in Indiana has a degree program in Irish language and literature, and its website provides many useful links.

www.pobail.ie: The Department of Arts, Heritage and the Gaeltacht is responsible for the government's *20 Year Strategy for Irish*, which can be accessed in English at http://www.pobail.ie/en/20YearStrategyfortheIrishLanguage/Publications/. In the same section, the authoritative *Comprehensive Linguistic Study of the Use of Irish in the Gaeltacht* by Conchúir Ó Giollagáin, published in 2008, is also available.

www.tg4.ie: TG4 is a television station broadcasting a few hours in Irish each day (along with unrelated programs in English which provide commercial income for the station). Irish-language programs other than news are subtitled in English, and can be viewed "live" online; many are also available online for subsequent viewing.

www.udaras.ie: Údarás na Gaeltachta's statutory remit is the economic, social and cultural development of the Gaeltacht areas where Irish remains the majority or significant community language. The Údarás (Authority) funded a six-minute video on the history of the language which can be viewed in both English and Irish on the following links: http://www.youtube.com/watch?v=9U0v9LHgyRY&feature=related; http://www.youtube.com/watch?v=bzH1phxBEEQ (in Irish)

Publishers of Irish-Language Books

Most of the following websites are in both English and Irish.
An Gúm: www.gaeilge.ie/angum
An Sagart: www.ansagart.ie
An tSnáthaid Mhór: www.antsnathaidmhor.com
Cló Iar-Chonnacht: www.cic.ie
Cló Mhaigh Eo: www.leabhar.com
Cois Life: www.coislife.ie
Coiscéim: www.coisceim.ie
Futa Fata: www.futafata.com
LeabhairCOMHAR: www.iriscomhar.com/leabhair
Leabhar Breac: www.leabharbreac.com

The following companies publish a small number of noneducational Irish-language books in addition to their main output in English:
Mercier Press: www.mercierpress.ie
New Island Press: www.newisland.ie
O'Brien Press: www.obrien.ie
Veritas: www.veritas.ie

Fidelma and the Celts of Brittany: Ancient and Modern

Herve Latimier

Brittany (Breizh) is currently part of the French State having been absorbed into it by the Treaty of Union of Brittany and France in September 18, 1532. The Treaty of Union followed a long war by France to take over the country. The war was marked by the siege of Nantes (*Naoned*) in 1487; the battle of Saint Aubin du Cormier (*Sant Albin an Iliber*) in July, 1488, in which 6000 Bretons and their allies died; and then the death of the Breton ruler Duke Frañsez II in 1488. Brittany's younger ruler, Anna Breizh, Frañsez's daughter, tried to maintain Breton independence and married Maximilian of Austria, but Charles VIII and a French army invaded. Charles VIII persuaded the Pope to annul the marriage and then married Anna himself. Charles VIII died in 1491 and, after his death, his heir, Louis XII, married her in 1498. Her daughter Claude married Francois I of France. It was then decided by the French monarchy that the titles should no longer be separated, and the King of France would become Duke of Brittany.

The Treaty of Union, however, recognizes Brittany as an autonomous province still with its own parliament until the abolition of that parliament on September 6, 1790, following the French Revolution. From that time the Breton language and culture was severely discouraged, and today it is estimated that only 200,000 native speakers remain in a population of 4,365,500. Even today the Breton language is not recognized as an official language in France, and international pleas for the language to be taught in state schools and used in the media and in other aspects of public life are ignored. In July 2008, the French Constitution (Article 75–1) was amended to state that "regional languages belong to the heritage of France." This ambiguous statement does not give actual recognition, rights, or funding to the language. However, the regional authorities in official Brittany (the department of Loire–Atlantique,

Liger Atlantel, has been separated from the rest of Brittany since 1941) support the language as well as private schools to cater to the Breton speaking population. The Celtic Breton language is not the only language of Brittany. A predominately Romance language (Gallo) is also spoken in the eastern part of the country.

The Bretons are an ancient Celtic people, one of the Brythonic speaking group. This group consists of Welsh, Breton, and Cornish speakers, or "P" Celts. The "Q" Celts are those speaking the Goidelic group, which are Irish, Manx and Scottish Gaelic. "P" and "Q" are scholastic terms referring to the substitution of the sound *qu* in Goidelic for *p* in Brythonic. For example, the word for son in Irish is *mac* but in Breton is *mab* (indicating the mutation of p into b). It is thought that these two branches of Celtic began to diverge around 500 B.C.

Brittany was once called Armorica (land before the sea) and was part of Gaul; Gaulish was also a Celtic language whose written remains identify it closely with the Brythonic group. But from the fifth century there was a mass exodus from southern Britain, when the Angles and Saxons started to invade and form their kingdoms, driving the indigenous Celtic population out. Armorica was one of the areas in which they sought refuge, and these settlements continued for two centuries, changing Armorica into Brittany, or "Little Britain." In Breton, we use the word *Predeneg* when we speak of the common Brythonic language in Fidelma's time. Even after the language began to diverge to form modern Welsh, Cornish and Breton, it was mutually understandable until the late medieval period, and speakers can still communicate from a basic vocabulary. Readers should know that the Celtic peoples shared a civilization symbolized by the Druids, who had a similar organization of society, a philosophy, law, and art, as well as their related languages.

The purpose of this essay, therefore, is to try to answer why Sister Fidelma Mysteries appeal so particularly to Breton fans. Apart from the excellence of the stories themselves, Fidelma is placed in situations where she often interacts with Bretons and other Brythonic Celtic peoples.

Why are we, Breton speaking Bretons, interested in Fidelma's mysteries? First, there is no reason why the Breton population would have a different proportion of readers fond of mysteries and historical mysteries than any other nationality. Good novels with good characters and a serious historical background are naturally always popular, such as the stories of Sir John de Wolfe, Brother Cadfael, or Judge Dee. Good stories with a Celtic historical background have even more appeal to Breton readers.

I will demonstrate that Bretons, who often find their own ancestors in the Fidelma stories, are regarded by the title character as her own kin. This is already a good reason for Bretons to appreciate Peter Tremayne's books but, of course, it's not enough. I see three other reasons that I shall explain further. The first is the historical background, which can give us Bretons a kind of pride in the old civilization to which we are heirs, and in the values that it brought to Europe, and to mankind in general. I speak of a pride without any feeling of superiority. The second aspect is the relationship between the pre–Christian Celtic religion and Christianity, and the struggle between the Celtic doctrines and the Roman ones, which echoes to this day. The third aspect is Fidelma's own personality, her appeal to the modern world. There are many others, to be sure. Every reader has his own reasons to be a fan.

The first review of a Fidelma mystery I wrote, as a reviewer for the Breton literary journal *Al Liamm*, founded in 1946, was of *Absolution by Murder*. This appeared in October 2001 (issue no. 328), under the pen name Eflamm gKervilio. I must acknowledge I didn't know Fidelma before I read the novel, nor did I know Peter Tremayne. I had been looking for a novel by Richard Knight (one of the Crowner John's Mysteries; a half Norman-half Welsh hero able to speak Predeneg, or Cymraeg, his mother's language). I didn't find what I originally sought, but that's how I initially discovered Fidelma. I did not know then that readers of *Al Liamm* had already heard about Peter Tremayne, via one of his short stories, "The Singing Stone," which had been translated into Breton by Dr. Janig Bodiou-Stephens and published in the 240th issue of the same magazine under the title of *Ar Maen-Kanañ*. This fact was mentioned in *The Brehon* ("Peter Tremayne in Celtic Languages XVIII).

I became a fan and regularly wrote reviews of the Fidelma novels for *Al Liamm*. Soon I joined The International Sister Fidelma Society. I began to wonder if the author would be interested in the idea of the Fidelma short stories being translated into Breton. One day, I spoke to Bernez an Nail (1946–2010) about Peter Tremayne, and my hope to see Fidelma's mysteries translated into Breton. Bernez was a former director of Skol Uhel ar Vro — The Breton Cultural Institute — and then director of a publishing company (Les Portes du Larges), as well as author of a dozen books himself. Bernez knew Peter under his own name, Peter Berresford Ellis, the leading Celtic scholar, and had first met him in 1985 when Peter was chairman of Scrîf-Celt, the Celtic Languages Book Fair. We were traveling in Bernez's car to a meeting in Karaez. He told me about Peter, and about Peter's friendship with Professor Per Denez (1921-2011). Per Denez had been professor of Breton at the University of Rennes2 Haute-Bretagne (*Roazhon2 Breizh-Uhel*), and was one of the foremost Celtic scholars as well as the author of many books and papers in his subject. Per had known Peter from the 1960s.

The result of these contacts was that the summer issue of *Al Liamm* (n°363), August, 2007, was devoted to Fidelma with three short story translations, an article by Professor Per Denez about Peter, one by David Robert Wooten about the International Sister Fidelma Society ("Sister Fidelma in Breton"; "Tremaine Voted Best Mystery Series Author of 2007"). Jean-Michel Mahé, one of the translators who worked on this issue, later translated the novel *The Dove of Death* as *Koulm ar Marv*, published by ABER in 2010. I personally hope this will not be the last appearance of Fidelma in Breton.

Fidelma and the Brythonic Celts

The first important Brythonic Celts in Fidelma's life, of whom she often speaks, were Saint Patrick and Pelagius.

Patrick, *Pádraig* in modern Irish, *Padrig* in modern Breton and modern Welsh, was born about A.D. 385 or 387. Scholars debate whether he died in 461 or 493. He left an autobiography, his *Confessio*, from which we can be sure that he was a Romanized Briton. His father was Calporius, a deacon, who was son of a priest named Potitus, of the town of Banna Venta Berniae, thought to be near modern Carlisle. He is credited with bringing the New Faith (of Christianity), as people say in Fidelma's stories, to Ireland.

Pelagius is also mentioned as being a Briton, born about A.D. 354, and died sometime between 420 and 440. Fidelma often refers to his teachings (*The Spider's Web*, *Shroud for the Archbishop*, and in the short story "The Astrologer Who Predicted His Own Murder"). This mention is one of the reasons that led me to translate the aforementioned short story (*Ar steredour a rakwelas e vije drouklazhet*) for the special issue of *Al Liamm* (n° 363, August 2007). It appears to me that Fidelma prefers the teachings of the Celtic monk Pelagius, who was later regarded as a "heretic," than those of Patrick, who became, with Rome's blessing, the patron saint of Ireland. One of the main historical themes in almost every story is the struggle between the doctrines of Rome and that of the Celtic Churches. Pelagius is known through the writings of his "primary" opponent, Augustine of Hippo. However, a body of Pelagian writings does survive, and Rome frequently accused the "Celtic Churches" of Pelagian heresy.

A modern look at Pelagius and his influence on Brythonic Celts can be seen in the movie *King Arthur*. According to this interpretation, Pelagius is portrayed as the mentor of young Lucius Artorius Castus, otherwise Arthur (*Arzhur* in Breton). Pelagius's excommunication and murder is one of the reasons which led Arthur to break off loyalty with the declining power of the Roman Empire and help his fellow Britons fight the Saxon invaders. Who knows the truth about Arthur? Whether this film version is credible historically or not, I agree with the film's depiction of Pelagius' actions and his influence on Celtic Christianity. This is well depicted in the way Pelagius influences

Fidelma. Peter Tremayne, in his role as a Celtic scholar, has written extensively on Pelagius' influence on Celtic Christianity in several books, including *Celtic Inheritance* (1985), *Celt and Saxon* (1993), and *The Druids* (1994).

We know that the Abbey Landevenneg in Brittany (*Breizh*) obeyed the Celtic rule of Colmbanus, from Ireland, until A.D. 818. There were still strong links between all the Celtic peoples and lands at that time. It was often easier to travel by sea than by land. Therefore, we sometimes find that Fidelma, like many other Irish religious of her time, often travels to other lands and to other Celtic communities. Tremayne vividly describes her sea voyages in many of his books. Some of the mysteries take place in Brythonic Celtic lands, where she meets with Welsh, Bretons and even Gauls who are not completely Romanized.

In *Act of Mercy*, Fidelma makes a pilgrimage to Santiago de Compostela in Galicia. Galicia was also settled by large numbers of fleeing Brythonic Celts from southern Britain in the fifth and sixth centuries, and the area has a strong Celtic influence. She travels on a ship whose first mate is a Breton from Bro-Ereg, *Gurvan*. His adopted son's name is *Gwenvrid*. They make a stop in *Enez Eusa* (Ushant) and witness the wreck of a ship from Montroulez named *Morvaout* (*Cormorant*). Irish, Bretons and other Celts seem at home among Brittany, Britain, and Ireland. They do not have any difficulties in understanding or relating to each other.

Smoke in the Wind takes place in Wales, in the kingdom of Dyfed, which was settled by an Irish tribe called the Déisi, part of which remained in the land of the Déisi Muman in Fidelma's own kingdom of Muman. Cymru (*Kembre* in Breton) is like a second (or a first) home for Bretons. Many characters' names have a taste of Brittany: Goff (*Gov* in modern Breton) means a smith, Tryffin (*Trifin*), the abbot of Sant Dewi (*Divi*), Iestyn (*Jestin*), and Buddog (*Budog*). We also read about Boudicca (*Boudika*), Morgan ap Arthyrs (*Morgan mab Arzhur*), and Macsen Wledig. We learn about the link between Samhain and "The Eve of All Hallows" (*Gouel an Hollsent*), which was an important holy day for the Bretons until a few decades ago — and still is for some.

Fidelma shows a certain fluency in *Predeneg* (British Celtic) as we read in *Smoke in the Wind*. At the end of the third chapter, Abbot Tryffin says:

"I forgot. Among the nobles and the religious, we can speak the language of Éireann and, indeed, Greek, Latin, and some Hebrew, but the ordinary people speak only the language of the Cymry. You will need an interpreter."

"Your language presents no problem to me," Fidelma replied, lapsing into Cymraeg. "I served my novitiate with several sisters from the kingdom of Gwynedd and learnt from them" [31].

The author seems well aware of the interchanges between Ireland and Wales, which are ably outlined in *Ireland and Wales: Their Historical and Literary Relations* by Cecile O'Rahilly.

In the short story "The Lost Eagle," we are in Canterbury, in the part of Britain settled by the Jutes, the cousins of the Angles and Saxons. We hear about the fight of the British Celts against the Roman legions centuries before, and how Boudicca decimated the élite Roman legion, the IXth Hispana during her insurrection.

In *The Haunted Abbot,* Fidelma shows she knows the *De Excidio et Conquesta Britanniae* (On the Ruin and Conquest of Britain), the famous account written by St. Gildas (*Sant Weltaz* in Breton) concerning the massacres of the British Celts by the invading Saxons, which caused their mass exodus, many to settle in Armorica.

In *The Council of the Cursed,* there is enmity between Bishop Ordgar, bishop of Kent, and Abbot Cadfan of Gwynedd. When Ordgar is murdered during the Council of Augustodunum (Autun) in A.D. 670, the question is whether that conflict is relevant. We hear about the slaughter of a thousand brethren when the abbey of Benchoer in Gwynedd (modern Bangor in north Wales) was burned and destroyed by the Angles of Mercia. These are facts taken by the author from contemporary accounts of the time, such as St. Gildas' account, and the various chronicles of the Britons, such as Nennius's *Historia Britonum,* or *Brut y Tywysogion* (*Chronicles of the Princes*).

In *The Dove of Death,* the entire story takes place in Brittany, especially around Morbihan in the south. *Mor Bihan* in Breton means "The Little Sea." There is probably no need to explain the fascination for Breton readers for this novel. Fidelma's "father" gave a special meaning to this story by writing, after his dedication, a few words in Breton and in English. "*Gant ar spi e c'hello pobl Vreizh adkemer un deiz he flas e-touez ar bed gant he yezh hag e sevenadur.*" "'With the hope that the ancient Breton nation, its language and culture, takes its place once more among the nations of the world'" (v). For Bretons struggling to retain their language and culture, it is a kind and encouraging token of friendship. *The Dove of Death* demonstrates the author's knowledge of the landscape and seascape of the area, and a knowledge of the history of seventh-century Brittany and its rulers. The author has stated that it was his friend, the late Professor Per Denez, who had first suggested that he bring Fidelma to Brittany. The novel was translated as *Koulm ar Marv* into Breton by Jean-Michel Mahé and published in 2010 by Aber Publishers (*Fidelma in Breton*). It was the first Sister Fidelma novel to be translated into a Celtic language and, for Bretons, a boost to their ego because it appeared in Breton before its translation into French appeared.

When the fleeing Brythonic Celts settled in Armorica in the fifth and sixth centuries A.D. they were often led by religious who brought Christianity with them. At that time, the Angles and Saxons were still pagans. Brythonic Celts, such as Patrick, also had a hand in evangelizing Ireland before it became a great place of Christian education and sent missionaries all over Europe. Britain, that is the British Celts, were largely evangelized by the second century, and even the Picts in northern Britain. Three Brythonic Celtic bishops attended the Council of Arles in A.D. 314, and several were at the Council of Rimini in 359. Christianity was an important part of the Celtic civilization at this time. Five out of the seven "Founder Saints" of Brittany and first bishops were monks from Cornwall (*Kernev*) and Wales (*Kembre*): Maloù (of Sant Maloù), Samzun (Dol), Brieg (of Sant Brieg), Tudual (of Landreger), Paol Aorelian (of Kastell-Paol) and Kaourintin (of Kemper). One of them, Padern (of Gwened), was supposedly born in Armorica. There are three Saints *Paternus* in ancient records, and it seems difficult to tell one from the others. There are many "brothers and sisters" made saints by "*vox populi*": Budog, Eflamm, Enora, Karanteg, Iltud, Eneour, Kiwa, Gweltaz, Koupaia, Fragan, Ninnog, and Telo, among the countless religious who crossed what was called the *Mor Breizh*, the Breton Sea, which is now called The English Channel. And often they crossed in both directions.

These religious of what we now call "The Celtic Church" shared the same kind of Christianity as Fidelma. The author's description of this "Celtic Church" is very interesting for Bretons. Two questions find the beginning of answers through the Sister Fidelma stories. The first is about the difference between the organization and doctrines of a rural and abbey-based church, such as the Celtic one; and the urban and Episcopal one, of which the head served as a temporal prince, like the Latin Church. The second question involves the influence of pre–Christian Druidic culture on Celtic Christianity. One can be sure from the evidence that the first Celtic monks and abbots had been Druids. There are no accounts of violence in the evangelization of Britain or Ireland. Colmcille's famous sixth-century poem says it all: "My Druid, he will not refuse me, is the Son of God, and may he side with me."

There is no long line of martyrs among the Celts as there was in other parts of Europe. A lot of locations were "consecrated for the faith, for it was an old custom to go and offer prayers by it," as Tremayne's character Brother Metellus says, speaking about a menhir (*maen-hir*) on the island of Edig in *The Dove of Death* (22). It is fascinating to learn, or to be given the thirst of learning, by means of a story and its characters. The Celtic Church came to an end about the ninth century, but I believe that the traces of the Celtic civilization it carried remain in the Celtic peoples of the twenty-first century. Reading about the philosophies of the Celts in the Sister Fidelma novels can be very stimulating for contemporary society, as well as provide us with a vivid and positive look at the Celtic contribution to European civilization.

The ancient Irish law, the Brehon Law, lies at the centre of all the Fidelma mysteries. The author gives clear explanations where needed in his "Historical

Notes." But in the historical note in *Smoke in the Wind* we also read that the Welsh had a similar law system. "These law books were popularly known as 'The Laws of Hywel Dda.'" This is a reference to the Welsh king under whose authority the codification of the law system was made in the ninth century. The author continues: "However, they represented an ancient legal tradition among the Celtic peoples so that comparisons between the Brehon Laws of Ireland and the Laws of Hywel Dda can clearly be made. It was this common legal tradition that catches the interest of Fidelma in the current story" (x).

Certainly the Breton reader can spot the obvious similarities. In *Smoke in the Wind*, Fidelma travels with a Brythonic Celtic Brother (Brother Meurig) who is a judge, a *barnwr* (in Breton we say "*barner*" for judge). There is no reason to doubt that the Bretons came from Britain to Armorica with a similar system. In *The Dove of Death* Fidelma meets *Iarnbud*, the *bretat* to Canao, *mac'htiern* of *Brilhag*. And later, *Kaourentin*, *bretat* of Bro-Gernev. In modern Breton *breutaer* means advocate.

The Celtic Breton law system was codified too late to be useful if one wants to make close comparisons between the Irish, Welsh and Breton laws. The "Très Ancienne Coutume de Bretagne" (Very Ancient Custom of Brittany) was written when Yann III was Duke of Brittany between 1312 and 1341, just before the Breton War of Succession (which saw the de Montforts win with the help of the English against Charles de Blois and Jeanne de Penthièvre, who were allied with the King of France). The war ended with the Treaty of Guérande (*Gwenrann*) in 1365. Jean de Montfort became Yann IV. Yann IV founded Urzh ar Eminig (l'Ordre de l'Hermine) in 1381, a knighthood open to women and people of common birth, which I am sure Fidelma would entirely approve. However, the first known printed copy of these Breton Laws was published in 1480. It contains mainly rules of proceedings, and has clearly been influenced by other law systems. But it is a testimony to the existence of a "very ancient" law system. Most Celtic scholars would agree that all the Celtic peoples had similar systems in Fidelma's time.

When one learns about the Brehon Laws through Peter Tremayne's books, one is amazed. Law is a picture of the state of society, as the author admits in *Smoke in the Wind*: "Seen from today's perspective, the Brehon Laws seemed to enshrine an almost ideal society" (xi). The place of law and justice is, today, one of the criteria of democracy. The place of women under Brehon Law seems much better than in a lot of contemporary societies. If one adds to this the level of general knowledge of the people, the famous "abbey-universities" of Ireland, the way rulers were chosen, there are reasons to look at the Celts of that period with admiration. Perhaps we have reasons to be concerned about the regressions in history too. While reading the Fidelma stories, it occurred to me that ancient Celtic society seemed organized so that the king, chieftain, or *mac'htiern* must have been appointed by an agreement of the members of the family, the legal advisers, the religious and other members of the society. In other words, there is a kind of democracy at work, while in other European societies, feudalism, the rule of the strongest, is developing.

I confess that I am often envious of Fidelma as being too clever, too courageous, too highly knowledgeable, too honorable, as well as attractive and of noble birth. It is not by chance that the author makes her character far from perfect. She can be impulsive, too arrogant, too sure of herself. Her attitude towards Eadulf and their son, Alchú, is complicated. Her complicated attitudes are understandable to modern readers. Her ideas about religion and society seem very contemporary. My "dark side" asks whether they might be too contemporary, until one realizes that she is a product of the evidence presented by the Brehon law system, the legal texts and observations, and, indeed, her entire society. The author himself has often mentioned the two-volume *A Social History of Ancient Ireland* by P.W. Joyce, which he read as a young student. It is clear that the society depicted in the Fidelma books did exist, and is not a fabrication of the author's imagination.

What makes Sister Fidelma so "modern" is that she raises questions similar to those raised today on a variety of issues: the relation between men and women; relations to other people and to other cultures; how to hold fast to his/her opinions; career versus personal life; place of motherhood; religion; and many other matters. They are old questions, perhaps as old as mankind itself. Fidelma is educated, indeed, but if she seems so "modern" in her dealings with those problems it is because, perhaps, seen from today's perspective, the Brehon Laws seemed to enshrine an almost ideal society.

"Truth is great and will prevail," says Brehon Morann; in Irish, "*Mór í an fhirrinne, agus buaidhfe sí*" and in my own language of Brittany, "*Meur eo ar wirionez ha trec'h e vo*."[1] I am neither an historian nor a sociologist, only a literary critic for *Al Liamm*. My "truth" is the pleasure I get from the Sister Fidelma Mysteries. My only "victory" *(trec'h)* would be to have shown that the Sister Fidelma stories not only bring pleasure to their Breton readers, but are a source of reflection about the Celtic past and, importantly, about the Celtic future.

Note

1. The Brehon Morann quotation is discussed by Peter Berresford Ellis in *The Celts: A History* (174).

Works Cited

Colmcille. "Christ Is My Druid." *Annals of the Four Masters*. Corpus of Electronic Texts Edition. University College Cork. <http://www.ucc.ie/celt/published/T100005A/index.html>.

Ellis, Peter Berresford. *Celt and Saxon*. London: Constable, 1993.
_____. *Celtic Inheritance*. London: Frederick Muller, 1985.
_____. *The Celts: A History*. 1998 (as *The Ancient World of the Celts*). New York: Carroll & Graf, 2007.
_____. *The Druids*. London: Constable, 1994.
"Fidelma in Breton." *The Brehon: The Journal of the International Sister Fidelma Society* 9.3 (Sept. 2010): II–III.
Gildas. *The Ruin of Britain, and Other Works*. Ed. and trans. Michael Winterbottom. Totowa, NJ: Rowman & Littlefield, 1978.
Joyce, P. W. *A Social History of Ancient Ireland*. 2 vols. 1903. New York: B. Blom, 1968.
King Arthur. Dir. Antoine Fuqua. Touchstone Pictures, 2004.
Latimier, Herve. Rev. of *Absolution by Murder*, by Peter Tremayne. *Al Liamm* Oct. 2001.
Nennius. *British History; and the Welsh Annals*. Ed. and trans. John Morris. Totowa, NJ: Rowman & Littlefield, 1980.
O'Rahilly, Cecile. *Ireland and Wales: Their Historical and Literary Relations*. London: Longmans, Green, 1924.
Patrick, Saint. *The Confession of Saint Patrick and Letter to Coroticus*. Trans. John Skinner. New York: Image/Doubleday, 1998.
"Peter Tremayne in Celtic Languages." *The Brehon* 4.3 (Sept. 2005): VIII-IX.
"Sister Fidelma in Breton." *The Brehon* 6.2 (May 2007): XVIII.
Tremayne, Peter. *Act of Mercy*. London: Headline, 1999.
_____. "The Astrologer Who Predicted his Own Murder." *Whispers of the Dead: Fifteen Sister Fidelma Mysteries*. New York: St. Martin's Minotaur, 2004. 49–73.
_____. *The Council of the Cursed*. London: Headline, 2008.
_____. *The Dove of Death*. 2009. New York: Minotaur Books, 2010.
_____. *The Haunted Abbot*. London: Headline, 2002.
_____. *Koulm ar Marv* (*The Dove of Death*). Trans. Jean-Michel Mahé. Landeda: Aber, 2010.
_____. "The Lost Eagle." *Whispers of the Dead: Fifteen Sister Fidelma Mysteries*. New York: St. Martin's Minotaur, 2004. 343–66.
_____. *Shroud for the Archbishop*. London: Headline, 1995.
_____. "The Singing Stone." *Fantasy Tales* 8.16 (1986); reprinted in *Al Liamm* Jan. 1987 as *Ar Maen-Kanañ*, trans. Janig Bodiou-Stephens.
_____. *Smoke in the Wind*. 2001. New York: St. Martin's Minotaur, 2003.
_____. *The Spider's Web*. London: Headline, 1997.
"Tremayne Voted Best Mystery Series Author of 2007." *The Brehon* 7.1 (Jan. 2008): II–III.

Who Wears the Pants? Role Reversal in the Sister Fidelma Mysteries

M. E. Kemp

Peter Tremayne's series featuring Sister Fidelma and her partner, Brother Eadulf the Saxon monk, is certainly one of the best in the proliferation of medieval mysteries that continue to dominate the historical mystery genre. Accurate detail and excellent writing are hallmarks of the series. Tremayne is an expert in the field of Celtic Studies and it shows in the fictional but believable Sister Fidelma series set in the mid–six hundreds, a period of incredible culture in Ireland. Fidelma is actually a princess and sister to the King of Cashel, with a law degree and an insatiable curiosity to solve puzzles. She's the Will Shortz of the mid–eighth century. Brother Eadulf is also a puzzle-solver who has studied in the great Irish schools and has spent several years in Rome. In fact, it is because of their ability to solve puzzles that they are drawn together.

The two characters are introduced to each other (and to most readers) at an important religious conference featuring two opposing churches, that of Ireland and that of Rome. Sister Fidelma literally bumps into the young Saxon monk in the hallway at their first meeting and is rather taken with the young man. In fact, Eadulf is described throughout the series in rather more detail than Fidelma, who is repeatedly described as tall with green eyes and red hair. We know that Eadulf is brown-haired and brown-eyed with the strong build of a warrior, with a sense of humor and compassion. He usually wears a brown wool cassock.

Fidelma seems to be most associated with her sharp tongue. As the sister of the King of Cashel you'd think Fidelma would be described as wearing silken, embroidered robes, at least on special occasions such as the grand assemblies where she always reveals the guilty party, but all we know is that she wears a religious cassock, and a hooded cape when she travels. Practical, but not particularly entertaining. Fidelma is no fashionista. Surprisingly, she does don clothes reflective of her role as a king's sister in *The Chalice of Blood* and *Dancing with Demons*, her attire as shocking to readers as to some of those witnessing her within Tremayne's pages.

Fidelma has a sharp tongue and a short fuse, which seems to be associated with her red hair. Pity the poor redheaded person who has to contend with that myth. No wonder Fidelma has a temper. Brother Eadulf, on the other hand, complements her as the calm, good-natured partner that he is, even in the beginning of their relationship when he dares to suggest he be head of the investigation into the Abbess Étain's murder. Eadulf knows the laws and customs of the country, as he explains in what seems a reasonable request. Sister Fidelma nearly bites his head off. It is Eadulf who compromises by suggesting that no one be in charge, as they both bring different abilities to the quest. She gives in but with bad grace, although she feels a "strange chemical sensation" when he looks at her (*Absolution by Murder* 94). This "strange chemical sensation" is an unusual description for a perfectly normal attraction between a man and a woman and Tremayne uses the words in the early books. Sister Fidelma is an authority on Irish law and Tremayne is an authority on Celtic law and culture, which in the mid seven hundreds granted women legal rights on a par with legal rights for women today. So far as romance goes, one wonders if Sister Fidelma got stuck in science class or if she had a nun-teacher who held a ruler between her and her partner at school dances to keep them a set distance apart. Her emotions are under rigid control.

In the first book in the series she hesitates, naturally, to view the body of her friend, the murdered Abbess Étain. Eadulf offers to view it for her, and is again rebuffed. He is ordered to find a lamp and hesitates; he is not used to being ordered about by a woman. But he does as he is told, and it won't be the last time for that. Eadulf's willingness to compromise will prove his undoing as a man — at least the stereotype of a man.

Bishop Colmán and Abbess Hilda foresee this team's success. "It is like putting a wolf and a fox together to hunt a hare," Colmán says. And the Abbess replies: "It would be interesting to know which you see as the wolf and which as the fox" (*Absolution by Murder* 85). This is an astute observation by the lady abbess. With her red hair, green eyes and clever mind Fidelma has the physical appearance that would warrant her being described as a fox — even in today's slang she could be described as foxy. Yet her courage and tenacity reveal the heart of a wolf, and a wolf on the scent does not give up. Eadulf has the build of a warrior and no one can doubt his courage. David Nalle, in an Internet book review, calls him "the somewhat headstrong but very able Saxon monk Brother Eadulf with whom she [Fidelma] develops a close personal relationship." Now if anyone is headstrong it seems to be Sister Fidelma, who roams the countrysides of ancient Britain and Ireland with no retinue except a Saxon monk. But as the series goes on Brother Eadulf seems to lose his edge as a puzzle solver and becomes more of a spear-carrier, content to stand by while Fidelma bursts upon the stage for a star-turn, all spotlights directed upon her in a blinding display of her logic. The series is named for Sister Fidelma, after all. When does Eadulf's role change?

At the ending of the second book in the series, *Shroud for the Archbishop*, Fidelma climbs into the boat that will take her from Rome back to Ireland. Eadulf has come to see her off. Does he jump into the boat and sail off into the sunset with her in a romantic gesture of devotion and affection? No, he does not. He sensibly remains behind in Rome to complete some administrative work. He is, at this time, still his own man.

Eadulf plays little role in the third book, *Suffer Littler Children*, so we must examine his role in the fourth book, *The Subtle Serpent*. Eadulf only appears at the ending of this book, although it is made clear that Fidelma has been thinking about him with a kind of longing since she left him behind in Rome. Fidelma rescues him from slavers who captured the ship in which Eadulf was sailing to Ireland. Poor Brother Eadulf then gets conked on the head and hidden in the hold of another ship—you'd think he'd get the message that hanging with Fidelma is dangerous. Still, she has saved him from slavers so that must put him under an obligation to her, which may be the first step in their role reversal. Usually it's the man who rescues the helpless female from a fate worse than death.

In reviews of the series books it is primarily the *Yorkshire Evening Post* who pairs these two as a team, calling them "a splendidly entertaining double act" ("What Critics Say About the Sister Fidelma Mysteries"). Otherwise it is Fidelma who is praised in reviews, with little or no mention of her partner. Poor Doctor Watson, as sidekick to the great Sherlock, gets more attention than Fidelma's companion. Their creator, Peter Tremayne, himself seems to have little to say about Eadulf. In an interview with the Historical Novel Society's publication, *Solander*, he explains how the series came about. Umberto Ecco's *The Name of the Rose* had just come out and the Brother Cadfael series was taking off in sales. Tremayne was lecturing at Toronto University:

> After I had talked to the students about the role of women in Ireland, the ancient Irish law system, how women could be judges and lawyers and about the conflicts of the Irish, or what we now called the Celtic Church, and Rome, we adjourned across the campus to Dooley's Bar. One of the students, knowing that I wrote some fiction, said the subject of my lecture that day would made good background for a murder mystery in which the sleuth was a female Irish lawyer of the Celtic Church period [Cuthbertson].

Thus was Fidelma born of a few too many beers in a pub. He does not speak of Brother Eadulf, but he does go on to talk about the Celtic church and how clergy were allowed to marry — indeed, even the Roman clergy were allowed to marry until the eleventh century, well after Fidelma's time. There is also much talk in the series of a "soul mate," a person to whom one can bare one's thoughts and be met with understanding. There is no doubt that Eadulf plays this part. There is also no doubt that Eadulf falls in love with Fidelma and that Fidelma feels strong affection for him but is not "in love" with him. Fidelma loves The Law. Another example of role reversal, where a woman very often falls in love with a man while the man holds her in affection but not to the same degree, consumed as he is with his work.

As for children, don't even get me started on that. Sister Fidelma has to be the world's worst mother. As Philip Grosset notes in his review in *Clerical Detectives*, "The one person she never seems to spend much time with is her own son Alchú, but then he has a full-time nurse." A quick smooch and a hug for little Alchú and she's off on another adventure. One can just picture the teen-aged Alchú haranguing his mom with hands firmly planted on his hips: "Well you never loved me anyway! You were never there for me!" It's a good thing the kid has a loving nurse and an affectionate father. It's clearly Eadulf who can hardly wait to get back to see his little guy. Again, Eadulf plays the woman's role in child rearing, affectionate and nurturing, as is his nature.

It takes thirteen books into the series before Eadulf finally rebels against his role as second-hand man. In *The Leper's Bell* he lets it all out: "I was hereditary *gerefa*, magistrate, of the thane of Seaxmund's Ham. I have pride, Fidelma. I have self-esteem. I have the vanity of my race. It is sometimes hard for me to find myself here. I am a stranger in a strange land" (110).

He goes on to examine their marriage in this light, to the astonishment of Fidelma. "I cannot continue like this, Fidelma.... When we did not have any formal marriage between us, I did not feel the antipathy that I am now subjected to by the people who surround you. What I cannot understand is the way that your actions and attitude to me now seem to condone the antagonism that is ranged against me" (*Leper's Bell* 111). (A classic hissy-fit. Who gets along with their in-laws?)

Fidelma, of course, runs to the law books for her answer, for Eadulf is considered "a landless foreigner with restricted rights" (*Leper's Bell* 111). Heaven forbid she should run to her husband and throw her arms around him to console him. She does, however, come to examine her relationship with Eadulf and to realize: "She was not in love with him but something infinitely more real — she loved him and needed his companionship, wisdom and support. She had been looking for an *anam chara*, a soul friend, and she suddenly realized that there had been no need to look. What a fool she had been" (195).

Fidelma is prickly about her relationship with the young Saxon monk but even her brother, Colgú the king of Muman, has noticed her affection for Eadulf earlier in the series. In *Valley of the Shadow*, the sixth book, he teases her. "I simply observe that you have spent much time in the company of the Saxon. I see the way that you and he respond to each other. Am I not your brother and have no reason to be blind to such things?" (14–15). Colgú is more observant than is his sister, who blusters and protests that they are "just friends."

A prophecy of their future together is made at the end of the tenth book in the series, *Smoke in the Wind*. Eadulf asks Fidelma to explain the meaning of a ring he found in his piece of cake. Fidelma rather reluctantly tells him that the ring means whoever finds it will be shortly married, which news Eadulf receives with happiness. That's just fine with him. However, Fidelma has found a hazel nut in her piece of cake, which means she will never marry. Where does this contradiction leave the reader or the series?

Their relationship is further complicated in the next book, *The Haunted Abbot*, where they are engaged in a form of trial marriage and Sister Fidelma announces at the very end of the tale that she is expecting a baby. Thus the advent of little Alchú, who may well prove to be the turning point in their relationship.

Fidelma as Feminist

It should be noted that Sister Fidelma, a determined woman, is not the only strong woman on the medieval scene. Margaret Frazer, author of the Sister Frevisse series, writes in an author's note, "judging by intensive readings of documents & studies of late medieval England, there seems to have been a great many strong-minded, independent, capable women who took every advantage their world offered and made the most of it." Sister Fidelma, in an earlier time of Irish glory and independence for women, is certainly a strong woman and a feminist of the first order. It is heartening to know that she is not alone in her determination to bring law and order to the medieval frontier.

Besides Frazer's Sister Frevisse there is also Priscilla Royal's Prioress Eleanor, who solves puzzles much like Fidelma, has a high rank, and is very attracted to a handsome young man in her service. However, Prioress Eleanor has a much bigger problem with her man than Fidelma ever had or will have. Eleanor's love is doomed without her knowing why. Brother Thomas is gay.

However much a second fiddle Brother Eadulf plays in the series, not even his severest critic can call him homosexual. He likes women — Fidelma in particular, but he appreciates any pretty woman. Not that he flirts, but he is gallant in his own fashion.

Then there is Roberta Gelles' series featuring Magdalane la Batarde and her friend Sir Bellamy of Itchen. Magdalane solves mysteries while she runs a business, looks out for her dependents and romances two men at the same time. (Magdalane runs a whorehouse, but it's a respectable whorehouse authorized by the Bishop. Her "nuns" seem to be much nicer in disposition than the ones Fidelma has to deal with.)

In real life we have only to consider Eleanor of Aquitaine, whose strong character almost drove King Henry II insane. She was the mother of two kings, John and Richard the Lion-Hearted, and seems to have been a devoted mother. Eleanor was indefatigable in raising the funds to pay the ransom of Richard when he was captured on his way back from the Crusades. Fidelma lacks these motherly feelings. Not even her most devoted fan can accuse her of that. However, her sense of justice would ensure that she retrieve her lost son, as indeed she does in *The Leper's Bell*.

Fidelma's strong point is that her society allows her to be a staunch advocate for justice. Even without the advanced laws of her time, you just know she would stand up for the rights of the meek and the poor. She takes a back seat to no man, unless it be the High King of Tara. She openly questions the encroaching Church of Rome attitude towards women, which proclaims the subjugation of women to men. She regards Eadulf as a partner, even if she does sometimes run roughshod over his feelings. When asked to undertake an investigation she insists upon Eadulf's full participation in this work.

Fidelma is single-minded in pursuit of her career, which is to be an advocate of the courts. She is very good at her job. This sometimes interferes with her home life, which comes second to her career. This is a very contemporary situation that many women face.

Tremayne's saving grace as an author of historical mysteries is in his own words. "My characters can do nothing that is not consistent with the time, place and social system." Would that all writers of history would abide by that code. Tremayne is fortunate in that he chose a period in Celtic history when women's rights were contemporary with our own today. Sister Fidelma is a strong woman of action, with a logic that is calm and also deadly. No doubt that is why Brother Eadulf appears weak in comparison. If Fidelma can time-travel to our century and fit right in with contemporary women, Eadulf also reflects the dilemma of the modern male, once the breadwinner but now unsure of his role in society. One can argue that it is better to be weak and under the thrall of a bewitching red-headed woman than to be a muscle-bound, knuckle headed, booze-befuddled character like the detectives of today's cinema. *Hasta la vista, baby.*

WORKS CITED

Cuthbertson, Sarah. "The Fascination for Sister Fidelma." *Solander* 15 (Spring 2004). Historical Novel Society. May 2004. Web. 7 Nov. 2011. <http://www.historicalnovelsociety.org/solander/fidelma.htm>.

Frazer, Margaret. "Author's Note." *The Novice's Tale.* New York: Jove Books, 1992.

Grosset, Philip. "Sister Fidelma." *Clerical Detectives.* Web. 7 Nov. 2011. <http://detecs.org/fidelma.html>.

Nalle, David. "Book Reviews: The Sister Fidelma Mysteries." *Blogcritics Books.* <http://blogcritics.org/books/article/book-reviews-the-sister-fidelma-mysteries>.

Tremayne, Peter. *Absolution by Murder.* 1994. New York: Signet, 1997.

_____. *Badger's Moon.* 2003. New York: St. Martin's Minotaur, 2005.

_____. *The Chalice of Blood.* 2010. New York: St. Martin's Minotaur, 2011.

_____. *Dancing with Demons.* 2007. New York: St. Martin's Minotaur, 2008.

_____. *The Haunted Abbot.* 2002. New York: St. Martin's Minotaur, 2003.

_____. *The Leper's Bell.* 2004. New York: St. Martin's Minotaur, 2006.

_____. *A Prayer for the Damned.* 2006. New York: St. Martin's Minotaur, 2007.

_____. *Shroud for the Archbishop* 1995. New York: Signet, 1998.

_____. *Smoke in the Wind.* 2001. New York: St. Martin's Press, 2003.

_____. *The Subtle Serpent.* 1996. New York: St. Martin's Press, 1998.

_____. *Valley of the Shadow.* 1998. New York: Signet, 2001.

Yorkshire Evening Post Review. "What Critics Say About the Sister Fidelma Mysteries." *The International Sister Fidelma Society.* Web. <http://www.sisterfidelma.com/critics.html>.

The International Sister Fidelma Society

David Robert Wooten

The International Sister Fidelma Society sprang into existence at the end of 2001, providing a forum for fans of the popular historical crime series. The embryonic group had already begun life during the previous year. At that time, my business was based in Little Rock, Arkansas, and being a history major and graduate of the North Carolina State University — with a special interest in the ancient Irish Gaelic aristocracy — I was already very familiar with the nonfiction works of Peter Berresford Ellis, a Celtic scholar and historian who also specialized in the selfsame field. I had come into personal contact with him while including some of his academic essays in publications I was then editing. It took me a few years to realize that Peter Berresford Ellis was also Peter Tremayne, author of the seventh-century crime mysteries featuring Sister Fidelma — a fact unrealized by many of his readers to this day. By this time the books were becoming international bestsellers. I pointed out to Peter that, when exploring the Internet, I was astonished to discover there was no website devoted to his creation. I asked his permission to set up such a site as a resource for his ever-expanding fan base.

Within a short time of the website's inception in 2000, the site's guestbook began to receive queries about the establishment of a society, a forum through which people could join and exchange views about the series, as well as hear news about the publications and the author. Eventually, I set up a survey on-site to determine just how many readers would join such an organization. The response was overwhelming. I approached Peter again, asking his permission to establish the group. Furthermore, I asked him if he would become the organization's patron. He acquiesced to both requests, and by the end of 2001 I announced the creation of the simply, but appropriately, titled International Sister Fidelma Society.

It was an exciting period as I watched those first applications for membership coming in from various countries. We were able to launch the first issue of *The Brehon*, the Society journal, dated February, 2002. I had decided that, while the website was free to everyone, members would receive this print magazine three times a year. Apart from that first issue, we have produced it in January, May, and September. The journal consists of twenty pages of text and photographs. Initially, this was entirely in black and white, but as we expanded readership, we were able to use color covers starting with the May, 2007, issue. Under our title banner I put a quote from the semi-legendary Brehon Morann—"*Mór í an fhirrinne, agus buiadhfe sí* ... truth is great and will prevail." We felt this slogan would be very appropriate because of its relevance in the stories.

The moderate membership fee also covered the cost of administration, running the website, answering queries, and a plethora of other things necessary to maintain such an organization. Indeed, as the Society progressed, we were able to produce other related publications, posters, calendars, and items ranging from mugs to t-shirts, linking in with the retailer CafePress to provide oft-requested merchandise which our members could access and buy via the website.

Looking back at that first issue, it is interesting to see that we included short pieces from internationally known anthologists and writers such as Peter Haining (1940–2007), who wrote his memory on "The Naming of Sister Fidelma." Mike Ashley, the leading biographer, anthologist, and historian, wrote on "The Dawn of Fidelma." Both these editors and authors had been among the first to recognize that Fidelma was a new and exciting creation. We also reprinted an article by Peter Tremayne entitled "An Author's Cares" from the winter 1992 issue of the UK magazine *The Author*. We initiated a letters page, "Readerspeak," but had not yet progressed to "Editorspeak," wherein I could "sound off" in each issue. The first such editorial appeared in the May 2002 edition and then became a permanent column in the magazine.

Our inaugural back cover was a reproduction of one of the pages drawn by the UK artist Art Wetherell, originally destined for a proposed graphic novel based on a Fidelma story—truly great artwork. Sadly, Art Wetherell died of a heart attack on Christmas Day 2003, leaving this project uncompleted. Our back cover spot was subsequently devoted to reprinting the latest covers of Fidelma titles spanning the globe.

Member response was gratifying, and the Society started to attract a worldwide loyal following. During the second year members not only started to send in letters for "Readerspeak" but submit articles as well.

What sort of people joined/join the Society? All types. Although, I confess, our demographic is weighted toward a preponderance of lawyers, teachers and college professors, academics, librarians, writers, elected officials, and priests of many religious sects (from Catholics to Anglicans to nonconformists, and even a member of a Hindu religious community). They all come together, sharing their fascination for the Sister Fidelma stories and the background of same. Some of Fidelma's translators (into such languages as Portuguese, French, German, Dutch, Spanish, Italian, Russian, Greek, Estonian, and Polish, to name but a few) have even joined, such as Professor Marie Kai, who translates the books and stories into Japanese.

Of necessity, the *lingua franca* of the Society is English. We have delved into making the website more internationally friendly, including computer-aided online translation services (limited as they may be), as well as links where specific queries can be submitted in German and Dutch; at times, individual members help out when letters come to us addressed in several other languages. However, through the years, the membership has regularly been two-thirds USA/UK-based, and one-third from all other countries. We soon discovered that the Fidelma series had reached cult status in Germany and France, and we did our best to form active "chapters" of the Society there (as well as in other countries). While we have regularly retained "keen" individual members, some nations have not provided as many enthusiastic "joiners" of fan societies as the USA. *The Brehon* and website still use English as the primary medium.

It soon became apparent that our modest journal, *The Brehon*, was attracting some quality writer-contributors. One of the first academic analytical pieces came from Dr. Michelle Klingfus, then at the University of Northern Iowa, who wrote a two-part analysis of the books entitled "Finding Fidelma: History Within the Mystery." These appeared in the January and May issues of 2003. In May 2004, my current co-editor, Professor Edward J. Rielly, published an article on Fidelma — "A Woman for All Seasons." Another of our current contributors, Dr. John Scaggs, then at Limerick University, contributed "Mystery and Detection in the Sister Fidelma Novels" in the September 2005 issue. Even Celtic scholars added their analyses, including Dr. Andrew Breeze, of the University of Pamplona, Navarre, in Spain. He singled out one title, writing "*Smoke in the Wind*: Historical and Cultural Links of Ireland and Wales in the 7th Century" for the May 2007 issue.

Fidelma also caught the eye of several members of the legal profession. In our January 2005 and May 2005 issues, a distinguished attorney, Wallace Johnson, a prosecutor in the U.S. Department of Justice and a former special assistant to the President of the United States advising on legislation, wrote a two-part article on Brehon law. Mr. Johnson had been so intrigued by the Sister Fidelma stories that he had taken a sabbatical from his law practice. He went to University College Cork in Ireland to study Brehon Law and was able to share his knowledge with our readership. Another criminal defense attorney who joined the Society was Joe Scalzo, Jr., of Toledo, Ohio, a junior partner in the local law firm of Scalzo and Geller, who also taught law at the University of Toledo. Mr. Scalzo actually introduced the Fidelma stories into his classes, comparing modern U.S. criminal law and Brehon Law. He contributed an intriguing article on "Sister Fidelma and Modern Criminal Law" to *The Brehon* in May 2007. New Orleans lawyer Patrick O'Keefe, an honorary life member of the Dublin Solicitors' Bar Association, actually wrote a lengthy article on Fidelma in *The Federal Lawyer,* the journal of the U.S. Federal Bar Association, also in May 2007. *The Brehon* received permission to reprint this in its September 2007 issue.

A rather pleasant surprise came when the President of the Supreme Court of Argentina, Dr. Enrique Petracchi, made a speech in praise of seventh-century Brehon Law, prompting Fidelma's Argentine publisher, Maggie Tolderlund, of Peuco Editores, to write a piece for *The Brehon* quoting the speech in the September 2006 issue. And we had many regular contributors, like the late Maurice McCann (1938–2011), an Irish member with degrees in history, who wrote articles for us.

The Society not only attracted academics who contributed to *The Brehon*, but one of our English members, Peter Breheny, taking his degree in literature, decided to use the Sister Fidelma Mysteries as the subject of his dissertation and was successful in gaining his degree.

Since the second year of the Society's existence, many of our members suggested that the Society should organize a Fidelma convention, inviting the author to appear. Two-thirds of our membership was then based in the United States. Despite this, however, many members suggested that the logical place to hold such a gathering was in Fidelma's "hometown"—Cashel, in County Tipperary, Ireland. At the time, we felt there might be logistical problems with such a venue. As we considered the situation, fate, as they say, lent a hand.

Peter Tremayne had been invited to officially open the Cashel Arts Fest in November 2004. The organizers had realized that international tourists to Cashel had increased, with people eager to see where Fidelma came from, as well as the sites associated with her in the books. Therefore, not only was Peter asked to open the festival, but he was welcomed to Cashel Town Hall, where the mayor and town council unanimously voted him a civic reception and presentation—the highest accolade the town could bestow. The then Mayor of Cashel, Councillor Tom Wood, made the presentation.

Peter had also been asked to speak about Fidelma in the scenic setting of the fifteenth-century Vicar's Choral on The Rock of Cashel itself. At the end of the talk, Seamus King, a local author and broadcaster, proposed a vote of thanks, putting forward the suggestion that the town ought to hold a regular Fidelma gathering. *The Brehon* reported the possibility in its January 2005 issue. Shortly thereafter we were contacted by Seamus, on behalf of the Cashel Arts Fest committee, asking if we could help with the promotion of what would be called a Féile Fidelma in 2006. A *féile*, in Irish, is a festival or gathering. The history of the Féile will be found within this volume.

As its contribution, the Society undertook the production of a Féile Fidelma program booklet. To defray expenses of production, businesses in Cashel, as well as many of the Sister Fidelma publishers, took advertising in the booklet. For example, the 2010 Féile program booklet was 40 pages, plus a 4-page, full-color cover. Every Féile program started off with an official welcome to the town by the current mayor, as well as by the chairman of the South Tipperary Council. These program booklets—for 2006, 2008, and 2010—have become much sought after collector's items.

One interesting offshoot of the Féile was that one of our Cashel members, Olivia Quinlan, manager of the Cashel Heritage Centre, decided to relaunch her guesthouse as Bruden Fidelma—Sister Fidelma's Guesthouse. Naturally, this was done with the permission and participation of the author, who officially cut the tape to open the guesthouse in 2006. The rooms were named after characters in the books and decorated in keeping with the stories. Olivia even offered guests a seventh-century Irish organic breakfast, in keeping with the atmosphere. Fidelma's Guesthouse now acts as the official home of the International Sister Fidelma Society in Ireland.

Cashel certainly took Fidelma to heart, and on St. Patrick's Day, March 17, 2007, Ireland's national day, the town chose Sister Fidelma (in the person of local actress Fiona Hallissey) and Brother Eadulf (as portrayed by Tom Shanahan) to lead their St. Patrick's Day Parade on horseback through the town. Sister Fidelma was the "Grand Marshall" of the parade.

The Society also began to produce color maps of "Fidelma's World," with an indication of all the locations relating to the various books.

Dr. Gearóid Ó Laoi from Cork pointed out that no Fidelma story had ever appeared in her native language—Irish. Dr. Ó Laoi promptly translated the short story "A Scream from the Sepulcher," and, after some discussion with the author, the Society published it in booklet form in 2008 as *Screach ón Tuama*. Fidelma's Argentine publisher, Maggie Tolderlund, provided the superb artwork for the booklet, I contributed a foreword, and some of the critics' comments were included, with a list of the series to date. The prize-winning Irish language novelist Anna Heussaff believed it to be one of the best Irish-language fiction publications produced, and went on to write an analytical piece in *Comhar* (October 2010) berating Irish-language publishers for not issuing the series in Irish.

The same year, 2008, we were receiving mail from not only our members, but also from visitors to Cashel, with the complaint that, when they visited The Rock of Cashel, the guides dwelt solely on the surviving Norman ecclesiastical buildings — the only surviving buildings on the Rock. No one was mentioning that this was the site of the Eóghanacht Kings of Munster, from the third century, who were, of course, Fidelma's family. I approached Peter and asked him if he could write some short guide on the subject for our membership. Peter not only produced an essay but a fairly composite account, citing early texts. We published it in 2008 as *Sister Fidelma's Cashel: the Early Kings of Munster and their Capital.* I contributed a short introduction, the book carried illustrations, and Cashel Heritage Centre became the principal sales outlet.

We want our members to be as active as possible, and we encourage them to set up reading groups at their local libraries. We also set up a Sister Fidelma Yahoo Discussion Group, with one of our long time members, Mairéad Reidy, as the interlocutor. We enjoy a close contact with our patron, the author, and when, as sometimes happens, we cannot provide answers to the questions that come into us, the author is always willing to help us out. We try to keep abreast of matters relating to the books and their author, especially keeping watch over any misinformation about them that appears on websites, or elsewhere.

The Sister Fidelma Mysteries were taking us into a world that very few of us knew anything about. Even the author, in some of his early historical forewords to his books, admitted that few people knew about this world outside of the Celtic Studies departments of universities. Indeed, we began to receive a lot of inquiries about the background to the books. We began to receive some letters asking if the author had invented the Brehon Law system. We decided to put a "Frequently Asked Questions (FAQs)" page on the website where the facts could be detailed. Perhaps it was because of the publicity engendered by Fidelma that, in 2004, The Law Society of Ireland established a conference: "Brehon Law in Modern Times: A 21st Century Perspective on 7th Century Irish Law." Certainly, few people can argue that the ancient Irish law system had become popular through the pages of the Fidelma Mysteries.

Where does the Society go from here?

We frequently ask our members for feedback and input, and certainly members are not lacking in ideas. Some, sadly, are impractical because of finances. Others we have put on the shelf for future consideration. For example, in *The Brehon*, September, 2008, one of our German members suggested that the Society start to campaign for an archive of all the author's works. Another suggestion was that we should try to persuade Saxmundham, in Suffolk, England, to hold a similar function to Cashel in celebration of their famous fictional son, Brother Eadulf. This was outlined in the January 2011 issue of *The Brehon*.

The author is still writing Fidelma Mysteries, and *Atonement of Blood* (2013) will be the twenty-second novel in the series. There are two volumes of short stories already published, and several uncollected short stories, including a novelette.

One development that might lead to a new impetus and horizon for the Society would be if the series were translated to film or television. Members constantly contact the Society to see if this is a possibility.

At this time The International Sister Fidelma Society continues under the patronage of the author, and it continues to see itself as a forum for the enthusiasts of the series. Indeed, we find that those interested in other works of the author, especially his nonfiction works, also contact or join us. We are, however, basically a literary society, a society of enthusiasts whose prime interest is the Sister Fidelma Mysteries. That is our *raison d'être*. We are neither an academic nor a "pseudo-academic" group, nor are we a propagandist group for any particular set of beliefs, religious or political. We are simply people from all walks of life, and from all countries, who enjoy what we believe to be one of the best historical mysteries series currently being written.

Féile Fidelma:
Its Origins and History

Seamus J. King

Féile Fidelma, a literary weekend devoted to the fictional works of Peter Tremayne, has been held biennially at Cashel since 2006.

When the idea was first mooted, finding a name for such an event was one of the early considerations. No fewer than sixty "summer schools" are held in Ireland during the year, most of them devoted to historical, literary, and musical figures. They are usually held over the summer but the Sister Fidelma weekend was outside the season, so a different name had to be found. Eventually "Féile Fidelma" was decided on, which means something equivalent to "a festival devoted to Fidelma," even though it isn't strictly a festival! But the name sounded good and the alliteration was important.

The aim of the weekend was to explore the world of the Fidelma mysteries, the series of murder stories based in seventh-century Ireland written by Peter Berresford Ellis under the pseudonym Peter Tremayne. Since the main character in the mysteries was Sister Fidelma, who resided on the Rock of Cashel with her brother, King Colgú, and set out from there to solve the murder mysteries, Cashel was the appropriate place for such a weekend.

Genesis of Idea

The idea of holding a literary weekend devoted to the fictional works of Peter Tremayne originated with the Cashel Arts Festival, which was set up in April 2003, on the instigation of Cashel Heritage Trust. The aim of the festival was to emphasize the maximum involvement of the community in the development of an arts festival. Such a festival would become a catalyst for the general development of the arts in Cashel.

The first Cashel Arts festival ran November 13–15, 2003, and was a big success. It provided a series of platforms and opportunities for all sections of the community to engage with the arts in a meaningful and enjoyable way. There were also two major concerts. The official opening of the festival was carried out by Seán Donlon, Chancellor of the University of Limerick and former Irish Ambassador to Washington. In the course of his remarks he spoke of the role of communities in Ireland in the promotion of the arts and how they have acted as catalysts for developments in the arts.

The organizing committee was extremely happy with its first festival and immediately set about organizing a more extensive one for 2004. There was agreement that the choice of Sean Donlon to open the 2003 festival was an inspired one and his presence had added prestige to the event. It was agreed that the choice of person to open the second festival should to be equally inspired.

Peter Tremayne had a long association with Cashel as a visitor. He recalled that as a small boy his father, who was from Cork City, had told him that Cashel was once the ancient capital of the kingdom of Munster. Peter had, in fact, given a talk to the Cashel Writers Circle at the Cashel Palace Hotel in 1997 about his Sister Fidelma novels. As an Arts Fest Committee member, I had read and reviewed, for the local newspapers, a number of his mystery novels and believed he fitted the bill as the right choice to open the 2004 festival. He had recently opened the Rosscarbery Arts and Literature Weekend in West Cork (*Southern Star* 6 May 2000). Peter was contacted by the secretary of the committee, Emily Kirwan, and agreed to come to Cashel on November 11, 2004, to open the second Cashel Arts Festival. He also agreed to give a talk on the Sister Fidelma mysteries and to hold a workshop on creative writing during his visit.

Mayor Tom Wood of Cashel and the Cashel Town Council were unanimous in affording Peter a civic welcome on the evening following the official opening. In his remarks, Mayor Wood referred to the writer's speech when he opened the Cashel Arts Festival. In the course of that speech Peter referred to the rich literary heritage that was Cashel's. According to the Mayor we may have concentrated too much on our second millennium history, and the exploration of the literary heritage of the first millennium might now be a fruitful exercise. He congratulated the author on bringing that earlier millennium alive for us through his novels in the Sister Fidelma mysteries and presented the writer with a bronze piece of Celtic design (*The Nationalist* 20 Nov. 2004).

Following the civic welcome Peter then gave a talk on the Fidelma mysteries and their location in Cashel in the hall of the Vicar's Choral on the Rock of Cashel. The meeting was chaired by Seamus J. King, and during question time following the talk he suggested that a gathering of fans of Sister

Fidelma at Cashel might be considered for the future. There was an enthusiastic response to the suggestion ("Cashel Arts Festival Opened by Peter Tremayne").

During the following spring there was serious consideration given to the suggestion that some kind of literary weekend be organized. Correspondence was started with Peter. He agreed with the idea, but was of the opinion that plenty of time should be allowed to organize it. Following discussions it was agreed to hold the event in 2006. The Cashel Arts Fest members were of the opinion that any event that was organized would be under their aegis. Initially a date in November was proposed to coincide with the Arts Fest. There were second thoughts that the time of year might have a detrimental effect on the number of participants. May and September were considered as being before and after the tourist season when costs might be lower. Eventually early September was agreed on, with the dates from the 7th to the 9th.

The format of the weekend was set. There were to be seven lectures, commencing with an opening talk by the author on Friday evening, followed by three lectures on Saturday morning and a further three on Sunday morning. Peter provided hands-on assistance in this area, advising on a top range of speakers to ensure the prestige of the event. A coach trip between Cashel and Emly to places associated with the mysteries between Cashel and Emly was planned, as was a gala dinner on Saturday night. The name of the weekend was to be the Féile Fidelma. A registration fee of US$150 for participants was established. It was recognized that the registration fee might not cover all the costs of the weekend and that some extra funding could be required, so an application was made to LEADER, a funding body for local initiatives, which came on board with a promise of financial help for the event.

Once the date and the format were agreed on, Féile Fidelma had to be publicized. The Cashel Arts Fest got outstanding help in this area from David Robert Wooten, Director of the International Sister Fidelma Society and editor of his print journal *The Brehon*. David was added to the organizing committee to advise on the Féile and help promote the event to his membership.

Booking for the weekend was opened on the Cashel Arts Fest website with the incentive of a ten percent reduction in the registration cost for all bookings completed by May 1, 2006. The target number of registrations was achieved. Participants came from ten different countries including Argentina, Brazil, Germany, Spain, The Netherlands, Canada, United States, England and Ireland. A magnificent 32-page program booklet, supported by advertising from Fidelma publishers and local businesses, was edited and produced by David Wooten and his Society. This became not only a souvenir but is now a sought-after collector's item.

Eventually the dates of the first Féile Fidelma arrived and there was a certain amount of trepidation that the event would not be a success. The Cashel Palace Hotel, designed by Sir Edward Lovett Pearce and built in 1730 as a residence for the Archbishops of Cashel, was considered the best venue for the event. It's a beautiful building, small and intimate, and the participants were thrown together much more than they would be in a bigger, modern establishment. The bar, which is a vital part of any Irish get-together, is in the basement and not very large. People are in intimate surroundings in a small space and the place is fortunate to have an extraordinary barman, Denis Heffernan. He leaves his place of work behind the bar occasionally in order to break into song, and he has a fine voice and a good repertoire as well. In fact, he has also written a song, "Cashel: My Hometown," which has been recorded. Denis is a huge attraction in the hotel and did much to bring the Fidelma group even more together.

Even Peter himself was excited and described the event as "One of the greatest and most memorable experiences in a writing career stretching back nearly forty years. That is my assessment of the Féile Fidelma 2006! And my wife, Dorothy, has summed it up as 'a magical weekend.' We traveled to Cashel, a town we know so very well, on Thursday evening with my nephew, Paul. We arrived in some anticipation, as we had no idea how the Féile would turn out. Our old friend, Seamus King, met us and we went for a meal to discuss the weekend programme" (Remarks on The International Sister Fidelma Society website, about the Féile Fidelma, 2006).

Before the official opening, the new Mayor of Cashel, Councillor Patrick Downey, invited the organizers and main speakers to join him in a small reception in the Town Hall. Then we headed for the Cashel Palace where the Féile was officially opened by the Mayor, together with Councillor John Fahey, Vice-Chairman of the South Tipperary County Council. John Murray, the chairman of the Cashel Arts Fest, also welcomed those attending.

Peter gave the introductory talk on "Fidelma's World," and there could have been no better person to introduce the proceedings. He was introduced and his talk chaired by John Murray, with other Arts Fest Committee members introducing the remaining speakers. The Fidelma mysteries are part of the genre of crime fiction, and Dr. John Scaggs, then of Mary Immaculate College, Limerick University, was drafted to speak of the impact of Sister Fidelma on Irish Crime Fiction. Dr. Andrew Breeze of the University of Navarra, Spain, addressed the links between the cultures of the kingdoms of Ireland and Dyfed in Wales, as reflected in the Fidelma adventure, *Smoke in the Wind*. Dr. Dan McCarthy of Trinity College, Dublin, Ireland, an authority on astronomy and chronology in the ancient Irish annals and chronicles, spoke about how closely the knowledge of the annals has been substantiated by modern scientific investigations. Professor Máirín Ni Dhonnchadha, of University College, Galway, Ireland, spoke of a seventh-century love tale of Liadan and Cuirither, which parallels the story of Fidelma and Eadulf in the mysteries. As the mysteries had then been translated into thirteen languages, it was only appropriate to hear from someone in the area of translation. Hans van den Boom, the Dutch translator and publisher of the books, therefore had been invited to speak.. Finally, the person who had done more than anyone to publicize the Fidelma mysteries, David Wooten, spoke about the role of The International Sister Fidelma Society and its future (*The Nationalist*, 16 Sept. 2006; *The Tipperary Star*, 16 Sept. 2006).

There was an extra event which many of the participants attended. Cashel businesswoman Olivia Quinlan, in agreement with the author, redecorated her Georgian guesthouse in John Street, Cashel, and renamed it Bruden Fidelma: The Sister Fidelma Guesthouse. All the rooms were decorated with Fidelma themes and given names of characters from the books. Outside was displayed a magnificent illustrated sign giving details about Fidelma. Peter officially cut the ribbon to open the guesthouse, with guests welcomed by Ann and Philip Ryan dressed as Fidelma and Eadulf. There was a reception for guests afterwards (*The Tipperary Star*, 16 Sept. 2006).

On Saturday afternoon, participants boarded a coach to be driven to Emly (Imleach Iubhair), which today is just a little village but which in Fidelma's time was the site of the great abbey and cathedral of St. Ailbe, a pre–Patrician saint who brought Christianity to southwest Ireland. It also was the location of Peter's novel *The Monk Who Vanished*. The ancient abbey buildings were replaced in the thirteenth century by a cathedral which was destroyed in the Tudor Conquest at a time when Emly was still a "Cathedral city." A church was rebuilt there and today is worth a visit for its fine stained glass windows, one of which commemorates the famous King-Bishop of Cashel, Cormac Mac Cuileanáin (A.D. 836–908), who was also a poet and lexicographer. Peter came on the coach to explain some of the history and connection with Fidelma.

One of the social highlights of the weekend was the Féile dinner on Saturday. This was a most enjoyable event, and the enjoyment was reflected in the way the decibel level of the conversation rose as the meal progressed. Peter Tremayne added to the enjoyment with an entertaining after dinner speech. There was a late night for some afterwards in the bar. This social aspect of the weekend had its own importance. It provided the opportunity for networking and establishing Fidelma contacts. Such a good rapport was built up among the participants that many returned for the second Féile Fidelma two years later. A photograph of the group was taken and contact details exchanged.

Initial reactions to the weekend were very positive. The variety of participants from so many countries added to the international flavor of the event and reflected the worldwide appeal of "Fidelmania," an expression coined by the French literary journal *Livres Hebdo*. The quality of the lectures was of such a high standard that nobody could have been displeased with the weekend. The accessibility and affability of the author made a huge impact on the participants. The smallness of the town of Cashel gave an intimacy and cohesion to the event that helped make it special. One of the important matters discussed before the Féile ended was the possibility of holding a second weekend. The consensus appeared to be that there had to be another one at some time in the future, and that Cashel, Fidelma's "hometown," is the only place to hold it.

The Cashel Arts Fest Committee didn't have much difficulty in deciding to hold a second Féile Fidelma. I was more than willing to do the organizational work once again. The funding that had been received from LEADER had helped to defray the costs and there was even a small surplus. It was agreed that September had been a satisfactory time to hold such a weekend and it was decided to hold it between the 5th and 7th of September, 2008. The general consensus was that two years should elapse between events. It was agreed that the format used in the first Féile Fidelma was a satisfactory one and should be followed again with one exception. It was decided to do away with the coach trip on the Saturday afternoon as it took too much time, which could be spent with better results exploring Cashel, shopping, or just relaxing.

Cashel had certainly taken Sister Fidelma to its heart, and when the town was planning its celebration of St. Patrick's Day in 2007, it was agreed that there was only person to lead the parade as Grand Marshall — Sister Fidelma (*Tipperary Star*, 17 Feb. 2007). Local actress Fiona Hallissey took the part of Sister Fidelma, with Tom Shanahan as Brother Eadulf. They led the parade through the town on horseback, followed by a motorized unit of the Irish Army, and then floats from many organizations (*The Nationalist*, 24 March 2007).

The second Féile Fidelma was held in the Horse & Jockey Hotel on September 5–7, 2008. Situated eight miles north of Cashel, the hotel was chosen as the venue for the weekend because of the unavailability of the Cashel Palace Hotel. It turned out to be a very suitable alternative with plenty of facilities, a friendly staff, and good food and drink. Many of those who had attended the first Féile Fidelma registered for this one, and there was increased participation. Even more countries were represented, such as Sweden and France (*Tipperary Star*, 12 Jan. 2008, 5 Aug. 2008; *Irish World*, 5 April 2008).

Delegates were welcomed by the Mayor of Cashel, who at this time was

Councillor Martin Browne, and the chairman of the Cashel Arts Fest, John Murray, and, again, I was "master of ceremonies" ("Féile Fidelma 2008 — A Great Success"). The first talk of the weekend was given on the topic "An Author's Cares" by Peter. This was an informative and witty presentation on the trials and tribulations of being a writer and the difficulties he encounters in the course of his work. Peter held his audience spellbound for the hour and was delighted to answer their many queries afterwards. In fact, he proved then and over the course of the weekend that he is the most accessible of authors, spending much time talking to his readers, signing their books, and, on the Monday evening after the weekend, meeting his fans in the local library for another session.

Saturday introduced us to the heavier academic contributions of the weekend. Dr. Dagmar Ó Riain-Raedal, of University College, Cork, opened proceedings with a talk entitled "In the Sign of the Cross: The Secret History of the Rock of Cashel." Dr. O Riain-Raedal knows more about the Rock of Cashel than anyone in existence, having made it her life study, and she imparted her wonderful erudition with a leavening of dry humor.

Professor Dáibhí Ó Cróinín, of the National University, Galway, was the next to take the podium, and his topic provided the shortest title of the weekend, "AD 664." And what was the significance of that year? It was the year the Fidelma mysteries began with the setting of the first novel, *Absolution by Murder*, in which the Abbess Étain, a leading speaker for the Celtic Church, is found murdered in suspicious circumstances. Professor Ó Cróinín expounded on the significance of the year which saw the Synod of Whitby, where the murder took place, a major eclipse of the sun, and a plague as well. He pointed out that the reference to the timing of the eclipse had been given correctly in Peter's novel in spite of incorrect information given by the Venerable Bede. In fact, it was the Irish annals that had been more precise and accurate. Professor Ó Cróinín is, in fact, Ireland's expert on this period.

The third and final talk of the day was completely different, devoted to the musical instruments of prehistoric Ireland right down to the time of Fidelma. Simon and Maria O'Dwyer, from Galway, are an amazing couple who have made a study of these ancient instruments from archaeological remains as well as from paintings and engravings. Their study hasn't stopped there but they have reconstructed many of these instruments and were able to illustrate their talk by showing examples of them. Their real tour de force was to be able to play them as well, filling the theatre with ancient sounds and introducing us to the kind of music Fidelma would have listened to as she enjoyed her meal after a busy day.

Saturday evening was the occasion of the Féile dinner. This was a high point of the weekend. The bonding that had taken place up to then was firmed up as the participants ate and drank together in a convivial atmosphere. Everyone was welcomed by me, and the grace was said in Swedish by Ulla Trenter, the Swedish translator of Fidelma. John Murray proposed the toast to "Our Guests" on behalf of the Cashel Arts Fest, and Peter Tremayne suitably replied with a witty presentation.

The Sister Fidelma mysteries have made a huge impact in Germany, and Dr. Karola Hagemann gave the first talk on Sunday morning to examine why they had become so popular. Karola is part of a writing duo in Germany under the name "Malachy Hyde" and has published a series of historical mystery books featuring Silvianus Rhodius, a detective in Anatolia in the time of Mark Antony. She analyzed the reasons why novels based in Celtic Ireland should make such an impact in her country. According to her, one of the features of the novels that attracts the Germans is the wonderful open log fire that is a part of Fidelma's home on the Rock of Cashel and at which she unwinds with a mug of ale after a difficult day. According to Dr. Hagemann, all Germans dream of an open fire!

Morgan Llewelyn is Ireland's bestselling contemporary historical novelist, and her work has appeared in twenty-seven languages. Like Fidelma, she loves the countryside and is an expert horsewoman. Her talk was "Novelising Ireland." What better speaker for the task? In fact, contemporaneously with her appearance at the Féile Fidelma weekend was the publication of her latest book, on St. Brendan. She spoke of the importance of myth and how all myth is based upon some fact. She regaled us with stories of the lengths to which she has gone in researching her novels and the meticulous care with which she develops her plots. In addition, she has written in praise of the Sister Fidelma books and their historical background.

Last, but by no means least, was David Wooten, whose contribution to the success of the second Féile Fidelma was outstanding. As the director of the International Sister Fidelma Society, he had publicized the event over the past twelve months, exhorted members to travel to Cashel, kept people informed of what was going on, and did all in his power to publicize the Sr. Fidelma novels. He spoke about the Society, what work it does, and where it is going.

One of David's major contributions to the weekend was the production of the program booklet for the event. This time it was in full color with thirty-six pages plus cover, and lavishly illustrated, containing all the information required by those who attended the weekend. As well as the program, it included biographical notes on the speakers, welcome pieces by the Mayor, the Cashel Arts Fest Committee, and, of course, Peter and David Wooten. The booklet also contained the text of the talk given by Dr. John Scaggs at the first Féile Fidelma, "The Impact of Sister Fidelma on Irish Crime Fiction."

This publication is a collector's item and a valuable companion to a similar booklet produced by David for the first Féile Fidelma.

When the participants begun to disperse there was a distinct end-of-term feeling. Much was learned over the weekend, acquaintances were renewed, friendships were begun, and there was a feeling of general satisfaction that the visit was worthwhile. There was talk of a third Féile Fidelma in 2010 and even a suggestion that it might be held in the USA because of the big American following, but most people agreed that it would be difficult to take it away from Cashel with the city's many associations and historical resonances. Cashel, after all, was Fidelma's hometown.

The dates for the next Féile were fixed for September 10–12, 2010. One of the observations the organizers made from the two former weekends was that the event had become somewhat detached from the townsfolk. This was mainly because Peter had accepted invitations from the Cashel Library to talk after the Féile in the library at a free event, funded by the library. Local people had decided to attend that event rather than pay the registration fee to take part in the Féile itself. Peter decided to forego the library appearance in 2010, and local people were to be involved by introducing two changes to the weekend program. The first of these was the involvement of the local Choral and Dramatic Society in the dramatization of one of Peter Tremayne's short stories, "Invitation to a Poisoning." The second was an extensive tour of the town open to the townspeople and participants alike by local archaeologist Joanne Hughes.

The Cashel Arts Fest Committee and the International Fidelma Society had initial reservations about organizing the 2010 festival, given that the world economic state had deteriorated so much since the last Féile held in 2008. They set a target of a minimum number of registrations and were delighted with the response. The Fidelma fans are loyal but there were also many new faces. Once again, David and the Society produced a forty-page program booklet in full color, which included a short story, "Finbarr's Bell," which has once again made the program a collector's item for Fidelma's fans.

This Féile was officially opened by Dr. Seán McCarthy, the chairman of South Tipperary Council, who apologized for the absence of the Mayor of Cashel who had been called away to a business conference. The chairperson of the Cashel Arts Fest, Petronella Clifton-Brown, and I, as coordinator and master of ceremonies once again, also welcomed participants, as did Peter. After the reception, the evening opened with a new development, "An Evening with Peter Tremayne," a question and answer session chaired by David Wooten. David had collated all the questions beforehand from members of the Society, and Peter answered them, with the session proving a great success (*The Nationalist*, 16 Sept. 2010).

The weekend always includes a substantial academic input and 2010 was no exception. Professor Padraig Ó Riain of University College, Cork, one of the leading experts on the Fidelma period, spoke of the Psalter of Cashel. A most erudite man, he also revealed that he is no musty intellectual but an excellent communicator who made difficult academic information accessible to all. This was followed by a totally contrasting presentation. Irish actress Caroline Lennon is well known, having played the character of Siobhán in the BBC Radio's long running series *The Archers* for nine years. She also reads the Sister Fidelma mysteries on Audio Books. Her talk, on the experience of "Reading Sister Fidelma," made a big impact, probably fitting one's image of what the main character in the novels was like! Peter has declared that Caroline is his favorite reader of the stories.

Caroline also had a part to play in the next item on the program, a dramatized reading of Peter's short story "Invitation to a Poisoning" directed by the well-known Irish playwright and director Neil Donnelly (*Irish Independent*, 21 Aug. 2010). This new dimension to the weekend was well received by the audience. Seven actors were drafted in from the local drama group, Cashel Choral and Dramatic Society, to do a rehearsed reading, with Caroline playing the part of Sister Fidelma. Neil Donnelly brought them to a level of perfection, which was amazing in such a short time. Everyone enjoyed the production, and the general consensus was that such a production ought to be part of future programming.

In the afternoon the participants were invited to join local archaeologist Dr. Joanne Hughes, who concentrated more on the history of the town after the English settled, with an emphasis on the eighteenth century. Peter stepped in on Sunday afternoon and took a group to The Rock of Cashel. He was allowed to conduct his own guided tour of Fidelma's town and what it had been like in her day. One of the highlights of the weekend was the gala dinner, and, once again, Peter did not fail to have the audience in gales of laughter with his after-dinner speech about the problems facing a writer.

Sunday morning began with a talk by Irish-language novelist Anna Heussaff, who has won awards for her own mystery novels in Irish. She spoke about the problems facing the Irish language today and the difficulties and attitudes which beset Irish-language publishers. She believed that the Fidelma mysteries should appear in Irish but, in fact, The International Sister Fidelma Society, in response to queries from Irish fans, had published in 2008 its own booklet with a Fidelma tale in Irish. This was *Screach ón Tuama (A Scream from the Sepulcher)*, translated by Society member D Gearóid Ó Laoi.

The next speaker was to be the Italian editor of the Fidelma books talking about their popularity in Italy. At the last minute, he was unable to attend due to business reasons, and so three of the Fidelma translators, being in attendance, formed a panel to speak about the problems of translating the Fidelma books. These were Ulla Trenter Palm of Sweden, Hans van den Boom of the Netherlands, and Maggie Tolderlund of Argentina. Their contributions were well received, with audience participation, and the organizers felt they could inspire future talks! Once again the talks ended with David of The International Sister Fidelma Society, who brought the audience up to date concerning the Society. David does an amazing job running the Society website and editing and publishing the Society journal, *The Brehon*, which appears unfailingly three times a year and is twenty pages long, with a color cover. He also deals with the numerous questions that come into the Society from all parts of the world and keeps people informed about the world of Fidelma and the progress of the novels.

Fourth Féile Fidelma

Before the formal events were concluded, the question was raised about holding a fourth Féile Fidelma in 2012. Once again the response was positive, and once again it was decided that it should take place in Cashel. The plans were set in place at the start of 2012 and various speakers expressed their willingness to take part. As usual, the author agreed to attend and a program for the weekend was arranged along the lines of previous gatherings. As before, the speakers presented a balance from the world of academia, the arts, and literature.

Among them was the Irish novelist Cora Harrison, whose works included "The Burren Mysteries," featuring a sixteenth-century female Brehon. Her theme was the conflict between Brehon law and English law during the time of the Tudor Conquests of Ireland. Cormac Millar, the Irish crime writer and aficionado of the genre, agreed to talk about clerical crime fiction. Cormac Millar is the pseudonym of Dr. Cormac Ó Cuilleanáin of Trinity College, Dublin, and a member of a distinguished Irish literary family. His father was a famous professor of Irish literature, his mother was the bestselling novelist Eilis Dillon, and his sister is also a well known poet, while his great uncle was the poet Joseph Mary Plunkett, executed in 1916 as a signatory of the 1916 Proclamation of the Irish Republic.

A return guest to the Féile was Award-winning Irish language crime novelist, Anna Heussaff, speaking about the femininity of Fidelma, while another returning speaker was former Abbey director and award-winning playwright Neil Donnelly. Having dramatized and presented one of the Fidelma short stories at the 2010 Féile, Donnelly presented an analysis of the way to dramatize the Fidelma stories.

The program also included Dr. Damian Bracken, of University College, Cork, an expert on the conflict between the Irish churches and Rome during Fidelma's period; and archaeologist Richard O'Brien. O'Brien had been leading an excavation on a site called Rath na Drinne, just south of Cashel. Originally thought to date back to Fidelma's time as a fortified farmhouse, the location appears in the Fidelma's novels as the site of a tavern run by Ferloga and his wife, Lassar. O'Brien's excavations have now established the date of its original constriction was around 3000 B.C.

Once more the Féile organization has shown there are endless subjects for talks and discussion and many authorities who admire the work of Peter Tremayne in putting such subjects before a modern readership in such an exciting form. In February 2012, enthusiasts were already registering to attend. While the organizers realized that they were still in a world of international economic turmoil, perhaps even more so than they were in 2010, the committee believed, from past experiences, that the fans of Sister Fidelma are enthusiastic and eager to learn more about these exciting stories and their background. The ultimate success of the Féile Fidelma depends on the number of those readers of the Fidelma mysteries who can come to Cashel for a weekend of talks devoted to the works and their background. The organizers also believe that the presence of the author at these weekends is one of their strongest attractions, and as long as he is willing to return to Fidelma's "hometown," they will continue to be a success.

Works Cited

"Cashel Arts Festival Opened by Peter Tremayne." *The Brehon: The Journal of the International Sister Fidelma Society* 4.1 (Jan. 2005): XVII–XVIII.
"Féile Fidelma 2008 — A Great Success." *The Brehon: The Journal of the International Sister Fidelma Society* 8.1 (Jan. 2009): II–III.
"The Féiles." *The International Sister Fidelma Society.* <http://www.sisterfidelma.com/feile fidelma.htm>.
Livres Hebdo 5 May 2006. <http://livreshebdo.fr>.
Tremayne, Peter. *Absolution by Murder*. London: Headline, 1994.

Newspapers
Irish World 5 April 2008.
The Nationalist 20 Nov. 2004.
The Nationalist 16 Sept. 2006.
The Nationalist 24 March 2007.
The Nationalist 16 Sept. 2010.
Southern Star 6 May 2000.
The Tipperary Star 16 Sept. 2006.
The Tipperary Star 17 Feb. 2007
The Tipperary Star 12 Jan. 2008.

Interview with Peter Tremayne*

Edward J. Rielly

EJR: *In an interview a few years ago, you said that you wrote for three reasons: "because of an inner compulsion to write," "to get published," and "to earn a living." When did you first feel that inner compulsion? Did you write a lot as a child, for example? Can you explain a bit more what you mean by feeling compelled to write?*

PT: When I was twelve years old, the author Allan Campbell McLean (1922–1989), who wrote thrillers for younger readers, responded to my precocious statement that I wanted to be a writer. I had written a fan letter having admired his thriller *The Hill of the Red Fox* (1955). He talked of that "inner compulsion" and told me that no matter how many obstacles, hardships, rejections, lack of money, and all the criticism and naysayers, if I found that I still *had* to write, that it was as necessary as having to breathe, that was the inner compulsion.

I had certainly developed the "inner compulsion" by the time I was eight when I achieved my first publication—a letter in a children's newspaper. Indeed, I wrote a lot as a child, little books that I bound and illustrated myself. When I was fifteen, my mother bought me my own portable typewriter as a birthday present. There was no stopping me. What was, of course, of great help to me was that I came from a literate family. My father was not only a journalist but he wrote serials and short stories for "the pulps," although he never put anything between book covers. My mother was a prolific letter writer and eventually wrote a 90,000-word memoir when she was ninety years old that was published after her death. My siblings also wrote occasionally but never went into it professionally. I can never remember a time when I was not reading, writing and believing in my ability to use these gifts to earn a living. After all, at a tender age I learnt the words of Samuel Johnson —"No man but a blockhead ever wrote except for money."

I felt such a compulsion to earn my living by writing that I dropped out

*Email interview conducted on June 27, 2011.

of college at the age of sixteen to take a job on the local newspaper as a junior journalist. I weathered the parental storm that followed. However, I eventually returned to higher education to take my degrees in Celtic Studies but never regretted those years learning the craft of journalism.

EJR: *You have made a living for decades as a writer. Was it difficult to make that decision to rely totally on writing for a living? Or did you gradually move to that position?*

PT: When I decided in 1975 to leave the editorship of a weekly magazine and become a full-time writer, I put several "safety-nets" in place. The most important support was the approval of my wife. The next was that I was able to rely on regular journalistic work and, finally, I had some book commissions. My first nonfiction book had been published in 1968. By 1975 I had not published fiction, although I had several rejection slips for novels and plays. But my ambition to make it as a fiction writer had not been blunted. Within two years I had published my first fiction work and never looked back. I would never advise anyone to "give up the day job" before being assured of some financial backing. Always have some safety net before launching into the unknown.

EJR: *A lot of aspiring writers have the sorts of questions that you probably have been asked many times, but since most readers of this volume probably have not heard or read your responses to those questions, we are going to ask them again. First, did you face, as so many beginning writers do, a lot of rejection slips? What advice do you have for beginning writers as they start to accumulate rejections? At what point should one accept that publishing is not in his or her future?*

PT: The old saying is that everyone has at least one book in them. The crucial decision that the individual has to make is whether they are a person of only one book or whether they truly possess the inner compulsion that we have spoken of. Was it Raymond Chandler who advised that one has to write a million words before one begins to write? I certainly did my million. I wrote four novels and four plays, all rejected, before I had my first acceptance. Don't be dismayed by rejection slips and remember, publishers are just as subjective as readers. Never throw anything away because it comes back with a rejection slip. Back in 1967, I sent out an article to a magazine. It came back a few days later with a rejection slip. I immediately removed the slip and put it into an envelope addressed to another magazine. A few days later I received an acceptance and a very nice check. Stories abound in this profession of those who have become best-sellers after being turned down many times. It is often told that Frederick Forsyth sent *The Day of the Jackal* to eleven publishers and it was rejected by them all. Edgar Wallace told my father the story of how he wrote a thriller which no one would publish and so he decided to publish it himself. It was called *The Four Just Men* and became a classic of the genre. If you truly have the compulsion you will never accept a point where mere rejection slips influence you to give up trying.

EJR: *Teachers usually tell their student writers that they need to keep reading a lot. You have undoubtedly spent much of your life reading, but had you also read extensively in detective fiction before turning to that genre as a writer?*

PT: I am an admirer of Samuel Johnson and used to go regularly to the annual Johnsonian wreath laying at Westminster Abbey followed by the luncheon and lecture. Forgive me, therefore, if I trot out a Johnson quote. "The greatest part of a writer's time is spent reading in order to write; a man will turn over half a library to make one book." I agree absolutely. I grew up in a large family library and, thankfully, my parents had eclectic tastes so my reading was extraordinarily varied.

I read a lot of detective fiction from the time I could understand it. My father, when he settled in England, became a crime reporter in Fleet Street. He became quite friendly with Edgar Wallace. I still have my father's collection of Wallace's work. Another friend of my parents was Edgar Lustgarten (1907–1978) who is probably better remembered today not for his crime fiction but his crime film series *Scotland Yard* and *The Scales of Justice*. So the family home was filled with such books.

I cut my teeth on Andrew MacKinnon's boy detectives, the Monty Trio mysteries, when I was eight years old. I know the date because I still have the first title I read in the series, signed to me on that birthday by my sister. A few years later I was moving on to Conan Doyle, Wilkie Collins, E.C. Vivian, Raymond Chandler, Leslie Charteris, et al. It would take too long to name all the names that stand out in my memory. And today my library is such that our house is drowning in a sea of books.

Symbolically, there is one photograph in our lounge of me at the age of three years old, in what I recall was a red "siren suit" (a one-piece suit that I was bundled into whenever the air raids took place and the family had to head to the shelter). In one hand I hold a little book that my brother gave me for my birthday. It was called *Peggy the Penguin*. I still have it. The book is on the shelf next to the photograph. My first reading book. From such things mighty libraries grow. The main lesson to any aspiring writer is to read, read and re-read.

EJR: *Did you find yourself influenced by certain fiction writers as you began the Sister Fidelma stories?*

PT: To say a simple "no" may sound arrogant. I should add "not consciously" and this is not to say that I was probably subconsciously influenced from decades of reading and learning my craft before I created Fidelma.

EJR: *What led you to build your stories around a protagonist that some new readers might characterize as a seventh-century Catholic nun and find quite unusual as a detective?*

PT: Firstly, I would never describe Fidelma as a "Catholic nun." And, I would hope, by this time in the series, most readers have realized that she is not. She is a religieuse of the early Irish church which we retrospectively call the Celtic Church. Its liturgy, rituals, ideology were not the same as Rome and that was the cause for the intellectual conflict between them. Like the schism between Rome and the Orthodox churches, the Celts were also following a different path. In fact, while the Celts had retained the earliest concepts of Christianity it was actually the Roman church, through their various councils, who had been reforming the faith and making changes. Rome did not really dominate in Ireland until after the Norman invasion. The invasion of the Angevin emperor (now referred to as Henry II, King of England) was supported by the Popes, Adrian IV and then Alexander III, as a means of asserting their authority over the Irish church. Henry II agreed to pay a penny per household fee to the papal coffers for Rome's support. Ironically, it was the Synod of Cashel in 1172 that reformed the Irish church along Roman lines.

Fidelma is very much a religieuse of her time and culture. I never use the word "nun." I have fought with editors over the use of the term. A "nun" conjures a very late medieval Roman idea of a celibate female in holy orders usually in a confined community. I remember one Irish magazine, in describing Fidelma as "a sexually active nun," missed the whole setting of the stories. We surely all know the history of celibacy in the Roman church, even if we don't know it in the "Celtic Church." It was not until the time of Leo IX in the eleventh century that celibacy started to be enforced among the religious and it took some centuries to achieve. At one point, in 1095, Pope Urban II ordered all the wives of bishops and priests to be rounded up and sold as slaves for the benefit of the Lateran Palace (then the Papal headquarters).

When a reader follows the books, you will find that Fidelma has only joined a religious community on the advice of her cousin, Abbot Laisrán of Darú (Durrow), as a means of gaining security. This was before her brother became King of Muman or had even been considered heir-apparent (*tánaiste*) to it. She is first and foremost a lawyer, an advocate of the ancient Irish law system. Most Irish professionals gravitated to the religious as they had, in previous centuries, been numbered among the Druids (not pagan priests but encompassing all the professionals of Celtic society, much like the Brahmins of India). Such changes and conflicts were still happening in Fidelma's time. Fidelma even questions the New Faith in many of the stories.

So, how did I create Fidelma? It was as simple as this: Back in the mid 1980s I was giving a talk at St. Michael's College, University of Toronto, Canada, on Celtic women, their place in law, society and religion in seventh-century Ireland. The seventh century was a crucial and exciting period in Ireland with Rome making its first attempts to flex its muscles over the native church. Remember, Irish missionaries were spreading across Europe at this point, bringing their native ideas and concepts as they set up communities even in Italy — Bobbio, Lucca, Fiesola, and Taranto among them. Rome achieved its first check to the Celtic ideas at Whitby, other councils followed. One devastating for the Celts was Autun in A.D. 670. That is why I felt that the seventh century was an exciting period in which to set the stories.

I mentioned some of the female Irish lawyers of the period, like Dar í, known to have written a law text on cattle theft, and, the almost mythical Brig Briugaid and later Áine daughter of Iugaire. A student jokingly suggested to me that the idea of a female lawyer among the Celtic religious solving murder mysteries would make a great setting. The English translation of Umberto Eco's *Nome della Rosa* (*The Name of the Rose*) had just been published and he was inspired by that.

It was not until some years later that Peter Haining (1940–2007), the prolific anthologist and editor, who was an old friend of mine, phoned and asked me if I had ever written an Irish based detective tale. He was looking for a tale to complete an anthology he was working on. It was then Fidelma sprang fully formed in a short story. Well, perhaps not quite fully formed. I had to find a name and tried "Sister Buan" — a good seventh-century name meaning "victorious." Peter did not like it. It was not right for English ears. It sounded to him too similar to Bertram Atkey's comical crook "Smiler Bunn." When he asked me if I could change the name I realized that Fidelma was perfect. It was an ancient Irish name associated with the Eóghanacht dynasty of Munster (Muman) in southwest Ireland. It sounded easy on the ear and was easy on the eye.

Once I had Fidelma's year of birth fixed, her family background, all I had to do was go to the ancient Irish annals and chronicles. There it all was, the family, the religious conflicts, the cultural conflicts, the plagues, the jealousies, the fights between rival kings and chieftains, but towering above it all were the laws of the Fénechus, the Brehon Law system, reflecting its sophisticated social system.

Once the readers understand the time and place, and come to realize that they are in a different culture, a different social system, a world where Fidelma is neither a Catholic nor a nun in the sense we understand the terms today, and reject all their pre-conditioning, which centuries of colonial and religious propaganda has helped to create, then they can better enjoy the adventures that I am recounting.

EJR: *As most readers of this volume know, you are a highly respected historian, especially focusing on Celtic history. As you write the Sister Fidelma stories, do you ever have trouble balancing the demands of the historian with those of the novelist? To put it another way, do you find yourself at times donning the historian's hat, at other times the novelist's hat, or do you keep both on at the same time?*

PT: In the case of Fidelma, I balance both hats at the same time. Of course, theoretically one is freer as a novelist and you don't have to keep checking and inserting your sources as footnotes. But this is not to say that I do not employ the same methodology of research to ensure the background is as accurate as it can be. I still turn to the ancient texts, especially the legal texts. My library of Brehon Law texts books is less than an arm's length from my chair. Often readers, because of the nature of the Fidelma books, write in and some even think I am making up the ancient laws to suit the books. To answer them, the Frequently Asked Questions (FAQs) page on the website of the International Sister Fidelma Society has been very helpful in answering some of the points they raise.

EJR: *Many novelists of historical detective fiction do not have your professional background as an historian. In your own reading, how do you react when you find an otherwise engaging novel that has some historical lapses?*

PT: I have to admit that I find it hard to engage in a novel after I have realized that the writer has not done his or her research correctly enough. I know it is placing a lot on the writer to expect them to know all the minutia of the times they are writing about and one can turn a blind eye to certain errors. But if a writer goes into details, then the quickest way to turn off that "suspension of disbelief," which is an essential to all fictional story telling, is for the writer to mention something that is entirely anachronistic. I am afraid that this has led me to avoiding a lot of modern historical fiction work unless it comes highly recommended or from a writer whose work I know. I have enough high blood pressure moments from movies and television without having to throw books across the room in disgust.

There is an anecdote I tell which is associated with the movies. This dates back to the 1960s when I and a friend of mine (a Classics lecturer who later became a well-known Classics Professor) went to see the famous movie *Spartacus* with Kirk Douglas. It is the last scene and Spartacus is one of the thousands who have been crucified along the Appian Way. He is hanging on his cross breathing his last. Jean Simmons and her newborn baby arrive in a chariot driven by Peter Ustinov. She holds up the baby, Spartacus' son, and informs him that she is taking him to Gaul where he will be raised as a free man. She leaps onto the chariot and Ustinov heads off down the Appian Way watched by the dying Spartacus. There was not a dry eye in the cinema — sobs all around. Then my friend remarked in a loud voice: "For Christ sake! If they are going to Gaul, then they are heading in the wrong bloody direction." The Appian Way leads south from Rome towards Naples. To get to Gaul they would have headed north towards the Alps. I can never see the movie again without a chuckle.

EJR: *Do you ever assume any historical poetic license in your Sister Fidelma stories in order to make the novels more accessible to their readers? Can you give some examples if you do? You have said a number of times that the novels are fiction. Do you have any concern that a misguided reader overly concerned with the novels as history may forget the actual genre in which you are working?*

PT: I certainly do not dumb-down things. I have been amused by some critics who complain about this. Readers should be intelligent enough to take onboard information and process it or ask questions if they don't — these days most people have access to encyclopaedias and dictionaries. I shudder when I see writers refusing to accept their readers are intelligent. A nonwriting example lodges in my mind from my youth. Going round Pompeii I passed a guide showing a bunch of English-speakers around the place where the Romans sold wine. The guide obviously did not think much of the intelligence of his flock. He pointed to the place and said: "Now this was where the people in Roman times bought their Coca-Cola."

I have pointed out my novels are fiction because that is what they are. One Australian critic did suggest I was making nonsensical claims for the books, which I was not. It was a claim derived from their own imagination because they had their own axe to grind. While I endeavor to make the background as accurate as possible, and the details in keeping with what is known of the time, the characters and story are mainly fictional. I admit that I do incorporate known historical characters in the stories. For example, Colgú, Fidelma's brother, was an historical King of Muman, ruling from A.D. 664/5 to 678, and his father (Fidelma's father), Failbe Flann mac Aedo Dubh, also ruled from 628 to 637/9 (remember Fidelma is born in 637). Their characterization and most personal events are products of my own imagination. Sometimes I am able to incorporate information about them from the annals or texts. An example is in *Dancing with Demons* where Sechnussach, the High King, is murdered in his bed. This is actually recorded in the annals. But I make no pretense about writing these books other than as historical murder mysteries set in seventh-century Ireland.

Now and then I get letters asking why I put such unpronounceable names in the stories. Once or twice critics have bemoaned my use of ancient Irish names. They do not seem to understand that they are the names of the period. Usually, I find these protests come from English-speakers and never from those who read the books in other languages. Some critics even ask why I don't use Irish names like Pat, Mick, Liam, Shawn and Shamus — all anglicized versions of much later Irish names. Sometimes I am forced to wonder if some of these "critics" realize that the Irish ever had their own language.

Well, heaven forefend that these same protesting readers try their hands at reading translations of foreign literature — the Russian or French novels, for example. Indeed, what about reading fantasy novels written by English writers — do they have problems there? Burroughs in *Tarzan and the Ant Men*, as example, has names like Adendrohahkis, Trohanadalmakus, and Komodoflorensal. Tolkien's *Lord of the Rings* has Elrond of Imadris, Galadniel, Boromir, Thrunduil or even Gimli son of Gloin. I don't think the names in the Fidelma stories are any harder.

I did once reluctantly accept a publisher's request to put a pronunciation guide in some of the books and it has remained on the Fidelma Society website as it became too distracting in the books. But my advice has always been — pronounce the names as you feel, just as you do with the strange names in foreign literature or in fantasy novels. If you are that particular, then there are some good Fidelma audio books read by Caroline Lennon, or try the pronunciation guide or even an Irish language course. One point about the latter, however ... I am using the Old and Middle Irish of the early period! Doubtless like reading Classical Greek on the basis of Modern Greek.

The Irish names that I use must be names that existed during the period. As a rod for my back, being aware of pronunciation difficulties, I try to keep these names as simple as possible. This presents problems. Should I try to ensure that I use a name only once in the entire series — apart from the principal characters? Impossible. Like modern times, there were popular names; so many people had the same name. There is the famous story in the early texts of how St. Cárthach (Carthage) had some monks working by a stream and something needed securing. He shouted: "Colmán get into the water!" At once twelve of the brethren leapt into the river. We are told that there were 234 saints of that name. To use the same name only once during the series would not be an accurate reflection of that world, any more than it is of this one. So I am happy using the same name in various books when they clearly belong to different characters.

EJR: *Popular culture studies now abound in colleges and universities, and the study of popular culture appears to have gained considerable academic respectability over the past twenty years or so. Have you found that change impacting your reception as both a historian and a writer of popular fiction?*

PT: As Popular Culture has such a multiplicity of definitions I am never sure what is meant. In literary terms is Literature (capital L) classed, as some critics suggest, as something different to genre fiction, which is regarded as popular culture? Did H.G. Wells (*War of the Worlds*), Aldous Huxley (*Brave New World*), George Orwell (*1984*), or Kurt Vonnegut (*Slaughterhouse 5*) write science fiction or Literature? So much depends on definition. I know that critics have been the worst offenders at providing differentiation.

Literature (capital L) has often been classed as something "superior" to genre fiction, and one still sees the prejudice in many book review columns of newspapers. Books hailed as Literature receive columns of analysis while genre fiction is ignored. Cynical publishers have told me they usually define Literature as books that sell 600 copies in hardcover, whereas genre fiction will sell 25,000.

If Popular Literature studies now means an end to this type of discrimination and that all types of fiction are encompassed for serious study, then this is surely a good thing. Would I be cynical to say, that from the writer's perspective, while it is nice to have critical and academic recognition, the most rewarding aspect for the writer is the royalty cheque from the publishers?

My advice to those ambitious to succeed as writers is do not think about critics, classification or even achieving a place in the literary world. I remember the words of one of my literary mentors, Eric Hiscock (1900–1989), once doyen of book trade critics. Eric's London based "Whitefriar" column was avidly read (and with fear and trembling) by publishers on both sides of the Atlantic. He had first encouraged Peter Cheyney to write, also Howard Spring (who dedicated *My Son, My Son* to him) and also discovered Len Deighton. I worked with Eric on the same weekly back in the 1960s and had just had my first book published. We were having a bottle of champagne in El Vino's in London's famous Fleet Street, then the center of the UK publishing world. I was bemoaning the critics and feeling down. "Dear boy," Eric said, "forget them. If they spell your name right, get the title of your book correct, get the publisher and the price correct, then everything else is a plus." As someone who has had all four things wrong in the same review, I came to respect Eric more. Alas, even he is forgotten now that he has passed into the literary Valhalla. I still enjoy turning back to his two volumes of memoirs and so pass on his words of wisdom for those who are worried about the judgment of the reviewers and achieving a place in the literary world, popular or otherwise.

Don't go into this business thinking that you are destined for literary immortality. I once wrote a biography of a favorite boyhood adventure writer, Talbot Mundy. During the research I went to his UK publishers, Hutchinson, for whom he had made a fortune, his books selling by the hundreds of thousands, four of them filmed. I wanted to see if the publishers had kept any archival material, letters and other material. The managing director admitted that he had never heard of Talbot Mundy. So if there is now a little niche to remember those whose work is classed as "genre fiction" in the new popular literature studies, that, in the view of this literary mortician, is no bad thing.

As for the historian's view, I have always seen myself as writing popular history — by which I mean that I am a translator between the academic historian and the general reader. I am unsure how that fits into studies in popular culture. The "academic historian" will always express superiority to the "popular historian." That is par for the course. Anyway, historians of academic or popular persuasion are always divided into two warring groups depending on their standpoint. There is "the bottle is half full" historian and the "bottle is half empty" historian. Like witnesses at an accident, they will never agree exactly on what they have seen.

EJR: *Writing a series of stories about the same main character must involve both some advantages and some difficult challenges. On balance, do you find it easier or more difficult to keep coming back to the same protagonist?*

PT: Fidelma and I have almost grown up together as the stories have proceeded. Although she emerged fairly fully formed in the first short stories, as the stories continued I found I was learning more and more about her. With each story she has revealed more about her life, her past love and what has shaped her character. The same applies to Eadulf. Therefore, it is easy to continue to accompany Fidelma and Eadulf on their adventures almost as if they are dictating the stories to me and showing me where they are going and why they react in such a manner. As readers know, sometimes they are unsure themselves and the road they travel is not any easy one. At the start of each new story, I am impatient and excited to find out where they will lead me.

EJR: *How do you approach the challenge of writing for two different types of readers: the one coming to your series for the first time and the one who has been reading the novels sequentially? How do you strike the balance between repeating enough to give the new reader the background he or she needs and yet not holding back the veteran Fidelma reader? A lot of aspiring writers hope someday to develop a series. Especially for them, perhaps you could give some specific examples of how you handle this "enough yet not too much" issue of giving background, describing recurring characters, etc.*

PT: Oh dear. This is one of those questions like asking the centipede how it walks. It is not a matter that I spent a great deal of time thinking about. Reintroducing the characters in each story is easily done, a brief conversation exchange between characters, a few words here or there. In the novels there are opportunities where this arises in the early chapters. What was difficult was doing this in the very early short stories. These were published in a variety of magazines and anthologies. When the publishers decided to print them in book collections (*Hemlock at Vespers* and *Whispers of the Dead*) a degree of repetition of introduction emerged. Of course, one critic picked up on this, apparently not realising the stories were collected from a variety of publications.

Perhaps, in retrospect, one should have edited and rewritten the stories especially for the book appearance. But the critic in question was the only one who seemed bothered by references to Fidelma's unruly red hair that cropped up in several of the tales.

As for the recurring characters, my advice to aspiring series writers is be sure of your continuity. The example that is often presented is Conan Doyle's "Case of Dr. Watson and His Travelling Wound." In *A Study in Scarlet* Watson mentions that he was wounded by a bullet in the shoulder in Afghanistan. In *The Sign of the Four*, the wound has moved to his leg. In "The Noble Bachelor," the wound is "in one of his limbs." Then there is the case of Watson's wives. Keen Sherlockians argue a minimum two wives and some as many as six. This is not to mention the argument over Watson's first name — Conan Doyle used both James and John. The lesson for the careful writer engaged in a series is to make sure that the same character's continuity is maintained. Keep a notebook with their description, previous references and any information that is likely to be referred to again.

EJR: *The many Fidelma fans obviously want her stories to continue. Do you ever get tired of her and perhaps just want to send her off on a vacation for a while?*

PT: I have never tired of Fidelma and Eadulf as yet and fully intend that they will be around for some time yet. But, as readers will know, I have also written in other periods and cultures. There is the short story series of Elizabethan detective tales centred on The Globe theatre in London. I have even written Sherlock Holmes pastiches. Some of these have been collected in *An Ensuing Evil* (2006). For example, of the ninety-six Tremayne short stories only thirty-five have been Fidelma stories. Of fifty-one Tremayne novels only twenty-four have been Fidelma novels.

EJR: *Another question with young writers and students in mind: Do you experience the infamous writer's block? Hemingway, for example, said that he usually tried to stop writing at a point where he still knew what he wanted to say next. That way, he could quickly get started again the next day. Do you have any tricks of the trade for avoiding that block?*

PT: Writer's block can take several forms. I have only experienced the trivial form which is a temporary difficulty associated with the task in hand. Essentially, this is a practical problem rather than an inspirational one. What I mean by this is, when constructing the story suddenly something does not feel right. For example, the characters have been taken to a place, a situation, and the writer comes to an abrupt halt not being clear how to take them further. The writer may have to spend a few hours, perhaps a day or maybe it is several days before they realize what is holding them up. This has happened to me and it was some time before I realized that a character — who I believed had an essential role in presenting some clues — was superfluous to the story. His small role could be fulfilled by another.

Hemingway had the right formula for tackling the morning blank page (or screen) syndrome. This is when you sit down at your desk, stare at the blank space and your mind is also blank. I certainly make some notes at the end of the day so that I know where I am heading when I sit at my desk in the morning. This, of course, does not deal with the hitches that arrive in the practicality of the writing.

EJR: *Is there any type of writing that you have not done yet but want to try?*

PT: I have tackled most forms of writing during my career, although I have not been successful in every field. I have written history nonfiction, biography, historical novels, sword and sorcery fantasy, supernatural tales, detective fiction, adventure thrillers, plays for theatre, for radio and, last but not least, published poetry. There have also been academic papers, journalism and book reviews. I have learned enough from the experience to know what I can do and what I can't do so, short of writing an autobiography, I don't think there is much left.

Sister Fidelma Bibliography

Sister Fidelma Books
- *Absolution by Murder* (1994)
- *Shroud for the Archbishop* (1995)
- *Suffer Little Children* (1995)
- *The Subtle Serpent* (1996)
- *The Spider's Web* (1997)
- *Valley of the Shadow* (1998)
- *The Monk Who Vanished* (1999)
- *Act of Mercy* (1999)
- *Our Lady of Darkness* (2000)
- *Hemlock at Vespers* (collection of short stories) (2000)
- *Smoke in the Wind* (2001)
- *The Haunted Abbot* (2002)
- *Badger's Moon* (2003)
- *Whispers of the Dead* (collection of short stories) (2004)
- *The Leper's Bell* (2004)
- *Master of Souls* (2005)
- *A Prayer for the Damned* (2006)
- *Dancing with Demons* (2007)
- *Council of the Cursed* (2008)
- *The Dove of Death* (2009)
- *The Chalice of Blood* (2010)
- *Behold a Pale Horse* (2011)
- *The Seventh Trumpet* (2012)

Sister Fidelma short stories (year of first appearance)
- "Hemlock at Vespers" (1993)
- "The High King's Sword" (1993)
- "Murder in Repose" (1993)
- "Murder by Miracle" (1993)
- "A Canticle for Wulfstan" (1994)

- "Abbey Sinister" (1995)
- "Tarnished Halo" (1995)
- "The Horse That Died for Shame" (1995)
- "The Poisoned Chalice" (1996)
- "At the Tent of Holofernes" (1997)
- "A Scream from the Sepulchre" (1998)
- "Invitation to a Poisoning" (1998)
- "Holy Blood" (1999)
- "Our Lady of Death" (1999)
- "Those Who Trespass" (1999)

The above were collected in *Hemlock at Vespers: A Collection of Sister Fidelma Mysteries* (2000)

- "Like a Dog Returning" (2000)
- "Who Stole the Fish?" (2000)
- "Scattered Thorns" (2001)
- "Corpse on a Holy Day" (2001)
- "The Astrologer Who Predicted His Own Murder" (2001)
- "Death of an Icon" (2001)
- "Whispers of the Dead" (2002)
- "The Blemish" (2002)
- "Gold at Night" (2003)
- "The Lost Eagle" (2003)
- "Dark Moon Rising" (2003)
- "The Banshee" (2004)
- "Cry 'Wolf!'" (2004)
- "The Fosterer"
- "The Heir Apparent"

The above were collected in *Whispers of the Dead: A Collection of Sister Fidelma Mysteries* (2004)

- "The Spiteful Shadow" (2005)
- "Does God Obey His Own Law?" (2006)
- "Sanctuary" (2006)
- "Finnbarr's Bell" (2008)
- "The Night of the Snow Wolf" (2011)

About the Contributors

Mitzi M. **Brunsdale** is a professor of English at Mayville State University, North Dakota. She is the author of *Sigrid Undset: Chronicler of Norway*; *Dorothy L. Sayers: Solving the Mystery of Wickedness*; *Gumshoes: A Dictionary of Literary Detectives*; and *Icons of Mystery and Detection: From Sleuths to Superheroes*, among others. Her academic field is comparative literature, focusing on modern and contemporary literature, with a special interest in contemporary crime fiction.

Richard **Dalby** is an antiquarian bookseller, bibliographer, writer, and editor of many anthologies, including *The Mammoth Book of Ghost Stories* (two volumes, 1990 and 1991) and *Chillers for Christmas* (1989). He has written 300 articles for *Book and Magazine Collector* (1984–2010), including a fiftieth birthday tribute to Peter Berresford Ellis, which covered all the pre–Fidelma books by Peter Tremayne (*BMC* 108, March 1993). He lives in Scarborough, North Yorkshire, UK.

Patricia C. **Flynn**, RSM, is a member of the Institute of the Sisters of Mercy of the Americas and is an assistant professor in the philosophy department at St. Joseph's College, Standish, Maine, teaching courses on the history of philosophy and ethical issues. An avid mystery reader, she is particularly fond of those historical novels, like Tremayne's, that provide an opportunity to experience another time and culture through the unraveling of intrigue and murder.

Anna **Heussaff** is an award-winning Irish-language writer. She has had four novels published to date, including two contemporary murder mysteries set on the southwest coast of Ireland, *Bás Tobann* (2004) and *Buille Marfach* (2010). She also teaches short writing courses to schoolchildren and college students and has translated factual books for children from English to Irish. She lives in Dublin.

M. E. **Kemp** writes an historical mystery series featuring two nosy New England Puritans, Hetty Henry and Increase "Creasy" Cotton, as detectives. Henry is twice widowed and wealthy, while Cotton is the nephew of the famous clergyman Increase Mather. Her latest book is *Death of a Cape Cod Cavalier*, the fifth in the series. Kemp has published many nonfiction articles and short stories in journals, magazines and anthologies.

Christine **Kinealy** is a professor of Irish history at Drew University in Madison, New Jersey. Since completing her Ph.D. at Trinity College in Ireland, she has worked in educational and research institutes in Dublin, Belfast, and Liverpool. She has written a number of books on modern Ireland, including *This Great Calamity: The Great Irish Famine 1845–52* (1994 and 2006), *Repeal and Revolution: 1848 in Ireland* (2009), and *War and Peace: Ireland since the 1960s* (2010).

Seamus J. **King**, a native of County Tipperary, Ireland, is a retired secondary teacher. After earning two degrees in Ireland, he completed an M.A. in political science at Western Reserve University in the United States. He has written 16 books, mostly on sports; his *History of Hurling* is the definitive work. He was one of the organizers of the first Féile Fidelma in 2006, and of the subsequent weekends in 2008 and 2010. He lives in Cashel, the "hometown" of Sister Fidelma.

Hervé **Latimier**, after taking his degree at the Institut d'Études Politiques de Paris, joined the French Ministry of Education, becoming a senior administrator before retiring in 2011. He is very active in the movement to secure rights for the Breton language and for self-government for Brittany. He is also vice-president of Roc'h Diwan, part of the Breton language schools founded in 1977.

Christiane W. **Luehrs** taught high school American history and college-level Western civilization, and English composition, world literature and multiculturalism at Fort Hays State University. Now retired, she teaches online for the Fort Hays State English Department; her favorite course is one on classics of detective fiction. She has also written articles and papers on fictional detectives.

Robert B. **Luehrs** (Ph.D., Stanford) was for almost forty years a professor of history at Fort Hays State University, teaching courses in early modern Europe and European intellectual history. Officially retired, he serves as Teaching Excellence Coordinator at Fort Hays, counseling young instructors. His publications include articles on witches, deism, utopianism, religious skepticism, L. Frank Baum's Oz books, and, in collaboration with his wife, Christiane, detective fiction.

Jennifer **Molidor** received her Ph.D. in Irish studies from the Keough-Naughton Institute for Irish Studies at the University of Notre Dame in 2008 and completed doctoral work on the mother-daughter relationship in Irish literature. She teaches courses in writing, literature, and film at Kansas State University, Salina.

Patrick **O'Keefe** practices admiralty and maritime law in New Orleans. He is recognized as a proctor in admiralty by the Maritime Law Association of the United States. In 1992 he was made a lifetime honorary member of the Dublin Solicitor's Bar Association. He is the present chairman of the International Law Section of the Federal Bar Association and serves as a Commissioner on the Louisiana Judicial Compensation Commission.

About the Contributors

Mairéad Ní **Riada** is a writer and founding member of The International Sister Fidelma Society. Born and brought up in Fidelma's Munster, she lives not far away from Saxmundham, Suffolk, in East Anglia — Brother Eadulf's "hometown." She became a research officer with HM Custom and Excise, contributing numerous research papers to technical journals, one of which won the 2004 "Excellence in Research to Practice" award from the American Society of Training and Development.

Edward J. **Rielly** is a professor of English at Saint Joseph's College in Standish, Maine. He teaches a wide variety of literature, writing, and popular culture courses. His publications include 23 books, among them a dozen volumes of his own poetry, a biography of F. Scott Fitzgerald, studies of American Indian history and culture, and books on baseball and football. His previous McFarland books are *Baseball in the Classroom* (2006) and *Murder 101* (2009).

Frank A. **Salamone** is an emeritus professor of anthropology and sociology at Iona College, New Rochelle, New York. He has conducted fieldwork in Nigeria, Venezuela, and East Africa, has written more than 100 articles and is the author, editor or coeditor of 15 books. His most recent are *The Lucy Memorial Freed Slaves' Home*, with Virginia Salamone (2007); *The Italians of Rochester 1940–60* (2000); and *The Culture of Jazz: Jazz as Critical Culture* (2008).

John **Scaggs** is a professor of English at Southwestern College in Chula Vista, California, where he is the coordinator of the English program. His main research interests are crime fiction and modern American fiction. He has published articles on Raymond Chandler, James Crumley, Cormac McCarthy, and Donna Tartt, and he is the author of *Crime Fiction* (2005).

Anita M. **Vickers** is an associate professor of English at Pennsylvania State University where she teaches courses in comparative and fantasy literature, and classical and Celtic mythology. She is the author of *The New Nation* (2002) and contributed to *Great Women Mystery Writers* (1994), *Cordially Yours, Brother Cadfael* (1998), and *The Detective as Historian* (2000). She has published articles on Charles Brockden Brown, Zora Neale Hurston, and poetry of the early nationalist period.

David Robert **Wooten** is the director of The International Sister Fidelma Society and editor of its magazine, *The Brehon*. Now a Charleston, South Carolina, businessman, he previously worked in the State Archives and serves as the executive director and member of the board of the American College of Heraldry. He is the author of *We All Become Forefathers* (1993) and was specialist editor (heraldry) for *The New Oxford Dictionary of American English* (2001).

Index

abbeys: Ard Fearte 76; Ard Finan 75; Benchoer 177; Blessed Ruan 13; Blobium (Bobbio) 7, 78–79; Coldingham 41; Durrow 62–63; Fearna 74–75; Fermoy 79; Imleach 75; Lios Mór 8, 14, 72–73, 114, 154; Lismore 79; St. Ailbe 200; St. Brigid of Kildare (Cill Dara) 5, 11, 15, 92, 99, 113, 120, 125, 132–33; St. Finnbar 75; Streoneshalh 7, 15, 39
Absolution by Murder 1, 3, 6, 9, 10, 14–16, 17, 30, 32, 34–42, 50, 60, 64, 65–66, 69, 98, 99, 100, 109, 113, 120, 134, 143, 145, 146, 153, 154, 155, 174, 183, 202
Act of Mercy 10, 56, 69, 74, 105, 111, 112, 113, 126, 127, 147, 176
Adrian IV, Pope 53, 112, 211
Aedh, Saint 75
Aiden of Lindisfarne 15
Ailbe, Saint 73
Alchú 11, 66, 75, 98, 114, 115, 123, 126, 136, 154, 180, 185, 186
Aldrith 63
Alexander III, Pope 211
Allingham, Margery 29, 138, 146
Anglo-Saxon Chronicle 15
Anglo-Saxons (cultural influence on Ireland) 65
Aquinas, Thomas 131
Arles, Council of 178
Arthur, King 175–76
"The Astrologer Who Predicted His Own Murder" 152, 175
Atkey, Bertram 212
Atonement of Blood 195
Auden, W.H. 118
Augustine of Canterbury 34, 38
Augustine of Hippo 105, 106, 131
Autun, Council of 121, 177, 212

Badger's Moon 11, 75, 99, 100, 102, 103, 114, 135–36
bardic schools 111–12
Barr, Nevada 37

Bede, the Venerable 15–16, 62, 63, 65, 202
Behold a Pale Horse 7, 9, 69, 78–79, 99, 115
Beowulf 63
Binchy, Maeve 167
"The Blemish" 153
Boudicca 176, 177
Bowen, Rhys 37–38
Brecain, Saint 64
The Brehon 2, 27, 174, 191, 194–95, 198, 206; *see also* International Sister Fidelma Society
brehon law 6, 8–9, 22, 51–53, 55, 57, 80–87, 111–12, 132, 194, 212; brehons 85–87; compensation 82–83; contrasted with Roman law 83–84; heirship 84–85; origins 80; restitution 84; updating of the law 81
Breizh, Anna 172
Brendan, Saint 76
Breton (language) 172–73
Bretons 172–75
Brigid (Brigit), Saint 54, 57, 99, 101
Brittany 172–80
Brontë, Emily 166
Bruden Fidelma (Sister Fidelma's Guesthouse) 193, 200
Bruen, Ken 31
Bryant, Sophie 55
Brythonic (P) Celts 173; *see also* Fidelma: and Brythonic Celts
Burroughs, Edgar Rice 215
Byron, George Gordon, Lord 115

Caedmon 15
Caesar, Julius 88, 94, 100, 101
"A Canticle for Wulfstan" 62
Carthach, Saint 72, 215
Cashel *see* Fidelma: locations in Ireland
Cashel, Synod of 211
celibacy 11, 12, 36, 53, 105, 110, 116 n. 2, 119–25, 131, 133, 134, 153–54, 211
Celtic Church 3, 5, 13, 14–15, 34–36, 51–54, 58, 64–65, 96–97 n. 8, 110, 119–24, 130–32, 133–36, 175, 178, 211

227

The Chalice of Blood 8, 9, 11, 13–14, 17, 52, 72, 75, 78, 79, 98–99, 114, 115, 126, 183
Chandler, Raymond 29, 32, 158, 209, 210
Charles VIII 172
Charteris, Leslie 210
Chesterton, G.K. 118
Cheyney, Peter 216
Christie, Agatha 48, 138, 139, 142, 145, 146–47, 149, 155
Cian 10, 56, 110–113
Coel, Margaret 37–38
Colgú 7, 9, 14, 70, 72, 82, 92, 103, 109, 126, 127, 149, 186, 196, 214
Collins, Michael 75
Collins, Wilkie 28–29, 159, 210
Colmcille, Saint 62, 178
Columbanus, Saint 78
communities, religious 35, 51, 122–25, 126–27, 131, 134
Conan Doyle, Arthur 29, 32, 37, 46, 138–40, 158, 159, 166, 210, 218
Cornwell, Patricia 155
"Corpse on a Holy Day" 74
Council of the Cursed 64, 69, 105, 114, 115, 120, 121, 154–57, 177
Cromwell, Oliver 162

Dancing with Demons 77, 100, 101, 104, 105, 114, 214
Day, Dorothy 34
"Death of an Icon" 91–92, 152
Declan, Saint 74
Deighton, Len 216
The Detection Club 142
detective fiction (rules) 142–46
Deusdedit 15, 40–41
Donaldson, Julia 167
Douglas, Kirk 213–14
The Dove of Death 11, 13, 69, 74, 100, 126, 175, 177–79
Doyle, Roddy 167
druids 12, 52, 76, 88–97, 173, 211; arbiters of justice 100; as characters in Fidelma stories 90–93; druidism and Christianity 93, 94, 178; guardians of heritage 100–1 relationship to Christian brehons 89, 111; *see also* Fidelma: as druid

Eadulf 3, 62–63; an Angle 61; biographical background 61, 95, 113; common sense 144; as a Dr. Watson 138–40, 144, 154; medical knowledge 62–64, 113; physical description 60, 182; religious vocation 62, 113; role reversal 182–88 in Rome 64–65, 113; Seaxmund's Ham (Saxmundham) 6–62; study in Ireland 62–64; study of law 65, 66; *see also* Fidelma: and Eadulf relationship

Eco, Umberto 3, 54–55, 184, 212
Edwards, Ruth Dudley 29
Eleanor of Aquitaine 187
Eliot, T.S. 28–29
Elizabeth I 162
Ellis, Dorothy 22, 23, 27, 77, 199
Ellis, Peter Berresford *see* Tremayne, Peter
Emerson, Kathy Lynn 49

fair play (in detective fiction) 142, 145–46
Féile Fidelma 2, 4, 27, 166; Féile 1 (2006) 198–201; Féile 2 (2008) 201–4; Féile 3 (2010) 204–6; Féile 4 (2012) 206–7; origins 192–93, 196–98; participants *see* individual Féile; Peter Tremayne's involvement 197–98, 199–200, 202–5
female detectives (early) 44–48
Fénechus, laws of *see* brehon law
Fidelma: as anruth 53, 85, 99, 127, 151; and Brythonic Celts 175–80 (*see also* Brythonic [P] Celts); childhood 111; as dálaigh 5, 6–7, 8, 32, 35, 52, 85, 96 n. 1, 127, 132, 151; as druid 94–96, 98–106; and Eadulf relationship 3, 10–11, 13–14, 40, 42, 56, 66, 110, 113, 114–15, 120, 134, 140, 148, 154, 182–88 (*see also* Fidelma: marriage, below; and motherhood, below); and feminism 56, 186–87; and horseback riding 102; investigative methods 140–41, 152–53; locations in Ireland 68–79, 192–94, 196, 200; marriage 11, 66, 101, 114, 120, 126, 154, 185, 186 (*see also* and Eadulf relationship, above); and motherhood 11, 13, 14, 114, 126, 136, 154, 156, 185–87 (*see also* and Eadulf relationship, above); physical description 9, 32, 56, 60, 109, 110, 125, 155, 182–83; religious attitudes 12–13, 35, 94–95, 98–106, 120–23, 125–26, 143, 157; and self-defense 9, 102; and sexuality 9–10, 11, 56, 112, 120–23 (*see also* celibacy); as a Sherlock Holmes 140
Fidelma stories: detective genre 28–32, 36–42, 44–49, 138–49, 154–55; Golden Age detective fiction 146–49; historical background 11–12, 14–17, 58, 89, 158, 194, 211–13, 213–15; modern media 27, 195; popularity with Bretons 173–75, 181; teaching 33–42, 158–59, 174–75, 192; translations 26, 161, 166, 169–70, 177, 191, 193, 200, 203
Fidelmania 1, 2, 27, 201
"Finbarr's Bell" 204
Fodhla, Ollamh 80
Forsyth, Frederick 209
"The Fosterer" 81, 156
Franco, Francisco 168
François I 172

Frañsez, Duke, II 172
Frazer, Margaret 49, 186
Fursa 62

Gelles, Roberta 187
Gerritsen, Tess 155
Gildas, Saint 177
Goidelic (Q) Celts 173
"Gold at Night" 81, 153, 158
Grace, C.L. 49
Grafton, Sue 155
Greene, Graham 34
Grisham, John 139

Haining, Peter 212
Hamilton, Steve 37
Hammett, Dashiell 32, 37–38
Harrison, Cora 4, 57, 206
The Haunted Abbot 61, 69, 78, 99, 105, 120, 177, 186
"The Heir Apparent" 85
Hemingway, Ernest 218–19
"Hemlock at Vespers" 6, 17, 26, 125, 132
Hemlock at Vespers 53, 78, 98, 99, 102, 104, 105, 109–10, 113, 138, 218
Henry II 53, 112, 187, 211
Henry VIII 162
Heraclitus 99
"The High King's Sword" 26, 78
Hiscock, Eric 216
Holmes, Sherlock 29, 36, 37, 47, 60, 102, 107 n. 2, 116 n. 7, 138–40, 154, 158, 169, 184, 218
Honorius, Emperor 106
Huxley, Aldous 216

International Sister Fidelma Society 2, 4, 27, 166, 175, 189–95, 198, 200, 203, 204, 206, 212; membership 190–91; memorabilia 190; website 27, 189, 191; *see also The Brehon*; Féile Fidelma
"Invitation to a Poisoning" 204, 205
Irish crime fiction 28–32; Fidelma's relationship to 30–32
Irish cultural renaissance 57
Irish Free State 50–51, 163
Irish language: attacked 162; book publishers 165–68, 171; Catholic Church 162; compared to other languages in translation 168–69; contemporary usage 164–65; Fidelma stories 166, 169–70; historical change 160–62; revival 163–64; subordination to English 162–63

James, P.D. 154
Jerome, Saint 106
John, King 187

John, Saint 133, 134
John XXIII, Pope 36
Johnson, Samuel 208, 210
Joyce, James 31
Juvenal 152

Kesey, Ken 167
Keyes, Marian 167
King, Laurie 37
Knight, Richard 174
Knox, Father Ronald 142–46

Lennon, Caroline 205, 215
Leo IX, Pope 11, 211
The Leper's Bell 11, 74, 75–76, 94, 98, 100, 102, 104, 105, 114, 123, 185, 187
Lewis, C.S. 34
"The Lost Eagle" 78, 177
Louis XII 172
Lovesey, Peter 30
Lustgarten, Edgar 210
Luther, Martin 131–32

Mac Art, Cormac 76, 86–87
Mac Cuileanáin, Cormac 200
MacKinnon, Andrew 210
Markievicz, Countess Constance de 50–51
Marsh, Ngaio 29, 146
Martel, Yann 167
Master of Souls 27, 76, 83, 85, 101, 105, 114
McCann, Maurice 27, 192
McLean, Allan Campbell 208
Millar, Cormac 31, 206
Mitchell, Gladys 48
Moling, Saint 75
The Monk Who Vanished 73, 74, 93, 99–101, 104, 114, 140, 141, 143–46, 148, 149, 200
Mundy, Talbot 216–17
"Murder by Miracle" 26
"Murder in Repose" 9, 26, 56, 90–91, 102, 109–10, 125
Murder She Wrote 57

Nennius 177
"Night of the Snow Wolf" 78

O'Connell, Daniel 162
Ó Cróinín, Dáibhí 65
ogham (ogam) 17, 74, 91, 96 n. 5, 104, 145, 161
Orwell, George 216
Oswy 7, 10, 14, 35, 39–42, 63, 65, 134, 155–56
Our Lady of Darkness 10–11, 74–75, 82, 83, 102, 114, 144–45, 154

Parker, Robert 32
Patrick, Saint 17 n. 1, 52, 70, 73, 80, 91, 94–95, 96 n. 6, 111, 116 n. 3, 132, 175, 177–78
Paul, Saint 105, 153
Paul VI, Pope 125
Pearl 34
Pelegius 95, 96 n. 7, 105–6, 135–36, 175–76
Peters, Elizabeth 49
Peters, Ellis 1, 20, 34, 173, 184
Poe, Edgar Allan 28, 32, 44, 138, 152, 159
A Prayer for the Damned 11, 76–77, 100, 105, 114, 120, 121, 126
Proclamation of the Irish Republic 50–51

Richard I (the Lion-Hearted) 187
Rimini, Council of 177
Roberts, Les 30
Roman Church 3, 14–15, 34–35, 53–54, 64–65, 95, 96–97 n. 8, 119–21, 124–25, 131, 134–35, 157–58, 178
Rowling, J.K. 167
Royal, Priscilla 186

St. Benedict, Rule of 121
"St. Finnbar's Bell" 75
Sayers, Dorothy 29
"Scattered Thorns" 152
Scréach ón Tuama 161, 166, 193, 205; *see also* "A Scream from the Sepulcher"
"A Scream from the Sepulcher" 78, 86, 193, 205; *see also Scréach ón Tuama*
Shadow and Light 34
Shakespeare, William 166
Shroud for the Archbishop 7, 9, 10, 12, 15–16, 17, 30, 32, 54, 69, 94, 102, 104, 105, 114, 141, 144, 145, 175, 184
Simmons, Jean 213–14
Smith, Alexander McCall 155, 159
Smoke in the Wind 11, 69, 100–2, 105, 114, 176, 179, 186, 199
soul mate (soul friend) 12, 14, 185–86
Spartacus 213–14
The Spider's Web 72, 82, 92, 99, 101–5, 114, 140, 141, 143–45, 147–48, 175
Spring, Howard 216
Stabenow, Dana 37–38
Stoker, Bram 167
Strabo 100, 101
Stuart kings 162
The Subtle Serpent 9, 17, 30, 71–72, 104, 114, 120, 123, 141, 143, 144, 154, 184
Suffer Little Children 7, 9, 12, 16–17, 27, 30, 69, 70, 74, 95, 100, 102, 104, 105, 120, 141, 145, 184
Sutton Hoo 61
Symons, Julian 142
Syrus, Publilius 101, 152

Tolkien, J.R.R. 215
Tremayne, Peter: awards 1–2, 21, 23, 25, 27, 80; biography 21–27, 208–19; childhood 208, 210; early writing 208–9; fiction (exclusive of Fidelma stories) 25–26, 27, 72, 174, 218; Fidelma's origins 26, 184, 211–13; nonfiction publications 2–3, 6, 22, 23–24, 36, 62, 63, 70, 77, 80, 89, 99–101, 105, 106, 122, 176, 189, 194; parents 21–22; professional background 21, 22–25; pseudonym 20, 25; reading interests 210, 213; *see also* Fidelma stories: historical background
Turow, Scott 139

Urban II, Pope 211
Ustinov, Peter 214

Valera, Eamon de 51
Valley of the Shadow 60, 64, 65, 92–96, 101–3, 114, 120, 143–47, 149, 186
Vatican Council, Second 36, 119, 126
Vivian, E.C. 210
Vonnegut, Kurt 216

Wallace, Edgar 209, 210
Watson, Dr. 60, 102, 116 n. 7, 138–40, 142, 144, 154, 184, 218
Wells, H.G. 216
Wentworth, Patricia 48
"Whispers of the Dead" 153
Whispers of the Dead 78, 83, 99, 100, 101, 104–6, 151, 218
Whitby, Synod of 3, 14–15, 35–36, 65, 98, 121, 134–35, 154, 212
"Who Stole the Fish?" 82
Wighard 15–16
Wilde, Oscar 27
women's rights 6, 8–9, 50–51, 53–55, 57, 111–12, 132, 156–57, 187
women's studies 51, 55

Yann III 179
Yann IV 179
Yeats, William Butler 115
yellow plague 15–16, 40–41, 156

Zosimus, Pope 106

www.ingramcontent.com/pod-product-compliance
Lightning Source LLC
Chambersburg PA
CBHW051220300426
44116CB00006B/659